Praise for *The Greek Doctor's Diet*

"It's the latest weight loss revolution… healthier than Atkins, just as effective as GI and, best of all, it's really simple." *Daily Mail*

"It's not a quick fix: it's a nutritional system designed to keep you naturally slim, which you should follow for the rest of your life." *Grazia*

"…this is a really good approach." Breda Gajsek, principal of the UK College of Nutrition and Health, quoted in the *Daily Mail*

"Dr Fedon Lindberg is not trumpeting any new and faddy gimmick. His book brings together his experience running one of Europe's most successful health clinics, where his unique approach has led thousands of patients to adopt lifestyle changes and – crucially – enabled them to stick to them." *The Independent*

"…solid, sensible advice based on the way the Mediterraneans – in particular the Greeks – have been eating for years." *Daily Mail*

THE GREEK DOCTOR'S DIET

A SIMPLE, DELICIOUS, SLOW-CARB, MEDITERRANEAN APPROACH
TO EATING AND EXERCISE DESIGNED TO KEEP YOU
NATURALLY SLIM AND HELP YOU TO AVOID:

DIABETES
HEART DISEASE
INSULIN RESISTANCE
SYNDROME X

DR FEDON ALEXANDER LINDBERG

RODALE®

This edition first published in the UK in 2005 by
Rodale International Ltd
7–10 Chandos Street
London W1G 9AD
www.rodale.co.uk

© 2005 Fedon Alexander Lindberg
www.drlindberg.com
www.greekdoctorsdiet.com

Printed and bound in the UK by CPI Bath using acid-free paper from
sustainable sources.

 3 5 7 9 8 6 4

A CIP record for this book is available from the British Library
ISBN 1-4050-7749-2

This paperback edition distributed to the book trade by Pan Macmillan Ltd

Notice
This book is intended as a reference volume only, not as a medical manual. The information
given here is designed to help you make informed decisions about your health. It is not
intended as a substitute for any treatment that you may have been prescribed by your doctor. If
you suspect that you have a medical problem, we urge you to seek competent medical help.

Mention of specific companies, organizations or authorities in this book does not imply
endorsement by the publisher, nor does mention of specific companies, organizations or
authorities in the book imply that they endorse the book. Addresses, websites and telephone
numbers given in this book were accurate at the time the book went to press.

CONTENTS

INTRODUCTION

I was born in Greece at the beginning of the 1960s. There I learned to appreciate the simple things in life – the sunlight, the blue sea and Greek food. I watched and learned while my grandmother prepared one great dish after another. She was a fantastic cook, and she was also quite overweight. When she was in her fifties, she was diagnosed with type II diabetes, often known as 'adult-onset' diabetes. Her blood pressure was high, too. My grandmother liked good food, but did not eat large amounts. My grandfather ate exactly the same food, yet he was always slim. Neither of them was particularly physically active, and neither exercised on a regular basis. Why was only my grandmother overweight? Why did she develop diabetes and high blood pressure?

Before long my father also was diagnosed with diabetes and high blood pressure. Just like grandmother, he was in his early fifties and had gained 13kg (2st) in a relatively short period of time; almost all of this excess weight was concentrated around his waist. Later, even my mother, who has always been of normal weight and exercised regularly, developed mild diabetes when she was 70.

Grandmother suffered her first stroke at the age of 65. Another soon followed. It was a tragedy for the whole family. I watched as the health of a person dear to me gradually deteriorated. It didn't take long before her heart began to fail, and she died before she was 70. Why did this happen? Could she have done something to prevent it? Many members of my family are doctors, including my father and three of my siblings. I studied medicine and developed an early interest in diabetes and obesity. After all, it is well known that both disorders are genetically determined. If you have one parent with type II diabetes, you have a 40 per cent chance of developing the disease yourself at some point in life. I wondered whether I could do anything to prevent this from happening to me.

Both in Norway, where I moved to in the early 1980s, and in the United States, where I lived for two years, I carried out research in the field of diabetes and insulin resistance (the underlying cause behind type II diabetes and a major contributing cause of obesity). In 1987, after undergoing an euglycemic clamp test, I was diagnosed with moderate insulin resistance. (The euglycemic clamp test is used in medical research to quantify the degree of insulin resistance. Due to its complexity, it is not used as a routine test in clinical practice.) I wasn't overweight, but I was predisposed to developing type II diabetes. The message was clear: I had to find out what I could do to prevent this.

I have always enjoyed good food and have a sweet tooth. Although I have never been significantly overweight, I have always monitored my weight carefully. I knew it wouldn't take much before the scales shifted upwards and my waistline increased. Did I have a lower metabolism than other people? Or could it be that some foods did not agree with my body chemistry?

Through my medical specialization, I gained a better insight into obesity, diabetes and other lifestyle diseases. This left me increasingly frustrated about how little doctors have done to inform the public about preventing these conditions.

We know that disorders such as obesity, diabetes, high blood pressure and high cholesterol are genetically inherited, but lifestyle is what determines who will become ill and when. I have seen many diabetics whose health has gradually deteriorated prior to diagnosis; they then go through a period of so-called dietary management. Almost without exception, the disease will progress and will require treatment with oral medications and, later, even insulin injections, unless a significant change in lifestyle takes place. Until a few years ago, the only medicines available increased the body's production of insulin (the hormone responsible for regulating blood sugar levels, which is already high in the early stages of type II diabetes and in most cases of obesity). These medicines do improve the control of blood sugar levels, but almost without exception they lead to weight gain (80 per cent of type II diabetics are overweight or obese to begin with), increased blood pressure and increased levels of triglycerides and cholesterol in the blood. Eventually, insulin-injection treatment becomes inevitable, resulting in even further weight gain and metabolic disorder. The obvious conclusion: too much insulin makes us fat!

What affects our insulin levels? The answer is very simple: the food we eat – not so much the quantity we eat, but what we eat.

While I was in the United States, I came across two terms in particular that have had a great impact not only on me personally but also on many people around the world: Glycaemic Index (GI) and Glycaemic Load (GL). The Glycaemic Index is a scientific method that can help you choose the right carbohydrates; Glycaemic Load relates the GI to the amount of carbohydrate eaten in a normal serving, or in 100 grams, making comparison between foods possible. The right carbohydrates, coupled with the right quality and quantity of proteins and beneficial fats, will allow your body to reach a healthy balance. I soon realized that this was one of the most important milestones in modern nutrition. Used correctly, this nutritional principle can prevent obesity and help overweight and obese people achieve gradual weight loss and better health. Diabetics can stabilize their insulin and blood-sugar levels, at the same time as losing weight and feeling great. Using the GI and GL principles can help to control blood pressure or even eliminate high blood pressure completely, and prevent cardiovascular disease. And eating foods that have a low GL can increase metabolic rate and improve overall performance – endurance performance, or stamina, in particular.

During recent years scientists have conducted a great deal of research on the Glycaemic Index and Glycaemic Load and how food affects our blood sugar, our hormones and, through them, our health. There is substantial evidence that even chronic inflammatory diseases such as asthma and rheumatic conditions, as well as cancer, immune disorders and female infertility, have a great deal to do with the kind of food we eat. It almost goes without saying that we are what we eat – but it is perhaps less obvious that we are also what our predecessors have eaten throughout the evolution of our species. One doesn't have to be a rocket scientist to realize that food can prevent and treat disease – FOOD IS MEDICINE!

In 1999, I set up the first clinic in Norway specializing in the prevention and treatment of lifestyle disorders such as obesity, diabetes, cardiovascular disease and other degenerative conditions. The clinic is called 'In Balance' and it offers multidisciplinary treatment through patient education in nutrition and cook-ing, organized exercise sessions to improve metabolism, support in managing lifestyle modification and, if necessary, the use of dietary supplements and/or medications. For more information, visit *www.drlindbergs.com*

As you read this book, you will learn how you can eat your way to better health, lower weight and higher performance by correctly applying the best med-icine we know of: food. You can eat great-tasting food that just happens to be healthy, without counting calories or feeling deprived, and you can eat as much as you want to feel comfortably satisfied – if you choose the right foods and combine them appropriately.

CHAPTER 1

WHAT THIS BOOK CAN DO FOR YOU

Do you enjoy great-tasting food? Of course you do. Anything else would be unnatural. A positive attitude towards food is of the utmost importance, even if you are overweight or have diabetes, and this positive relationship with food is characteristic of the way people around the Mediterranean have traditionally eaten. The traditional Mediterranean diet, especially the Greek diet (typically high in olive oil, fish, vegetables, beans, lentils and fruit, and low in potatoes, red meat and dairy foods), has been known for the past 40 years to be particularly healthy, and is the starting point for this book.

Our bodies are literally made of the food we eat, and we need the right type of food and in adequate quantities in order to be healthy. This book will teach you to make the right choices from the many types of food available. By making better choices, you will reach a hormonal balance and enjoy better health. Remember, your future health depends on the choices you make today.

Are you overweight?

This book is especially suitable for anyone who has a tendency to put on weight easily or who is already overweight or obese. Maybe you have other family members with the same problem. Or perhaps you eat the same food as your partner or your siblings, but only *your* weight is increasing. Do you tend to put on weight around your waist in particular, while your arms and legs are thinner in comparison? Your doctor may have told you that you should lose weight, eat less and exercise more. You may have tried countless diets and 'slimming' products, or joined weight-loss support groups. Well, yes, you always managed to lose weight to begin with, and maybe some diets were more effective than others. But it didn't last long. Maybe you couldn't stand the monotony of restricting the types of foods you ate, or the endless calculations of calories, carbs or points, and went back to what you used to eat before you started dieting. Regardless, you ended up weighing as much as or more than you did before the diet. Is your willpower as tired as you are? Do not despair. It is not your fault. This book will grant you diet amnesty. You do not necessarily gain weight because you eat too much, but mainly because you eat the wrong food. By choosing the right food – and with a little bit of planning – you can lose weight permanently while eating well and becoming healthier with every bite.

This is not a quick-fix diet but a nutritional concept you can and should follow for the rest of your life. You should not expect to lose more than 1–1.5kg (2–3lb) per week if you are overweight; if you lose more than this it will affect your fat-free (muscle) mass, which is not good, because it is muscle that keeps your metabolism active. This level of weight loss may seem slow to some, but by following these guidelines you will experience increased feelings of well-being and vitality that will stimulate you to continue.

Are you predisposed to heart disease?

If you have high blood pressure, elevated cholesterol or triglyceride (blood lipid) levels, or have already developed angina or had a heart attack or stroke, it is more than likely that food has contributed to your problems, due to a series of hormonal disturbances. Along with quitting smoking, mastering stress and leading a physically more active life, a balanced diet will have an enormous impact on your health. Not only will you feel better, but your blood pressure will improve and – with the agreement of your doctor – you may even require fewer medications. In addition, arteriosclerosis can be reversed, and nearly-blocked arteries can open up again. Our body has a fantastic ability to heal itself, if only it is given the chance.

Are you predisposed to diabetes?

If you have diabetes in your immediate family, this book can greatly reduce your chances of getting the disease yourself. If you are one of the 130 million people in the world with type II diabetes (adult-onset diabetes), you can achieve better control of your blood-sugar levels and prevent a series of complications related to this disease (the damage it causes to blood vessels and nerves can result in blindness, amputation, impotence, kidney disease, heart disease and stroke). As an added bonus, you will gradually lose excess body fat if you are overweight. You may experience reduced cholesterol and triglyceride levels and your blood pressure will improve. You may even manage without oral medications or insulin injections, need lower dosages than you used to, or be able to switch from insulin injections to the new medications that improve insulin action rather than increase insulin levels. I have had many type II diabetic patients who no longer require insulin injections, even though they have undergone many years of such treatment. It is well known that insulin and medications that increase insulin production lead to weight gain, higher blood lipids, high blood pressure and an increased risk of premature cardiovascular disease.

If you have type I diabetes, you will find you have steadier, more predictable blood sugar and the need for insulin will be reduced, but you will still be dependent on insulin shots; you will also avoid developing complications linked to the disease. A diet based on the principles of the Glycaemic Load and a few modifications to your lifestyle can give you a new and better life.

Can you avoid syndrome X?

Some of you will be wondering what this is and if it is something you should be worried about. Syndrome X is a hormonal disorder that accounts for more than half of all deaths in developed countries every year. Syndrome X puts you at increased risk of type II diabetes, obesity, heart attack, stroke and several forms of cancer, as well as inflammatory diseases such as asthma, allergies, psoriasis, migraine, rheumatic diseases, muscular and skeletal pain, Crohn's disease, ulcerative colitis, irregular menstruation, infertility and pre-eclampsia.

The terms syndrome X, metabolic syndrome and insulin resistance are used interchangeably, however it is important to note that many people have some degree of insulin resistance but do not have full-blown insulin resistance or syndrome X. How can you tell if you have insulin resistance? The easiest way is simply to look at yourself in the mirror. If your belly is bulging even though the rest of your body looks normal, then you are probably predisposed to hyperinsulinemia (increased production of insulin) and you may have already developed insulin resistance (the body's defence mechanism against increased insulin). If you are very overweight or obese, you almost certainly are insulin-resistant. The same is true if you have type II diabetes or if your doctor has tested your cholesterol levels and found you have increased triglycerides and reduced HDL cholesterol. High blood pressure is another likely indicator.

Even if you are of a normal weight and shape, you may have insulin resistance; in the developed world around 10 per cent of the population have insulin resistance without any other health or weight problems.

Some of us have a genetic predisposition to becoming insulin-resistant, but our eating and exercise habits determine whether or not we actually develop the syndrome, so the answer is clear – change your habits and change your life.

Stressed out?

Warning: stress can seriously damage your health. In nature, stress is a necessary survival reaction, but the stresses of modern life have nothing to do with real danger – you can't run away from them! So the hormones that nature intended to help us deal with stress remain in the bloodstream, causing chronic stress, with symptoms such as weight gain, low libido, difficulty in concentrating and poor memory, as well as more serious problems, including heart disease, diabetes, osteoporosis, skin conditions and inflammatory bowel disease.

Stress often affects the way we eat: we skip meals, or turn to 'comfort food'. But the high-carb, high-fat foods we generally choose as 'comfort' send our blood sugar soaring then plummeting. Unfortunately, the body interprets rapidly falling blood sugar levels (which also occur when we skip meals) as a stressful situation and secretes even more stress hormones. This vicious circle of chronic stress is something we all need to deal with urgently, and we can start by eating the right foods.

Always tired and sluggish, even depressed?

Have you been feeling abnormally tired and sluggish for a long time? Do you lack concentration and feel irritable? This may be due to a hormonal imbalance caused by your diet and lifestyle. Today's foods are a far cry from what we are genetically designed to eat, and some individuals tolerate a modern diet better than others. If you have symptoms that suggest low blood sugar an hour or two after eating a meal high in sugar, potatoes, white bread or pasta, you may suffer from what is called 'postprandial reactive, or rebound, hypoglycaemia'. Foods that cause a rapid increase in blood sugar cause a corresponding sharp increase in insulin (the hormone that controls blood sugar levels), followed by a rapid drop in blood sugar. When this happens, you will probably feel tired, irritable, hungry and lacking in concentration.

In this situation, grabbing a cup of coffee to wake yourself up is not a good idea: the caffeine in coffee increases the secretion of the stress hormone adrenalin, which raises your pulse rate and blood pressure and can have a negative effect on your heart, as well as contributing to your stress levels.

The answer is to eat differently. You will enjoy increased mental alertness if you choose more natural whole foods, such as vegetables and fruit, and increase your intake of foods containing omega-3 fats: the latter have been shown to lift depression and elevate mood.

Are your cravings out of control?

Are you one of those people who craves sweets, or bread, potatoes or other types of starchy food? When you start eating something sweet, or a savoury snack like potato crisps, do you find you must finish the whole pack? Do you experience mood swings and varying performance levels during the day? After lunch you feel tired, even lethargic, your concentration is poor and you may become irritable. You grab some chocolate, or maybe a sweet drink, feel better quite quickly, and have more energy, but an hour or two later you feel tired and hungry again. This pattern is repeated after dinner, which is often a big meal and eaten quite late. Maybe you even wake up during the night and raid the fridge. If all that rings a bell, it is possible that you are a carbohydrate addict.

Sugar addicts and anyone who is stressed or depressed is likely to turn to chocolate or other sweet and fatty or starchy foods because, by increasing the levels of serotonin and endorphins in the brain, they provide a soothing and calming effect. But they also cause high insulin levels, which can lead to obesity, type II diabetes, high blood pressure and cardiovascular disease. Alcohol addiction works in a similar way, so beware if you often feel you 'need a drink'.

You might be suffering from a hormonal imbalance, which could explain your eating and drinking patterns. By learning a little more about the way food and hormones such as insulin work together in your body you can control your cravings – rather than them controlling you.

Do you suffer from an inflammatory condition: skin problems, rheumatic conditions, allergies, asthma?

Inflammation is a natural part of the body's repair function, but when the inflammation process becomes chronic it causes disease. Inflammatory diseases – such as dermatitis, psoriasis, migraine, osteoarthritis, asthma, intestinal disorders and certain types of heart disease – have increased dramatically over the past 50 years, in parallel with the increased consumption of junk food, trans fats, refined carbohydrates and sugars, and the decline in consumption of natural whole foods. The good news is that by increasing our intake of foods high in omega-3 fats, together with antioxidant-rich foods, while reducing omega-6 fats, trans fats and high-glycaemic carbohydrates, we can redress the balance and reduce inflammatory problems.

Women: do you have PMS or infertility problems?

If you suffer from pre-menstrual syndrome (PMS), you already know that your hormones are to blame. By eating the right foods to correct the hormonal imbalance, you can greatly alleviate many of the symptoms. And although chocolate provides short-term relief – by releasing serotonin, the brain's 'feel-good' chemical – you will feel better in the long run by increasing your intake of foods rich in omega-3 fats, which boost the body's own anti-inflammatory response and relieve cramps, bloating and headaches.

Polycystic ovary syndrome (PCOS) is the major cause of female infertility; it affects between 5 and 10 per cent of all women of childbearing age in the western world. Like many other 'modern' disorders, it is linked to insulin resistance and can be treated through diet, by choosing the right types and quantities of carbohydrates, and exercise.

Can you reduce your risk of cancer?

Cancer is caused by damage to the genetic material, the 'software' of body cells, so they don't die or replicate as normal. This damage may be triggered by anything that increases oxidation: a low intake of antioxidants and essential nutrients; high intake of sugar and high-glycaemic foods; high intake of processed fats; environmental pollutants, stress and smoking.

Syndrome X (see page 13) is also known to increase the risk of several forms of cancer, including breast cancer. While no one is immune to cancer, you can certainly reduce your risk by paying greater attention to what you eat and how you live.

Can you slow down the ageing process?

Chronological ageing is unavoidable and equal for all. Every minute, hour and year is equally long for everybody. Biological ageing on the other hand is the result of the way we choose to live our lives. When you are 15 or 20 years old, you usually have the body your genes determined for you. But by the time you are 40, you usually have the body you deserve. It's like training a dog: you can think of chronological and biological ageing as yourself and your dog respectively; your dog may walk ahead of you, beside you, or behind you. It is within your power to control the ageing process – by training your dog to walk beside or behind you.

Physical signs of ageing, such as wrinkles and age spots, are partly genetically determined, but what we eat and drink can affect how we look in the months and years to come. A combination of healthy fats, antioxidants from vegetables and fruit, high-quality protein, plus plenty of water to drink, can help to keep our skin smooth and supple.

The invisible symptoms of ageing can be devastating, but even degenerative diseases of the brain and eyes can be prevented and to some extent improved by choosing the foods your body needs and avoiding those that will certainly make matters worse.

Want to improve your stamina or sports performance?

If you are involved in sports or lead a physically active lifestyle, you know how important it is to exercise and eat appropriately. You know that your performance depends on how efficiently your muscles work. Muscles depend on a steady supply of energy before, during and after exercise. Full glycogen stores in your liver and muscles, along with efficient fat burning, are essential. Maintaining a balanced diet and choosing low-glycaemic foods before and during exercise and high-glycaemic foods soon after exercise (for rapid recovery) will maximize your performance and increase your endurance.

Do you want to boost your vitality and improve your general health?

You need not be overweight or have a medical problem in order to be interested in achieving optimal health. Low-glycaemic foods and the correct balance of nutrients are of equal importance for everyone. Over millions of years, our bodies have evolved to handle natural whole foods, not the highly processed food of our modern diet, which contains high levels of high-glycaemic carbs and unhealthy, unnatural fats. This book may prove to be an eye-opener and will help you and your family to feel full of energy and glowing with health.

CHAPTER 2

LET FOOD BE YOUR MEDICINE

Let your food be your medicine and let your medicine be your food.
Hippocrates, *c.* 460 BC–*c.* 377 BC

nce, there was a time when our bodies were in peak condition because they got what they needed. We ate food that was simple but good for us, and exercise was a necessity in our daily lives. We have more than 100 trillion cells in our body, and in each cell there are more than one billion biochemical reactions per second, every day throughout our lives. Food is involved in all of these reactions. Unfortunately, today's highly processed food rarely supplies us with everything we need to be truly healthy. It provides the energy to survive and function on a day-to-day basis, but it leaves a lot to be desired if we want optimum health and vitality. Much of the food we eat consists of empty, useless calories, with ingredients that have been processed beyond recognition.

We need food that gives us nourishment, not just energy. We also need food that stimulates our intestinal flora (for more information, see page 31, under the heading lactose). Did you know that each and every one of us has about 1 kilogram of intestinal bacteria? We have a greater number of these bacteria than we have body cells. These bacteria produce important vitamins and fatty acids and are vital to our immune system. An imbalance may lead to a number of ailments, infections and inflammatory conditions. But while our food choices clearly affect our health, food should not be merely something you have to eat in order to survive or function well. Food should be a positive part of your life, something to look forward to, something that will enhance your family and social life. Food should not only be good for you, but should also appeal to your senses of sight, smell and taste.

Until a few decades ago, good doctors were 'craftsmen'. They had to use all their medical knowledge, but most of all they had to use good judgement and intuition to find out what ailed their patients and how they could best treat them. Often, they had no idea what actually caused a disease, but strangely enough, their remedies – which to modern doctors might sound like old wives' tales – did the trick. Observation was a key word – and was how the greatest discoveries and inventions came about. You did not need to know why cod-liver oil, vegetables and pulses were good for you; that was just the way it was.

In my childhood home in Greece, we had lentils, beans or chickpeas every Monday and Thursday. Fish was served every Tuesday, while on Wednesdays and Fridays the focus was on fresh vegetables. At the weekends, we had chicken or meat, mostly lamb. It was pretty predictable. There was always a bottle of wine on the table – grown-ups had a glass or two and the rest was saved for the next day. And we always had a Greek salad, with sweet sun-ripened tomatoes, chopped green peppers, cucumber, feta cheese (made from sheep's milk) and wonderful Greek oregano. The olives were served on the side, because my mother did not like them. A small bottle of olive oil, vinegar and wedges of lemon always accompanied the salad. Greeks use lemon on everything, even grilled meat, and it tastes really good.

Now, everything has changed. Many people eat without really thinking about it, and spend as little time as possible cooking. A hectic morning may mean you are worn out by lunchtime, so you grab a cheese and ham roll and a can of cola. In the evening, you make do with a 'dinner' of ready-made pizza, eaten while you watch your favourite TV show.

At the same time, we are concerned about keeping up to date with all the latest health claims and the specific benefits of eating, say, tomatoes or spinach, so that we can buy a vitamin supplement to provide these benefits – our nod in the direction of good health. Does this sound familiar? Food has become medicine, in the shape of a pill. But why do we need evidence that this or that food substance is beneficial to our health? After all, man has survived millions of years by eating natural produce – and we are the living proof.

Food is medicine, the best medicine we know of. In the past, we did not know how it worked as well as we do today. But as with all medicine, the wrong kind or the wrong dosage can have unwanted side effects or even cause illness.

Macronutrients and micronutrients

The food we eat is made up of macronutrients and micronutrients. Macronutrients provide energy, and they constitute the bulk of our food. They can be divided into the following categories: protein, carbohydrates, fat, alcohol and fibre (dietary fibre). Protein and carbohydrates provide approximately 4 calories per gram (114 calories per ounce), alcohol 7 calories per gram (199 per ounce) and fat 9 calories per gram (256 per ounce). Chemically speaking, fibre is mainly composed of carbohydrates, but very little of it is actually digested and converted into energy in the body. Nonetheless, it is very important to our health.

Micronutrients, such as vitamins and minerals, are found in very small amounts in our food. They do not contribute energy, but they are vital to our bodily functions.

What is protein?

Protein is crucial to our bodies. The word is derived from the Greek word *protos* and means 'the first' or 'the most important'. All life on earth contains protein. Our cells, hormones and immune system are all based on and communicate through proteins, so obviously we must ensure that we get enough of this nutrient. Proteins are made up of smaller compounds called amino acids, of which there are about 20 different kinds. Eleven of these can be produced by the human body. The remaining nine cannot be produced in the body, so they have to be provided by the food we eat. These are called 'essential amino acids'. If we do not get enough essential amino acids, our bodily functions will deteriorate. No bricks, no building!

Where do you find protein?

There are two sources of protein: animal protein and plant protein. Animal protein is found in milk and other dairy products, eggs, all meats, poultry, fish and shellfish. Note, it is the saturated fat in dairy products and meat that may be less healthy in large quantities, not the protein! If you choose lean meats and low-fat dairy products, fat is not an issue. For guidelines on choosing healthy sources of protein, see chapter 11.

Plant protein is mainly found in nuts, pulses such as beans, lentils and chickpeas and, to a lesser extent, in vegetables. Soya beans are a very good source of protein and have many other health-promoting qualities. They have been used in China, Japan and South-East Asia for thousands of years, but are seldom eaten in their natural state – instead they are transformed into a number of other products, such as tofu (bean curd), soya milk, tempeh, miso, fermented black beans and soy sauce. In recent years there has been an explosion in the number of soya products available, from soya flour and soy-based cheeses to meat and bacon substitutes – but some of the latter are very highly processed and not necessarily the healthiest option.

How much protein do I need?

As a rule of thumb, you need a daily minimum of about 1 to 1.2 grams of pure protein per kilo of body weight (based on a 'normal' weight, or a Body Mass Index, or BMI, of 23) if you are not particularly physically active. If you weigh 70kg (11st), you will need a minimum of 70 to 84 grams of pure protein a day. And if you are physically active, whether at work or in sports, or are pregnant or breastfeeding, you will need more. You can find more details about how to calculate the amount you need on page 147.

Note that we are talking about pure protein here, not the amount of food: since meat, chicken, fish and certain nuts (almonds, cashews, peanuts) contain approximately 20 to 30 per cent protein, you would need to eat 350g (about 12oz) of these foods to get 70g of pure protein. The body's need for protein does not change if you are vegetarian. Most cooked beans and lentils – and tofu – contain about 8 per cent protein, so to get your protein from these sources you'd need to eat about 900g (2lb) of beans. Vegetarians should eat onions and garlic together with their protein, as these foods contain sulphurous amino acids that are also among our most important antioxidants. Spirulina (an algae) is another good protein source from the plant world; it can be bought in powder form from health food shops and added to soups, salads and sauces.

What happens if you eat too little protein?

Too little protein can lead to loss of lean body mass, or muscle. Muscles, large and small, are important for movement and because they protect our vital inner organs. The muscles also constitute the part of the body that burns the most energy; so less muscle mass means a slower metabolism. Many age-related illnesses are strongly linked to the loss of lean body mass.

Many protein foods are also a source of important vitamins and minerals. For example, vitamin B12 (used for the formation of blood cells and in the digestive and nervous system) is found in meat, fish, poultry and eggs (but not in plant proteins).

The amino acids methionine and L-cysteine, and taurine (a derivative of methionine, cysteine and vitamin B6), also play an important part in the body's antioxidant system. A low intake of these amino acids may result in a lack of antioxidants produced by the body – and these are part of our defence against premature ageing and illness.

Animal-based protein is relatively expensive to produce, but in the industrialized world there is more than enough protein available. Underconsumption of protein may be a problem for less well-off members of society, because it is more expensive than carbohydrates and fats. However, as protein has a potent satiety effect it would be a better investment in terms of both money and health than cheap, highly-processed carbohydrate foods.

What if you eat too much protein?

The body does not store amino acids for later use. This means that any superfluous protein will either be converted slowly to blood sugar or be stored as fat. Too much protein will also, to a certain extent, stimulate the production of insulin, because some amino acids stimulate insulin secretion.

Whether excessive consumption of protein might put a strain on the kidneys has been debated for years. It seems that healthy kidneys adapt to a higher protein intake without harmful effects. However, people with renal failure or nephrotic syndrome should try to avoid too much protein in their diet.

Protein itself is very satiating and it is difficult to overeat on protein alone – it's the bread or burger buns, potatoes and chips that go with it that cause many of today's health problems.

Protein's role in metabolism

The breakdown of protein into amino acids occurs in the stomach and small intestine, and the production of protein needed by the body takes place in the liver. The process is rather energy-consuming and it also leads to the release of heat. Approximately 25 per cent of the protein from our diet is used in this process, which means that we are left with less energy derived from protein than the number of calories (4 per gram) indicate.

Protein is a key element for an efficient metabolism, and our consumption of protein has an effect on a number of hormones. Most importantly, protein stimulates production of the growth hormone IGF-1 and a hormone called glucagon. The growth hormone increases muscle mass, while glucagon not only increases our sense of fullness after a meal; it also, most importantly, promotes the burning of body fat to provide energy. Glucagon's main function is to increase blood sugar if it is falling (for instance, during fasting or between meals), thus ensuring a steady energy supply for the body. Blood sugar is released from the liver's sugar supply (glycogen) and is also produced from proteins and fat. When the body is producing glucagon it is not producing insulin – which means less fat storage and more burning of body fat. In chapter 5, which concerns food and hormones, you can read more about how different nutrients affect our metabolism.

PROTEIN AND FAT BURNING

Eating a certain amount of protein with every meal and snack will enhance your body's ability to burn fat and will satisfy your appetite far better than carbohydrates alone.

• For breakfast, yogurt or cottage cheese will boost your metabolism and the protein they contain will stimulate glucagon production.
• Nuts and seeds provide both protein and healthy fats, so they are a great choice for a snack, along with a piece of fruit.
• Bean, lentils and chickpeas provide both protein and healthy carbohydrates; soya beans and foods made from soya, such as tofu, are particularly high in protein.

What are carbohydrates?

Carbohydrates are generally divided into two groups: sugars (simple carbohydrates) and starches (complex carbohydrates). Both sugars and starches provide our bodies with the same amount of energy (4 calories per gram).

Most people associate carbohydrates with bread, cereals, rice and pasta, while potatoes, apples and carrots, for example, are considered separately, as vegetables and fruit. But vegetables and fruit also contain carbohydrates, in addition to water, fibre (a non-digestible carbohydrate), vitamins and minerals. Sweet foods, such as sugar, honey, biscuits and ice cream, are also carbohydrates.

How many, and which, carbohydrates do we really need?

Here is an interesting thought: we need a certain daily intake of protein (amino acids) and certain types of fat (essential fatty acids) because we are not able to produce them in our bodies. This is why we talk of *essential* amino acids and *essential* fatty acids. Essential carbohydrates, on the other hand, do not exist. The body is capable of producing all the carbohydrates it needs from protein and fat. We can survive without eating carbohydrates, even though this is not generally considered very healthy, because many whole foods that contain carbohydrates also provide useful and healthy micronutrients of plant origin.

The Eskimo diet is a good example of this. Traditionally, Eskimos have survived on a diet based on proteins and fat from fish and seals. You have probably heard that the Eskimos have a very low occurrence of heart disease. This is partly due to a high consumption of omega-3 unsaturated fat from fish, and also because of an extremely low consumption of carbohydrates.

However, carbohydrates are the body's – and in particular the brain's – preferred source of energy, mainly because we can store only a minimal amount of them. After they have been digested, more or less all carbohydrates end up in the blood as glucose – hence blood glucose, or blood sugar, as most people call it. The blood contains about 5 grams (one teaspoon) of glucose, which is used by all our organs to supply energy for our daily needs. The surplus is stored, as glycogen, in the liver and muscle tissue. Our brain is absolutely dependent on a stable supply of blood sugar, and it uses about 75 per cent of all the glucose that circulates in our blood. This explains why a low blood sugar level, known as hypoglycaemia, leads to considerable discomfort. At this point, the brain signals that there is danger ahead. It tells us to eat something sweet or starchy, because this is the quickest way to increase blood sugar.

By eating the healthy types of carbohydrates, such as lentils and beans, vegetables and fruits, in combination with the right sorts of proteins and fats, we can keep our blood sugar level stable and thereby reduce feelings of discomfort and hunger, and cravings for sugar and starch. The Glycaemic Index (see chapter 4) can be very helpful in determining which carbohydrates are beneficial and which are not.

Problem carbs

Less favourable carbohydrates (those that are highly processed and have a high Glycaemic Index) cause a rapid rise in blood sugar and stimulate the pancreas to produce a lot of insulin, the hormone that regulates blood sugar levels. If you eat refined, high-glycaemic carbohydrates often, or in large amounts, the pancreas will have to produce a lot of insulin in response to the high levels of blood sugar. This can ultimately lead to exhaustion of the pancreas and can cause all the health problems related to a high insulin level and insulin resistance. If you are not doing enough physical activity to use the energy these carbohydrates supply, the glycogen stores in your liver are almost always full, so excess carbohydrates will be converted into body fat. Unfortunately, high-glycaemic carbohydrates and foods containing them are very often among our favourites: potatoes, especially French fries; products made from refined grains, such as many types of bread, corn flakes, pastry, biscuits and cakes; beer; soft drinks; anything sweetened with sugar. By reducing the intake of such foods, and by combining them with the right amount of protein, unsaturated fat and dietary fibre, we can prevent negative consequences to our health.

But surely potatoes are a vegetable? Yes, but the human body lacks the enzymes to digest raw potato; in order to become digestible, potatoes must be cooked – in other words their starch structure is altered, and it is this starch that causes a rapid rise in blood sugar. The trouble is, they are now so popular that we eat them to excess – baked, boiled, mashed and above all fried.

What about wheat? Well, yes, cereal products (and this includes beer!) have been part of our diet for 10,000 years. Genetically speaking, this is a comparatively short time, but the real problem lies in the way most of our wheat is now processed. Since the middle of the nineteenth century, steel roller mills have been used throughout the world. They quickly and efficiently separate the white flour (almost pure starch) from the bran and germ – the parts of the wheat that contain most protein, fibre, vitamins and minerals and the parts that slow down absorption. Before the invention of roller mills, grains were ground between stones: stone mills are still in use, and stoneground wholewheat flour is a healthier, if slightly more expensive, option than ordinary white flour. Other types of grain, such as rye, barley and oats, and various ancient types of wheat, such as spelt, emmer and kamut, are more likely to be grown organically and processed in traditional ways. Perhaps not surprisingly, they also cause fewer allergic reactions and intolerance problems than ordinary wheat.

Pasta made from durum wheat and certain types of rice (especially brown basmati and the American-style easy-cook/parboiled long-grain rice) have a lower Glycaemic Index than potatoes and flour (in other words they do not have

CINNAMON

A lot of research is being carried out on antioxidants in food as we become increasingly aware of their importance in slowing down the ageing process and preventing many chronic diseases. Antioxidant-rich foods include vegetables and fruit, olives, nuts and seeds, coffee, cocoa and, last but not least, herbs and spices. Cinnamon is so powerful an antioxidant that, when compared with six other antioxidant spices (anise, ginger, licorice, mint, nutmeg and vanilla) and three chemical food preservatives, cinnamon prevented oxidation more effectively than the chemical antioxidants and all the other spices, except mint.

Cinnamon – the bark of the cinnamon tree – has a long history as a spice and as a medicine. Cinnamon is anti-microbial, and can inhibit the growth of both bacteria and fungi, including the yeast Candida, which causes thrush. Cinnamon's unique healing abilities come from its essential oils, which contain active components called cinnamaldehyde, cinnamyl acetate and cinnamyl alcohol, plus a number of other volatile substances. Cinnamaldehyde makes blood platelets less sticky and prevents blood clots. It also reduces the formation of arachidonic acid (see page 104) and therefore acts as an anti-inflammatory.

Cinnamon can be of significant help to people with type II (non-insulin dependent) diabetes by improving their ability to respond to insulin and increasing cells' ability to use glucose, thus normalizing their blood sugar levels. A recent joint US/Pakistani study included 60 volunteers with type II diabetes who were not taking insulin. Subjects were divided into six groups. Groups 1, 2 and 3 were given 1, 3 or 6 grams of cinnamon daily, while groups 4, 5 and 6 received a placebo. After 40 days, all three levels of cinnamon reduced blood sugar levels by 18–29%, triglycerides by 23–30%, LDL cholesterol by 7–27% and total cholesterol by 12–26%, while no significant changes were seen in those groups receiving placebo. Even the lowest amount of cinnamon, 1 gram per day (approximately 1/4 to 1/2 teaspoon), had a significant effect. When daily cinnamon was stopped, blood sugar levels began to increase.

The researchers' conclusion: including cinnamon in the diet of people with type II diabetes will reduce risk factors associated with diabetes and cardiovascular diseases.

such a dramatic effect on blood sugar) but should still be eaten in limited quantities, because they are very rich in carbohydrate.

Sweet but dangerous

Is there room for sweet things in a book such as this? Of course there is. Food should be about pleasure, and sweet foods – in moderate quantities – may contribute to the quality of life. However, the source of sweetness you choose is very important. In nature, there are five basic, commonly found types of sugar: glucose, fructose, lactose, sucrose and maltose, and each has a different effect on blood sugar levels.

Nutritionists often describe sugars as intrinsic (i.e. sugars that are part of the cellular structure of foods such as whole fruit and vegetables) and extrinsic (i.e. sugars that are not part of the cellular structure). Milk sugars (mainly lactose), although not contained within the cellular structure of the food, are considered to be intrinsic sugars. Non-milk extrinsic sugars – often called 'added sugars' – include those found in honey, table sugar (and all other sugar types such as demerara, cane sugar, muscovado), fruit juices, baked goods and confectionery. As a rule of thumb, no more than 10 per cent of your daily energy intake should come from added sugars. With an intake of 2000 calories, that would mean a maximum of 50g (1¾oz) of added sugar a day. To give you an idea of what this means, a 150g pot of unsweetened yogurt contains 14g of sugar (in the form of lactose, or milk sugar) and a 200ml glass of fruit juice contains about 20g of sugar. On the other hand, if you eat 100g of fresh strawberries, you get just 6g of natural, intrinsic sugar – along with healthy dietary fibre and vitamin C. In fact, by following the Greek Doctor's Diet, you will get an average of 12g of added sugars daily, as low-glycaemic fructose – which is much lower than the official recommendations.

The daily intake of sugar in the western world is far greater than the amount recommended for optimum health: average daily consumption in the US is 178g; in the UK it is 83g. World 'added' sugar consumption has been steadily increasing in recent years, but production exceeds demand and there is a global surplus of sugar, so it is a cheap ingredient for food manufacturers.

Honey: the first sweetener

Historically speaking, honey was the only sweet additive available. It was not found everywhere, and certainly not in large quantities. Fruits, including dates, satisfied man's need for sugar. Honey does not have a standard chemical structure – it is composed of water and varying proportions of glucose, fructose and sucrose, as well as minerals, vitamins and several healthy bioactive components – and its effect on blood sugar (Glycaemic Index) varies, depending on its composition. If you wish to lose weight or gain control of your blood sugar levels, you should avoid honey.

Glucose

Glucose (also called dextrose) is found in varying amounts in some fruits, and in honey. This is also the type of sugar that the body uses as energy currency. The mouth, stomach and small intestine easily absorb glucose – it needs no digestion and goes directly into the blood, so it is instantly available as energy. It causes a quick rise in blood sugar and stimulates the pancreas to produce insulin, which, in turn, ensures that glucose enters the cells. There, it may be burned to provide a source of energy or stored for later use, either as glycogen (the storage form of glucose) or converted into fat.

Glucose is what we use as a point of reference when we compare different foods and their blood sugar-increasing effect – that is, their Glycaemic Index (GI). On a scale of 0 to 100, glucose has a GI of 100.

Glucose is about 30 per cent less sweet than ordinary sugar, but it is widely used in the food industry in the form of concentrated syrup (glucose syrup or corn syrup), which is inexpensive to produce. Most people should avoid all products that contain glucose, glucose syrup and corn syrup: always read the label. (Diabetics who need insulin injections or oral medications to lower their blood sugar are the only exception to the rule. They should always carry glucose tablets with them, in case they get hypoglycaemia.)

Sugar

Sugar (also called sucrose, or table sugar, to distinguish it from other sugars) is the most common sweetener. You might think that it is quite natural. After all, it comes from the sugar cane or sugar beet, doesn't it? Yes, but it is not a fruit or vegetable; the sap of the sugar cane or sugars extracted from the beet must be processed to achieve the familiar crystalline form. Each sucrose molecule consists of a glucose molecule and a fructose molecule joined together. When we digest sugar, it is split into its two components, glucose and fructose. Glucose is absorbed by the blood and leads to a rapid rise in blood sugar, whereas fructose only slightly affects blood sugar. Because of its composition, regular sugar has a Glycaemic Index (GI) of 68, which is lower than the GI of glucose (100), but higher than fructose (19). If people consumed only a small amount of sugar, there would not be a problem. Many of today's health problems arise because we consume vast amounts of sugar, most of which comes from drinks and processed foods – and I am not just referring to sweet items but also savoury foods such as sauces and canned vegetables, even canned fish.

The human body does not need sugar. Apart from energy (calories), sugar contributes nothing: no protein, no essential fatty acids, no vitamins or minerals. Sugar – in crystallized, granulated, powder and syrup form – is an additive. The same is true of white flour and salt. We do not eat them on their own; they are added during food preparation. In many ways, sugar and – to a somewhat lesser extent – white flour are 'anti-nutrients': in order for the body to use them they require vitamins and minerals which they 'steal' from our body's reserves, short-circuiting our metabolism and increasing our need to compensate by consuming even more nutritious foods.

Remember, too, that sugar is often found in cakes, biscuits and other baked goods together with white flour and processed fat, which makes the situation even worse. Should we then stop eating sugar altogether? Well, it is the safest thing to do, but small amounts every now and again will not do much harm. In the long run, it is what you do every day that counts.

Fructose

Fructose is found in all fruit (and in honey). It is 30 to 50 per cent sweeter than ordinary sugar (it tastes sweeter in powder form than in liquid form), so you use 30 to 50 per cent less to obtain the same level of sweetness. It also provides 30 to 50 per cent fewer calories than ordinary sugar and causes considerably less tooth decay. Due to its ability to absorb water better than sugar, products containing fructose stay fresh longer.

Most importantly, fructose reacts differently in the body from other kinds of sugar. It is absorbed more slowly in the small intestine and cannot be converted into energy immediately. First, it has to go through the liver, where it is turned into glycogen and stored. Fructose has a very small effect on blood sugar, and it has a low Glycaemic Index of 19.

At the end of the 1960s, fructose was extracted from sugar (sucrose) for the first time. It can be bought as a powder for use in cooking, and is available from health food shops and major supermarkets. In recent years, it has become increasingly popular as a sweetener for products such as chocolate, low-fat yogurt and jam (but note that some products may contain a combination of fructose and sucrose or glucose). Basically, all products that are sweetened with sugar can be made with fructose instead. You might very well ask, 'Then why on earth is fructose not substituted for all sugar?' The main reason is that fructose is about four to five times more expensive to produce than sugar. If fructose was used instead of sugar, either food prices would have to be raised or the profit margins in the food industry would go down. The second reason is that the production of fructose on a global basis is relatively small compared to the almost unlimited access to sugar, which is a commodity. The truth of the matter is that unless we as consumers demand better food, the food industry is not going to produce it.

Don't be fooled by the term high-fructose corn syrup, which is used as an ingredient in cereals, sauces, soft drinks and confectionery. It is a variation on glucose syrup (see Glucose on page 28) in which some of the glucose is converted to fructose. It still contains around 50 to 70 per cent glucose.

Excessive intake of fructose may increase the level of triglycerides (fats) in your blood, but the same thing happens when you consume an excess amount of any carbohydrates. I recommend that, wherever possible, you should substitute fructose or no-cal sweeteners for other sugars, but also that you reduce your consumption of sugar in all forms. In fact the less you consume the better. Fruit is not recommended in unlimited quantities; in particular limit your intake of high-glycaemic fruits such as bananas and mangoes. In general I recommend no more than two pieces of fruit a day.

Fructose and diabetes

Eating fructose in small amounts is unproblematic for type I (insulin-dependent) diabetics. Very little insulin is needed to metabolize fructose – about five times less than for glucose. It is important to note that fructose will not treat hypoglycaemia, simply because it does not provide a quick elevation in the blood sugar level.

Type II diabetics should limit their fructose intake to no more than 50g (1¾oz) a day. The best way for all of us, diabetic or not, to maintain a stable blood sugar level is to get the majority of our carbohydrates from fruit, vegetables and pulses.

Lactose, yogurt and good bacteria

Lactose (milk sugar) is found in milk and other dairy products. It is considerably less sweet than sugar and has a lower Glycaemic Index (GI 46), which is why dairy products such as milk and ice cream have a low GI. On the other hand, dairy products contain saturated fat, of which we should eat less. Furthermore, 80 per cent of adults worldwide cannot tolerate lactose, because they have a low level of lactase, the enzyme needed to break down lactose.

There is a big difference between fresh milk and cultured or sour dairy products such as yogurt, buttermilk and cheese. In these fermented dairy products, the lactose has been broken down by the enzyme lactase. This makes these products easily digestible even for most people who have lactose intolerance. The bacteria in these products are 'probiotic', or beneficial, bacteria. A regular intake of these products promotes good intestinal function, inhibits the growth of disease-causing bacteria and is crucial to the immune defence system. The intestinal function is enhanced even more if you combine these foods with sufficient 'prebiotic' fibre (from vegetables, pulses, oats and barley) – non-digestible ingredients that stimulate the growth of good intestinal flora. Cheese contains little or no carbohydrate and quite a lot of protein and calcium, but it is also high in saturated fat, which is less desirable, especially not in combination with a diet rich in high-glycaemic carbohydrates.

Maltose

Maltose (malt sugar) is the kind of sugar that is found in beer. Malt sugar is composed of two glucose molecules chained together, and it leads to a higher rise in blood sugar than glucose does. Maltose has a Glycaemic Index of 105 to 110, which is one of the highest GIs. So if you are struggling with overweight or have diabetes, it is not a good idea for you to drink beer. It is much better to have a glass of wine with your meal. Alternatively, you may wish to have a low-carbohydrate beer.

Alternative sweeteners

Many sugar-free products today are sweetened with synthetic, non-caloric sweeteners, such as aspartame, sucralose/Splenda and acesulfame-K. Other sweetners are the polyols or sugar alcohols. e.g. lactitol, maltitol, isomalt, xylitol. These cause a very small, almost insignificant, blood sugar rise and can be healthier alternatives to sugar, as long as they are used in moderation.

What is fat?

Fat is our densest source of energy: it contains more energy per gram (9 calories) than any other macronutrient. Among other things, it is an important source of the fat-soluble vitamins A, D, E and K. In food, fat is found in the form of triglycerides, and when you eat fat, these triglycerides are split into their components: glycerol and three fatty acids. Nature contains numerous fatty acids, but not all of them play an important role in nutrition. Nothing is as important to our health as eating the right kind of fat.

Some fatty acids are important because they are building blocks for substances that are part of our immune system and have a positive influence on inflammatory reactions (you can read more about this in chapter 7). Others are vital to a well-functioning metabolism, because we need the right kind of fat from our food in order to burn fat. Obese individuals often lack essential fatty acids, or the relationship between the types of fats they eat is wrong, and they have too much stored saturated fat (originating both directly from the diet or converted from excess carbohydrate). In combination with antioxidants (see chapter 10), fatty acids influence our defence mechanisms against cancer, while others are important in preventing illnesses such as diabetes and heart disease. So, you see, there's more to fat than meets the eye.

All fatty foods contain both saturated and unsaturated fatty acids, but are usually described as either saturated or unsaturated, depending on the proportions of fatty acids present. Butter, for instance, is usually thought of as a saturated fat because it consists of 60–65 per cent saturated and 30–35 per cent unsaturated fat. Within the unsaturated category are two types of fats – monounsaturated and polyunsaturated.

The human body is able to produce saturated and monounsaturated fatty acids, but not some types of polyunsaturated fatty acids. Some of these, however, are essential for good health; the only way we can obtain these is through our diet. These are called essential fatty acids, usually referred to as omega-3 and omega-6 – and they are polyunsaturated. Omega-3 fatty acids (alpha-linolenic acid, eicosapentaenoic acid/EPA and docosahexaenoic acid/DHA) and omega-6 fatty acids (linoleic acid, gamma-linolenic acid and arachidonic acid) are, among others, an integral part of all cell membranes. The brain and the nervous system mainly consist of these essential fatty acids, which provide electrical insulation for the nerves in the brain and for the synapses (connections) between nerves, allowing rapid communication between them.

Depression and many disorders of the nervous system, including multiple sclerosis, are linked to a low intake of omega-3 fatty acids. Omega-6 fatty acids, though essential, are consumed in far greater quantities than necessary in the modern world. Western diets generally are too high in omega-6 and too low in omega-3, and this imbalance promotes chronic inflammation, the cause of many painful and life-threatening disorders (see chapter 7).

What kind of fat do you need?

What you need is mostly unsaturated fat, both monounsaturated and polyunsaturated. What you do not need too much of is saturated fat. What you do not need at all are industrially-produced trans fats (trans fatty acids): these are man-made fats, also known as hydrogenated (or partially hydrogenated) vegetable oils and fats. They are found in many margarines, vegetable shortenings and yellow fat spreads, and are widely used in the food industry. The vast majority of ready-made foods contain significant amounts of trans fats so always check the labels and avoid foods that list 'partially hydrogenated (vegetable) fat' among the ingredients.

If you look at where in nature these different fatty acids are found, you can classify them in terms of animal fat and vegetable fat. Vegetable fat generally contains a high proportion of unsaturated fatty acids (both monounsaturated and polyunsaturated). There are exceptions, however: coconut oil is extremely high in saturated fat, but is still quite a healthy food. Our biggest source of vegetable fat is plant oils, nuts and avocados.

Animal fat is found in milk, meat, butter, cheese and egg yolks – and a large proportion of this fat is saturated. As well as animal sources, coconut milk and cocoa butter (found in chocolate) mainly contain saturated fat. Moderate

ESSENTIAL FATS

Bear in mind that all natural fat sources contain a mix of saturated, monounsaturated and polyunsaturated fat – it is the proportions of the different types that vary. By using cold-pressed oils and eating a handful of raw nuts and seeds every day, as well as eating oily fish three or four times a week and 1 to 2 teaspoons of cod liver oil every day, you will be doing a lot to secure your intake of essential fats.

amounts of butter and cheese will not do you any harm; it is when saturated fats are eaten to excess, as part of a high glycaemic diet, that problems arise.

Fish is an exception, because oily fish is very rich in polyunsaturated fatty acids. Salmon, mackerel, sardines and herring are oily fish, and contain a lot of omega-3 fatty acids, which are very beneficial and actually essential to health. But not all fish is high in fat: white-fleshed fish such as cod and sole are pretty lean. Some foods from the plant world – for example, flaxseeds – are also rich in omega-3 fatty acids.

Another naturally-occurring fatty acid, CLA (conjugated linoleic acid), has had a lot of attention recently, as it may have a positive effect on the burning of fat and on our immune systems. It is found in small amounts in grass-fed beef, lamb and goat meat, and dairy products from grass-fed cows, sheep and goats. Substantial research has been carried out, and is still ongoing, into the potential health effects of CLA. It is too early to say whether there is any health benefit to be gained from supplemental CLA, therefore I recommend you get your CLA directly from food.

Omega-9, monounsaturated fat

Almonds, avocados, Brazil nuts, cashew nuts, hazelnuts, macadamia nuts, olives, peanuts, pecan nuts and pistachio nuts are very rich in omega-9, monoun-saturated fat. This should be the type of fat you eat most of. Olive oil, rape-seed (canola) oil and groundnut (peanut) oil contain mainly monounsaturated fat. Extra virgin olive oil contains natural antioxidants that make this oil unique in terms of both taste and health benefits. Rapeseed (canola) oil has a more neutral taste and includes omega-3 fatty acids, which are not found in olive oil, as well as specific plant sterols (substances that reduce cholesterol) and antioxidants.

Always look for oils labelled 'virgin' or 'cold-pressed', which means they are are as natural as possible and have not been refined using heat or chemicals. Cold-pressed hazelnut and avocado oils have a delicate flavour that is perfect for salads and vegetables. Groundnut (peanut) oil, while it can be cold-pressed, is generally highly refined using high temperatures and chemical solvents, so should be avoided. Other oils high in monounsaturated fat are the so-called high oleic sunflower and safflower oils, which can be used in place of olive oil. These are not to be confused with the regular sunflower and safflower oils, which are very high in omega-6 and almost always refined.

Omega-6, polyunsaturated fat

Corn, evening primrose, grape seeds, hempseeds, pumpkin seeds, sesame seeds, soya beans, sunflower and safflower seeds are all high in omega-6 polyunsaturated fat. Over the past 50 or so years, our diet in the western world has gradually become too high in omega-6 fatty acids and too low in omega-3s, due to a high consumption of vegetable margarines and refined plant oils and the demonization of saturated fat. This imbalance is causing serious health problems. We should be getting only two to four times more omega-6 than omega-3 in our diet, but we get as much as 20 to 30 times more omega-6.

Most of the oils that you find in the supermarket are refined, i.e. they have been processed at high temperatures and subjected to extensive use of chemicals. Consequently, these oils contain varying levels of many toxic by-products. If you use oil for frying only now and again, it is hardly very dangerous, because your body can handle the toxins. However, if you consume these oils every day, as many people who eat fast food or pre-packaged foods do, the toxins will accumulate in your cells and can trigger illnesses such as heart disease and cancer. These oils are also often used in the production of margarine, and this further processing produces harmful trans fatty acids, which can cause a range of health problems, including heart disease.

Switch from using sunflower, corn, soya and other refined oils and margarines to cold-pressed or extra-virgin oils – mainly olive oil and rapeseed (canola) oil – and avoid eating fried foods too frequently. However, you do not need to avoid the natural raw nuts and seeds that these oils are extracted from.

Omega-3, polyunsaturated fat

Most of us get too little omega-3 fatty acids in relation to omega-6 fatty acids, and should increase our intake. The best source of omega-3 fatty acids is oily fish such as salmon, sardines, mackerel, herring and tuna, as well as cod liver oil (as a supplement). The omega-3 essential fatty acids found in fish oil are eicosapentaenoic acid (EPA) and docosahexaenoic acid (DHA), and the body can use these immediately, whereas omega-3 from plant sources (alpha linolenic acid, or ALA) first has to be transformed in the body to EPA and DHA.

Flaxseed is the richest source of omega-3 in the plant world, with as much as 58 per cent health-friendly omega-3 fatty acids (ALA). Seven per cent of the fat in rapeseed and soya beans and five per cent of the fat in walnuts is omega-3 ALA; in pumpkin seeds the amount of omega-3 fatty acids varies from 0 to 15 per cent of the total fat content.

Omega-3s are important for the formation of red blood cell pigment (haemoglobin) and for proper cell growth and division and normal wound healing. They are also required for protein metabolism, and to transport and metabolize minerals, thus helping to maintain strong bones.

An optimal supply of omega-3s also has important benefits for the heart. Both omega-3 and omega-6 fatty acids are necessary for the transport of cholesterol in the body. However, omega-3s can lower high blood triglycerides by 65 per cent – better than drugs and without side effects. They can prevent life-threatening arrhythmias, thus reducing the risk of sudden death from heart attack. They also act as mild blood thinners by making platelets less sticky, thus reducing the risk of blood clots, which cause heart attack and stroke.

Sixty per cent of our brain is made of fat, and one third of that is omega-3 and omega-6 (in the ratio 1:1). The foetus needs omega-3 in order for the brain to develop and depends on its mother's omega-3 supply; hence pregnant women with insufficient omega-3 in their diet may give birth to children with learning difficulties. Omega-3 depletion in pregnancy is also a major cause of post-natal depression. Omega-3s can also help children with learning problems – an increased intake can help them learn faster and focus better. Research shows that intelligence (defined as the ability to learn) may increase with an adequate supply of omega-3s. And the benefits don't stop there – omega-3s lift depression and elevate mood. In addition, recent research has shown that an increase in omega-3 intake can reduce the severity of symptoms of schizophrenia. Omega-3s have also been found to improve cognitive function in sufferers of Alzheimer's disease and senile dementia, and multiple sclerosis and Parkinson's disease have both been found to respond positively to a high omega-3 intake.

Omega-3s have important benefits in other areas too. They can help to prevent leaky gut syndrome and food allergies. They improve bowel flora (beneficial bacteria) and have a positive effect on irritable bowel disease, Crohn's disease and ulcerative colitis. They also satisfy hunger and suppress appetite and help prevent addictions to – and reduce withdrawal symptoms from – foods, cigarettes, alcohol and drugs.

Omega-3s also reduce the formation of histamines and other inflammatory-response mechanisms. (You will find more information on this subject in the section on inflammatory conditions – a major cause of ill-health – beginning on page 101.) They are also very beneficial for our joints and reduce the symptoms of rheumatoid arthritis.

Omega-3s and omega-6s are also very important for the human reproductive system in both men and women, and can prevent premenstrual syndrome (partly because of the anti-inflammatory properties of omega-3 fatty acids).

Omega-3s protect our cells from dehydration, so they are excellent 'edible cosmetics', making the skin soft, smooth and velvety. Dry skin is often a good indicator of a deficiency of omega-3s, and we need more of these fats during the winter.

Finally, omega-3s protect genetic material (DNA) from damage. Our cells use omega-3 and omega-6 fatty acids to make 'oxygen bullets' to kill infectious invaders like bacteria and viruses. By boosting our immune system, omega-3s also inhibit tumour growth.

Saturated fat

Many people eat more fat than they need, much of it in the form of saturated fats, from full-fat dairy products (milk, butter, cream and cheese), meat, cakes, biscuits and pastries. We also get a lot of highly processed fat through cooking – from fried foods, sauces and gravies.

One of the biggest sources of saturated fat in the body, however, is carbohydrates like sugar, white bread, potatoes, rice and pasta. If you are not physically active, your body cannot use the energy from these carbohydrates, so it transforms sugars and starches into saturated fat and stores it in the body. This process is controlled by the hormone insulin, which rises quickly when you eat high-glycaemic carbohydrates.

Fast food items, such as hamburgers, pizza and sandwiches with margarine or butter, cheese and ham, are worse still: not only do they contribute a great deal of fat, but the fat is combined with high-glycaemic carbohydrates. For people with a predisposition to increased insulin production and insulin resistance, this is the quickest way to obesity, diabetes and cardiovascular disorders!

Why does saturated fat have such a bad reputation? Well, many people have a mental picture of it literally clogging the arteries, but it is not that simple. An excess of saturated fat in the diet, combined with lack of exercise, contributes to a higher level of LDL cholesterol (the 'bad' form of cholesterol) in the blood. As LDL cholesterol passes through the arteries it can become trapped in lesions on the artery walls, creating the fatty plaque that blocks arteries. Here, the cholesterol is prone to damage (oxidation), which further damages the arteries. Smoking, stress, low intake of antioxidants (from vegetables, nuts, pulses, fruits and berries etc.) and a high intake of high-glycaemic carbohydrates have all been shown to increase oxidation in the body.

The saturated fat found in red meat and egg yolks also contains arachidonic acid, an omega-6 fatty acid. An excess of arachidonic acid causes the formation of inflammatory substances that can lead to high blood pressure, an increased tendency to blood coagulation and risk of thrombosis, and various inflammatory conditions. For more on arachidonic acid see page 104.

An excess of saturated fat also indirectly increases the level of insulin in the blood, because it affects the cell membranes in muscle cells, making them less flexible and more insulin resistant.

How much fat do you need?

A minimum of 30 per cent of your total energy intake should derive from healthy, minimally-processed fat. For an inactive person who weighs around 70kg (11st) this means about 60–75 grams of fat a day, or the equivalent of 4–5 tablespoons. Divided among four to five meals a day, we are obviously talking about moderate amounts. Quantities are not large because fat contains so much energy per gram. Around 2 per cent of this fat should derive from omega-3 fatty acids (oily fish, or vegetable sources such as flaxseed and nuts); 3 to 6 per cent should derive from omega-6 fatty acids (found in most vegetable oils, such as sunflower oil, and most nuts). Not more than 10–15 per cent should derive from saturated fat (animal fat, dairy products, chocolate) and the rest, the biggest part, should come from monounsaturated fat (olive oil, rapeseed/canola oil, almonds, avocados).

If you are a very physically active person and your energy requirement is, say, 4000 calories a day, you should increase the amount of fat accordingly (making sure it is mostly unsaturated fat). Athletes sometimes make the mistake of eating too little fat and too much carbohydrate, which has a negative effect on their performance and recovery.

Too little polyunsaturated fat (especially omega-3 fat), in particular, can be harmful to your health and will also make it difficult to lose weight.

Fibre

Although dietary fibre (an indigestible form of carbohydrate) contributes little energy, it plays a very important role in human health. Almost all the fibre that we get from our diet comes from vegetables, fruit, pulses, grains and nuts. There are two main types of fibre: soluble and insoluble. Soluble fibre ensures the proper digestion of nutrients, and means the bowels absorb carbohydrates more slowly and thus blood sugar rises at a steadier level over a longer period of time. Soluble fibre also lowers cholesterol and is prebiotic, i.e. it supports good intestinal health. Soluble fibre is found in beans and lentils, oats, vegetables and fruit. Non-soluble dietary fibre, which is found in whole grains, increases the volume of food and aids bowel function. It is also believed that the fibre in our diet can prevent some forms of cancer, such as colon cancer, but this might also be due to other substances in fruit and vegetables.

The modern diet contains considerably less fibre than that of our Stone Age ancestors. Most people in the western world consume less than 20g of fibre daily. The official recommendation is 20–30g daily. By following the Greek Doctor's Diet, you will be getting an average of 34g of fibre daily. An easy way to increase your intake of dietary fibre is to eat two fruits and at least three to four servings of vegetables a day. Eating lentils and beans instead of potatoes and bread, for example, will also increase the amount of fibre in your diet. Remember that when you increase the amount of fibre in your diet, you should also increase your water intake, to ensure regular bowel function.

Some foods have added dietary fibre. Examples include fibre-enriched yogurt, bread and pasta, in which inulin or another type of dietary fibre replaces some of the flour or sugar. Inulin is a natural fibre extracted from chicory, and it is now being used in a variety of foods in order to increase their fibre content. Such foods are commonly referred to as 'functional foods', because something that is not normally found in the product has been added in order to provide a beneficial effect.

Vitamins and minerals

Vitamins and minerals are present in food in minuscule amounts, but they are essential for good health. Their role is to enable numerous chemical reactions to take place within the body, and we are likely to become ill if we do not consume an adequate amount of vitamins and minerals. Among other things, they control the metabolism of carbohydrates, fats and proteins, and regulate the production of hormones such as insulin.

Vitamins A and D (found in oily fish and dairy products) and E and K (found in many vegetables, nuts and seeds) are fat-soluble vitamins. Vitamin A can also be made in the body from carotenoids, pigments found in many vegetables. Vitamin D is made in the skin when it is exposed to sunlight.

B group vitamins (found in meat, fish, yeast and whole grains) and vitamin C (found in vegetables and fruit) are water-soluble vitamins and are easily lost during food preparation upon exposure to heat, water, light and air. Processed foods (frozen vegetables and fruit being an honourable exception) are therefore likely to be low in these essential nutrients.

In many instances, vitamins and minerals (such as iron, calcium, magnesium and zinc) work together in the body. Yogurt, for example, is a good source of calcium and B vitamins, but adequate amounts of vitamin D, K and magnesium are just as important as calcium in order to secure good bone density.

A varied and well-balanced diet, in which no single food is eaten to excess, should ensure you have all the vitamins and minerals you need for weight control and good health. However, in the modern world, despite the seemingly wide variety of foods available in our shops, many people do not get enough variety in their diets – particularly when it comes to fruit, nuts, pulses and vegetables. How many of us can truly say we eat the recommended minimum of five portions of vegetables and fruit a day? In addition, nutrients have been processed out of many everyday foods, and fruit and vegetables often lose a high percentage of their vitamins during their journey from the tree or earth to our tables.

Excessive amounts of certain foods, particularly refined carbohydrates, can deplete your vitamin and mineral stores. Equally, if you eat refined, processed food that lacks vitamins and minerals, or food with many artificial additives, your metabolism will suffer and produce more toxic waste than the body can get rid of. The situation will be even worse if the body is attacked daily by harmful substances (environmental toxins) found in polluted air or water, tobacco, chemicals or radiation. Sometimes we have to put back what the modern world takes out, so I am not entirely against food supplements. For more details, see chapter 10.

CHAPTER 3

YOU ARE WHAT YOU DRINK

The bewitching wine, which sets even a wise man to singing and rouses him up to dance and brings forth words which were better unspoken.
Homer, 800 – 700BC, *The Odyssey*

'To your health' is a common toast in many cultures, yet few people are fully aware of the enormous importance of what – and how much – we drink for our health and well-being. However, our bodies are made of water and food, and it would be foolish to ignore the quality and quantity of what we drink. Around 60 to 70 per cent of our body consists of a lightly salty fluid, with a composition resembling that of ocean water, which gave birth to primordial life. All our cells and organs contain significant amounts of this fluid, the intracellular fluid, and are surrounded by extracellular fluids, such as blood and lymph fluid. The myriad substances needed to sustain life are transported through these liquid avenues. Almost all metabolic reactions in the body require water, and most toxic by-products of our metabolism are excreted in sweat or, via the kidneys, in urine, with water as their carrier. Burning the food we eat to produce energy requires water as well: roughly a litre of fluid for every 1000 calories metabolized. With an average energy requirement of between 2000 and 2500 calories a day, 2 to 2.5 litres (about eight glasses) of water are needed. But it is important to remember that when you deliberately restrict your calorie intake in order to lose weight, you still need the same amount of fluid to burn stored calories and ensure proper excretion of toxic by-products.

Water

Drinking water is by far the most important source of fluids for our bodies. Fruits and vegetables also provide fluid, together with many vitamins and minerals and other micronutrients. If you eat a lot of bread, rice, pasta, potatoes, sugar and meat, and fewer vegetables and fruits, you may be depriving your body of enough fluid.

Weather conditions have a great impact on our daily fluid requirement. We lose a substantial amount of fluid through sweat, in addition to that which we lose every time we exhale. When ambient temperatures rise, so does the need for water. Anything that increases your metabolic rate, i.e. physical exercise and food, increases your fluid requirements as well. The same is true when you have a fever or raised temperature due to an infection.

One of the most common questions I get asked in my clinical practice is what one should drink to remain healthy. The answer should be obvious. No other animal drinks anything but pure water, and that is what we should drink. Like oil to a car engine, it is essential to our body.

How much we actually need to remain healthy depends on our basal metabolic rate (women burn in general fewer calories than men), our level of exercise, the ambient temperature, and the type and amount of foods we eat. You should also be aware of the fact that some drinks, such as coffee, black tea, cola and other carbonated drinks, can have a diuretic effect, so you may need to compensate for this with extra water – in order to maintain your fluid balance. However, we do not need to calculate the exact amount we should drink: 2 litres, or eight glasses, is a minimum for most adults; if you're thirsty, drink more water.

Public water supplies in industrialized countries are generally safe, although the amount of chlorine may affect the taste of the water; if this is the case in your area, you may prefer to drink bottled mineral water. Bottled water does not necessarily guarantee quality, since far from all bottled water comes from the unspoiled natural sources portrayed in the advertisements. Water can be a a significant source of minerals for the body. Water from different sources carries different minerals, but in general it contains magnesium, calcium, sodium and potassium. In some parts of the world water is a major source of calcium, which explains why most people do not need to consume milk in adulthood.

Fruit juice

Is juice a healthy drink? Well, fresh fruit juice does supply you with vitamins, minerals and some fibre. A glass of juice a day should not be a problem for most people, unless you are very insulin-resistant, diabetic or obese. Drinking juice instead of water is not a good idea, however, since juice is high in simple sugars and calories. You get roughly the same amount of calories from 350ml of unsweetened orange juice as from two eggs or 150g of natural yogurt, either of which are much more satisfying and balanced choices. Remember: it is far healthier to eat one or two portions of fruit a day than to drink a glass of their juice. You should eat your calories, not drink them.

Recent research has found that drinking juice or other soft drinks does not give the same satiety signals (feeling of fullness) as solid food. This means that many people don't eat less to take account of the extra calories in the juice they drink, and thus increase their risk of weight gain.

Grapefruit juice is often considered particularly appropriate for slimmers. I should point out that although it is fine in moderation, grapefruit juice has been shown to increase substantially the risk of kidney stones. Another thing to bear in mind is that, for unknown reasons, grapefruit juice interferes with the way some people absorb and metabolize certain medications, listed below.

Drug (brand name)	Indication
Fenofenadine (Telfast)	Allergies
Digoxin (Lanoxin)	Heart failure, dysrhythmia (irregular heartbeat)
Losartan (Cozaar)	High blood pressure
Vinblastine	Cancer
Calcium channel blockers e.g Nifedipine (Adalat), Felodipine (Plendil)	High blood pressure, angina pectoris
Carbamazepine (e.g. Tegretol)	Epilepsy
Statins (e.g. Lescol, Lipitor, Zocor)	High cholesterol, prevention of heart disease
Cyclosporine	Immunosuppressant
Buspirone (Buspar)	Anxiety, panic attacks

Soft drinks

What about sweetened and/or carbonated drinks? From an evolutionary perspective, humans and animals alike are designed to drink water and no other drinks, certainly not the sugar-loaded soft drinks of modern times.

Did you know that a 330ml can of cola or similar sugar-sweetened drink contains between six and nine teaspoons of sugar? Did you know that the total of our normal blood sugar is a mere teaspoon? Now consider that many people – even children – consume at least three or four cans (well over a litre) of these drinks every day; that's 18 to 36 teaspoons of sugar a day! In the US, the average consumption of soft drinks is 200 litres per person per year. Ireland and Norway hold second and third place in soft drink consumption after the US. These drinks supply our bodies with a huge number of calories and no other nutritional benefits; they do not even give a feeling of fullness, but they represent an extreme glycaemic load. New research from the US has concluded that there is a strong relationship between the amount of sugar-sweetened soft drinks consumed and the risk of developing diabetes and syndrome X, or insulin resistance. In children there is a clear relationship between the consumption of soft drinks and overweight. That is in addition to the fact that sugar is bad for your teeth.

How about sugar-free/calorie-free soft drinks? Well, if you must consume soft drinks, choosing those without sugar/energy is definitely a better deal, but still not the ideal choice, which is water. Several sugar substitutes and alternative sweeteners exist and some of them, in particular saccharin and aspartame, have been accused of causing all kinds of health problems. These accusations are as yet unsubstantiated, but we do not know what effects a high consumption of such substances may have after several years of daily use, so try to keep your consumption low. This is especially important for children. On the other hand, most of the sugar-free and calorie-free drinks contain a mixture of several sweeteners, so at least our intake of each one is reduced.

Few people realize that most soft drinks (even the sugar-free variety) have a high level of acidity. This may reduce the calcium in your bones, since the body uses calcium in order to neutralize pH; in turn, this increases your risk of osteoporosis.

Some types of fizzy drinks may also contain a large amount of salt (sodium), which can pose a problem for people with high blood pressure or heart disorders.

Milk

Surely milk is a healthy drink, if the numerous advertising campaigns can be believed? Is it essential for health, or could a high consumption be harmful?

From an evolutionary perspective, we can see that milk was not part of the human diet before the domestication of cattle some 10,000 years ago. This means that during several million years of human evolution, we did not include milk in our diets, other than mother's milk. No other animal drinks milk from another species after its own lactation period is over. Tolerating lactose (milk sugar) in adolescence or adult life is in fact a pretty recent mutation, more common among the Caucasian population, and most frequent in northern Europe. Lactose intolerance is present in 80 per cent of the earth's population, but around 80 per cent of Scandinavians do tolerate lactose, which explains the very high milk consumption in those countries. We can easily conclude that humans can remain healthy without consuming cow's milk or other types of milk. After all, 1.2 billion people in China manage without dairy products.

But hey, isn't milk meant to be an important source of calcium, necessary in order to prevent osteoporosis? Well, judging from the frequency of osteoporosis in Scandinavia, it has not helped much, since these countries have the highest prevalence of osteoporosis in the world, despite their high milk consumption. The Chinese, on the other hand, experience little osteoporosis despite zero consumption of dairy products. The answer to the increasing rate of osteoporosis should thus be sought elsewhere.

The importance of calcium intake for the prevention of osteoporosis is exaggerated. Our bodies maintain a fine calcium balance, depending not only on how much calcium is taken in, but also on how much is excreted. To maintain a healthy calcium balance, one should not only increase the intake, but also the uptake, and reduce the excretion rate of calcium. In order to absorb calcium from our food we need vitamin D, which is produced in the body as a result of exposure to sunlight. In order for our bones to retain calcium they need vitamin K, which is produced in our intestines by the good bacteria there and is also found in green leafy vegetables. The combination of low sunshine exposure and low consumption of vegetables in northern latitudes, as well as declining levels of physical activity and increased consumption of acidic soft drinks, is a more likely explanation for the prevalence of osteoporosis in northern Europe than a lack of calcium. Healthy vitamin D and K levels and regular 'weight-bearing' exercise are far better strategies to prevent osteoporosis.

Milk and dairy products are far from the only sources of dietary calcium, but they are indeed the most efficient, since their calcium content is high and easily absorbable. Other good calcium sources include figs, tofu, soya beans and other beans, spinach, broccoli, mustard greens, butternut squash, oats and even water, although its calcium content varies greatly from source to source. By getting your calcium from a variety of sources, you will ensure that you get a broad spectrum of micronutrients.

Recently a lot of interest has been generated by research indicating that increased intake of calcium *and* dairy products may actually contribute to a leaner body. It is not yet known whether this is the effect of calcium in general or a combination of calcium and other substances found in milk and dairy products – such as protein or CLA (conjugated linoleic fatty acids, found naturally in milk fat when cattle are grass fed).

Can you consume too much calcium? It seems you can. New evidence links excessive calcium intake with an increased risk of developing prostate cancer (men) and ovarian cancer (women). Although we lack conclusive proof, it would be prudent to avoid excessive amounts of calcium.

Despite what you may have heard, it has never been shown that there is a relationship between dairy fat and an increased risk of heart disease. The fat found in dairy products does contain a large proportion of saturated fatty acids. In particular, three saturated fatty acids in milk and dairy products (those with 12, 14 and 16 carbon atoms) are known to increase the levels of blood cholesterol, both the 'bad' LDL-cholesterol and, to a lesser extent, the 'good' HDL-cholesterol. But increased cholesterol does not necessarily increase your risk of heart disease. The English and French have similar cholesterol levels on a population basis and a similar breakdown of good and bad cholesterol, but the French have four times less heart disease than the English. Almost half of all heart attack patients have high cholesterol while the other half have normal or low cholesterol. Heart disease is primarily an inflammatory disease *not* a 'cholesterol' disease. A recent study in Sweden showed that there was in fact an inverse association between the consumption of milk and dairy products and heart disease.

The conclusion is that although they are not essential for good health, dairy products in moderation can form part of a balanced diet, as long as your body tolerates them. Milk and other dairy products are a source of high-quality protein and several vitamins and minerals, including calcium. Cultured milk products like yogurt are also a source of probiotic bacteria that contribute to intestinal health. It is better to eat yogurt, cottage cheese, quark, fromage frais and low- or medium-fat cheese rather than drinking a lot of milk. Not only does milk contain a significant amount of sugar (lactose) but, being a liquid, it does not supply the same satiety as cultured and solid dairy alternatives. Remember that cow's milk is not a food item like any other: it has been designed by nature as the perfect first food for calves, not the ideal food for humans.

Coffee

Is coffee healthy or not? As always, there is no easy answer. Coffee contains several bioactive substances, apart from caffeine, and may have positive or negative effects.

Coffee is a source of antioxidants, and a significant source in some countries – Spain and Norway being good examples. However, the reason for this is not that coffee is a very rich source of antioxidants, but simply that it is consumed in such large quantities. Among other positive findings are that coffee drinkers suffer less asthma, and that caffeine (from all sources) is associated with a lower risk of developing Parkinson's disease. A study from Scotland also found that coffee drinkers had a lower risk of heart disease. However, this contrasts with the findings of a Norwegian study, which concluded that coffee drinking was associated with higher mortality from heart disease, but not a greater risk of getting heart disease.

Coffee has also been found to increase homocystein levels in the blood, which can increase the risk of Alzheimer's and cardiovascular disorders (an increased intake of folic acid and vitamins B6 and B12 may counteract this effect). Coffee has also been shown to impair fertility among non-smoking women. In addition, it contains acrylamide, a potentially carcinogenous substance that forms when coffee beans are roasted.

Taking all this into consideration it seems wise to heed the wisdom of the Ancient Greeks, who said *Pan métron áriston*, meaning moderation is best. Do not drink more than one or two cups of regular coffee a day. You may also want to use decaffeinated coffee instead of regular coffee or to mix them together and gradually increase the amount of decaffeinated coffee until you drink only that. There are plenty of good decaffeinated coffees to choose from, and the taste is equally good, because caffeine has no taste. Also remember that caffeine is very addictive – the same way sugar is.

Tea

Few people will have failed to notice the promotion of tea as a healthier alternative to coffee over the past few years. All tea plants belong to the same species – *Camellia sinensis* – but local growing conditions vary, resulting in an array of distinctive leaves. However, it is the way the leaves are processed that results in the characteristics of the three main types of tea: green, black and oolong. Green tea is the least processed and provides the most antioxidants. Black tea is fermented before drying and oolong is lightly fermented.

Green tea is particularly rich in healthy antioxidants of the polyphenol and flavonoid family, including catechins and their derivatives. Catechins have been found to be more powerful antioxidants than vitamins C and E. The most abundant catechin in green tea is thought to play a crucial role in green tea's anti-cancer and antioxidant effects. Green tea drinkers seem to have a lower risk of a wide range of diseases, from simple bacterial and viral infections to chronic degenerative conditions, including cardiovascular disease, cancer, stroke, periodontal (gum) disease and osteoporosis.

Green tea is without doubt a much better choice than coffee, but it is also preferable to black tea, which contains caffeine and does not have the wide range of benefits of green tea.

Alcohol

Alcohol consumption is often a topic of moral debate. When it comes to alcohol and health, many people have a biased view one way or another. In many countries, certainly in Europe and the US, there is a tendency to advise people to greatly reduce their alcohol consumption or not to drink alcohol at all.

It is true that the overconsumption of alcohol represents a public health hazard and causes many preventable deaths in industrialized countries, both because it is implicated in many traffic accidents and because it loosens inhibitions, which may lead to risk-taking or violence. Alcohol also increases the risk of liver cirrhosis and liver cancer. Too much alcohol over long periods of time causes both the brain and the heart muscle to deteriorate, leading to dementia and heart failure and increasing the risk of certain types of stroke.

Alcohol itself is toxic, but our liver can handle small amounts at a time without much difficulty. However, if you drink more than one or two units a day – or larger quantities over the weekend, as many people do – your liver will not be able to cope as efficiently. A high consumption of alcohol means that you are continually poisoning your body: this can damage your liver, heart and most other organs as well, including the brain. Pregnant women should avoid alcohol because of the potential damage to the developing organs of the foetus. Having said that, the occasional glass of wine during pregnancy is not a crime.

Alcohol contributes to obesity because the liver's fat-burning ability is impaired: as long as there is alcohol in the blood, the liver prefers to burn alcohol rather than fat. Drinking alcohol and eating fatty foods during the same meal means your liver is trying to do two jobs at once: it deals with alcohol as a priority and stores fat in its 'in-tray' to deal with later. Alcohol also contributes to obesity because it supplies 'empty' calories (in other words they contain no nutritional benefit). If you drink too much alcohol, seldom exercise, and eat unhealthy foods (a combination that is not entirely uncommon), you will increase your risk of developing lifestyle diseases.

Is there anything positive to say about alcohol? Of course there is. Alcohol is a natural substance present in small amounts in overripe fruits and berries, and our bodies have the necessary enzymes to deal with it and make use of the energy it contains. Wine was consumed by the ancient Greeks during their feasts, or *symposia*, which literally means 'drinking together'. Most of us have experienced the relaxed feeling we get enjoying a glass of wine with good food among friends, and this contributes to our well-being.

More importantly, moderate alcohol consumption has some more direct positive effects on human health. It has been proved that one or two alcoholic drinks a day – here we are talking about one or two units of alcohol, the equivalent of one glass of wine for women and two for men – can substantially reduce the risk of heart disease, ischaemic strokes (blood clots in the brain arteries) and diabetes. For men the risk reduction is about 30–40 per cent, which is as much as the expensive and widely used modern statin drugs (which are anti-inflammatory and reduce blood cholesterol at the same time). Women have almost the same risk reduction; however, there is evidence that premenopausal women also see a small increase in their risk of breast cancer if they consume more than one alcoholic drink a day, unless they compensate by increasing their intake of folic acid. As premenopausal women are advised to take a folic acid supplement anyway, this is another good reason for such supplementation. The beneficial effect of alcohol in terms of heart disease, stroke and diabetes is more relevant in middle-aged and older people, who are at greater risk of these diseases.

One or two alcoholic drinks may also substantially increase levels of beneficial HDL-cholesterol, in fact more than exercise does, but exercise has so many other positive health effects (see Chapter 6) that there is no excuse to skip it for a drink.

It is alcohol itself that creates these health benefits, not just wine. Red wine contains certain antioxidants (also present in grapes, by the way), substances that protect our cells against premature ageing and disease, but it has not been proved that these have a substantial effect on protection against heart disease compared to the effect of alcohol in general.

In terms of alcohol consumption, the key word is moderation. Obviously, if you are unable to limit yourself to one or two alcoholic drinks a day, then you would be better off quitting altogether. As alcohol intake increases, mortality from heart disease declines, but all other causes of death increase, slowly to begin with, then sharply. 'Optimal' alcohol intake depends on gender, age, intake of folic acid and other factors, such as genetic make-up. In general, men should limit their intake to two drinks a day and women to one.

The bottom line? Keep your alcohol consumption to a moderate level, if you already enjoy drinking it. If you don't, don't feel you have to start. There are many other ways to decrease your risk of heart disease, diabetes and stroke – exercise, a healthy diet, less stress and not smoking being top of the list.

Remember: there's no better drink than water!

CHAPTER 4

THE SLOW CARB REVOLUTION

he Glycaemic Index and Glycaemic Load are scientific principles that can help you choose the carbohydrates that, coupled with the right proteins and healing fats, will allow your body to maintain a healthy balance and stay naturally slim.

The Glycaemic Index and insulin sensitivity

The Glycaemic Index (GI) ranks carbohydrate foods according to their effect on blood sugar, which is of profound importance for hormonal balance, metabolism, body weight and health. Carbohydrates that are absorbed rapidly and converted into blood sugar have a high GI. Conversely, carbohydrates that are broken down and absorbed slowly have a low GI and cause a less pronounced, more stable rise in blood sugar. It is these 'slow' carbohydrates, with a low GI, that should form the basis of every meal and snack – always balanced by an appropriate amount of protein.

To understand how the Glycaemic Index can help you lose weight and become healthier, you need to understand the connection between GI and the hormone insulin. The production of insulin increases when you eat carbohydrates. Food with a low GI leads to a lower production of insulin. Food with a high GI will lead to a high level of insulin in the blood. The more insulin you have in your blood, the more fat will be stored, and consequently you will burn less fat.

Besides making it almost impossible to lose weight, too much insulin can also result in long-term damage to your body. The more often your body experiences a high level of insulin, the more difficult it becomes for insulin to lower blood sugar. The pancreas tries to compensate for this by secreting more insulin. The more high-glycaemic food you consume, the more insulin your body will produce, and as a result you soon become caught in a vicious circle of hyper-insulinemia (higher insulin production) and reduced insulin sensitivity (insulin resistance). When this happens, your insulin level remains high constantly, whether you have eaten or not. However, it is only the blood-sugar-lowering effect of insulin that has deteriorated. Insulin still continues to promote fat storage. You will gain weight and have a greater risk of developing type II diabetes, high cholesterol levels, high blood pressure and cardiovascular disorders, as well as certain types of cancer.

The Glycaemic Index – a revelation

Dr David Jenkins, professor of nutrition at the University of Toronto, introduced the GI concept in 1981. It was initially used for finding out which foods were most favourable to diabetics. Jenkins wanted to examine the effect of different foods on blood sugar, rather than using lists of carbohydrates measured in grams and the exchange system used by diabetics (this is still being used in the United States and in Germany, for example). He quickly found out that the variations were great, even with seemingly similar foods with the same amount of carbohydrates.

Before the Glycaemic Index was devised, carbohydrates were generally divided into two groups: simple and complex. Simple carbohydrates, or sugars (glucose, fructose, lactose, sucrose, maltose), are made up of one or two sugar molecules. Complex carbohydrates, or starches (found mostly in grain products, potatoes, pasta, beans and lentils) and dietary fibre, consist of many simple sugar molecules chained together. Starches were thought to be digested and absorbed more slowly than sugars, and nutritionists recommended a high consumption of starchy foods and a more restricted use of sweet foods. It has now been found that some foods that are relatively high in simple carbohydrates (e.g fruit) are digested more slowly than many foods that are mainly complex carbohydrates (e.g. bread). With the Glycaemic Index, we are now much better equipped to choose the right kind of carbohydrates in our diet.

Since the 1980s, this method has been tested and applied at renowned universities and research facilities around the world. A joint World Health Organization/ Food and Agriculture Organization of the United Nations expert consultation produced a report on carbohydrates in human nutrition, which recommends the application of the Glycaemic Index as a health-promoting tool. Official dietary guidelines for type II diabetics in Europe, by the European Association for the Study of Diabetes (EASD), also recommend the use of the GI. In Australia, the GI symbol is endorsed by the Australian National Diabetes Foundation and the GI of foods has been used on many food labels since October 2001. In the UK, Germany, the US and South Africa, more and more food products are labelled with their GI as consumer awareness of the advantages of low-glycaemic, 'slow carbs' increases.

What is the Glycaemic Index?

The Glycaemic Index (GI) is a method of ranking foods according to their impact on blood sugar. What determines the GI of a food is how quickly its carbohydrates can be digested and absorbed. The faster they are digested and absorbed by the small intestine, the faster and higher the rise in blood sugar, and the higher the GI. Pure glucose can be absorbed directly into the bloodstream, so it has an immediate effect on blood sugar: on a scale of 0 to 100, glucose has a GI of 100. The GI compares food based on equal carbohydrate content, not equal amount of food: 50g glucose is pure carbohydrate, whereas the GI for carrots is based on the amount of carrots that contains 50g of carbs.

Foods that do not contain carbohydrates do not have a direct influence on blood sugar, consequently their GI is zero. This is why there are no GI numbers for foods that consist primarily of protein, such as eggs, chicken, meat and fish. The same is true of foods that consist mainly of fat, such as butter, margarine and oils. Most non-starchy vegetables have a very low carbohydrate content, usually less then 5 per cent. You would therefore need to eat a lot of tomatoes or celery, for instance, in order to ingest the 50g of carbohydrate needed to measure their GI. For this reason, you will not find the GI of many vegetables in the lists at the back of this book.

A food's GI cannot be predicted; it has to be measured through tests on humans. The test procedure is expensive and demands eight to ten people in a test panel per food. Between six and eight hundred foods have been tested internationally.

I admit that the GI concept can sound a bit complicated, but it's really just a matter of becoming familiar with it. After all, you have heard of calories throughout your adult life; the GI is just another way of finding out which foods are healthiest.

Never judge a book by its cover

The Glycaemic Index can throw up some surprises. Glucose and fructose are both simple sugars. You can compare them gram for gram, because they are both pure carbohydrates. Both taste sweet but, despite the fact that fructose is 100 per cent sweeter than glucose, fructose has a GI of 19, whereas glucose has a GI of 100! So if you eat 50g of glucose, your blood sugar will increase five times more than if you eat the same amount of fructose (see graphs, left).

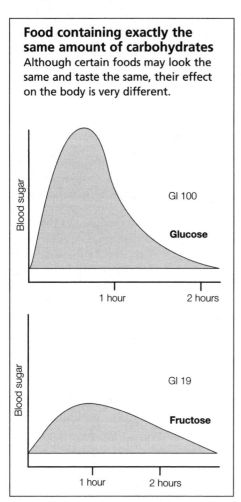

Food containing exactly the same amount of carbohydrates
Although certain foods may look the same and taste the same, their effect on the body is very different.

Blood sugar

GI 100

Glucose

1 hour   2 hours

Blood sugar

GI 19

Fructose

1 hour   2 hours

Mashed red lentils versus mashed potato is another good example. They look almost the same and have a similar taste. However, the lentil mash has a GI of around 30, while the GI of the potato mash is about 90!

What influences the GI?

Carbohydrates: The type of carbohydrates obviously has an impact – for example, sweet foods that are high in fructose have a lower GI than those that are high in glucose. Within plants there are two types of starch: amylose and amylopectin. Foods that are higher in amylose and lower in amylopectin will have a lower GI.

Cooking and processing: Starch changes its structure during cooking and processing, and becomes more easily digestible. Raw carrots, for instance, have a much lower GI than cooked carrots, but do not omit cooked carrots from your diet, as they are relatively low in carbohydrate and you would need to eat a considerable amount before they had a significant effect on your blood sugar.

Protein and fat: As it is only carbohydrates that have a direct influence on blood sugar, foods that combine carbs with protein or fat (such as chocolate) sometimes have a lower GI than foods that contain very little protein or fat (such as watermelon).

Fibre: Foods that are naturally high in soluble fibre, such as beans, lentils, oats and apples, tend to have a medium or low GI. Wholemeal flour and whole grains are preferable to refined flour and grains, which are practically devoid of fibre, although finely milled wholemeal flour has almost the same GI as white flour. In terms of grain flours, it seems that particle size, i.e. the degree of milling, is much more important for their GI than their fibre content. The reason for this is that most cereal grain, apart from oats, contain mostly insoluble fibre, which does not affect GI.

Acidity: Research shows that acid in food (for example, lemon and other citrus fruits, vinegar, sourdough bread) lowers the GI. This justifies all that lemon the Greeks put on their food – and chefs often use a squeeze of lemon juice to heighten the flavour of a sauce. Acid delays the emptying of the stomach and therefore also the absorption of carbohydrates in the intestine, and this leads to a lower GI. So use lemon on salads, squeeze it over grilled fish, vegetables, chicken and meat, and use lemon or vinegar in sauces and salad dressings. For best results, eat a salad with oil and vinegar or lemon dressing before you begin your main course.

Fruit

Many types of fruit have a rather low Glycaemic Index, both because they are high in fibre and because their natural sugar is fructose. Fructose, or fruit sugar, has a very low GI, 19, even though it is the sweetest natural sugar there is (glucose has a GI of 100 and table sugar 68). Bananas and some tropical fruits have relatively high GI, due to their high starch content; therefore you should not eat them as often as fruit with a lower GI such as cherries, strawberries and other berries, grapefruit, plums, peaches, pears, apples, oranges and grapes. But don't be afraid of watermelon: it has a high GI, but its high water content and low carb content means that a wedge of watermelon will not raise your blood sugar too much.

Bread

Whole grains and seeds weigh more than fine flour of comparable volume: the heavier the loaf, the coarser the bread, and the lower the GI. Even the coarsest bread, however, will generally not have a GI below 40–45, which means that bread can range from medium to high glycaemic but can never be low. The type of grain is also important: rye and barley have a lower GI than wheat. The addition of nuts and seeds such as sunflower, sesame, flax and pumpkin will reduce the GI of bread and at the same time add protein, healthy fat and fibre. Sourdough bread has a somewhat lower GI than regular bread, because acidity reduces the GI of foods. When choosing crispbread, look for varieties that contain rye, which has a lower GI than wheat.

Cereals

Corn, and therefore cornflakes, have a very high GI. It is important to find a cereal that has been minimally processed and is unsweetened. Cereals that are high in fibre, such as All-Bran, and unsweetened muesli (with a mixture of grains and seeds) are good choices. Their GI will be even lower if you add milk and berries, chopped almonds or other nuts, ground flaxseeds or soya flakes, and use fructose as a sweetener if you like.

Pasta, bulgur wheat and couscous

Many people are surprised to learn that pasta has a lower GI than bread (between 35 and 50). That is because pasta is normally made from durum wheat (semolina). Durum wheat pasta flour is coarser and contains a little more protein than regular wheat. Wholemeal durum wheat pasta contains more fibre, vitamins and minerals than regular 'white' pasta. The shape of the pasta also matters. Spaghetti has a lower GI than flat pasta, even though the ingredients are the same, because spaghetti is more elastic, and the digestive enzymes cannot break down the starch as quickly. Fresh pasta usually has a higher glycaemic effect than the dried sort.

The less you cook pasta, the lower its GI. Pasta 'al dente', which gives you something to chew on, is better for your blood sugar level than pasta that has been cooked for longer. Some types of pasta have a lower GI than durum wheat pasta. You may come across protein-enriched pasta, to which 20–30 per cent soya protein has been added. Pasta can also be made from other types of grain, such as barley and spelt, and from mung beans (cellophane or glass noodles).

Gluten-free pasta is normally made from corn, which gives it a higher GI.

Bulgur is actually coarsely chopped durum wheat that has been partially pre-cooked and dried; it is very quick to prepare and has a low to medium glycaemic effect. Couscous is a finer variety of bulgur.

Rice

The GI of rice ranges from around 40 to over 100, depending mainly on the type of rice but also on how it is cooked. The colour is less relevant, although brown rice is healthier in other ways, since it is higher in fibre, vitamins and minerals. As a general rule, the stickier the rice is after it has been cooked, the higher its GI. Short-grained, sticky Asian (jasmine and sushi) rice is high in the starch amylopectin, whereas 'parboiled' long-grain (American) rice and basmati rice have lower GI because they contain more of the starch amylose. Parboiled rice is also known as converted rice: it is steamed before it is processed further. Steaming forces the nutrients in the shell and germ into the grain, which enhances its nutritional value. The process also makes the rice less sticky and gives it a lower GI. You will occasionally see rice described as high-amylose, which means it has a lower GI.

Wild rice is not really rice, but the whole grain of a type of grass; it has a pleasant nutty taste, lots of fibre and a medium–low GI of 57.

Is ice cream better than white bread?

Dr Jenkins' findings have caused great interest and controversy ever since the GI concept was first introduced. For example, ice cream has a GI of about 40, while white bread has a GI of about 70. Remember, however, that we are not talking about 50g of bread and 50g of ice cream, but more like 100g (3 slices) of bread and 200g (2 tubs) of ice cream (because ice cream contains fewer carbohydrates per 50g than does bread).

The GI does not tell you anything about the qualities of the food other than its blood sugar impact. Some really unhealthy food is low GI, because fats have no direct effect on blood sugar. Therefore, even though oatmeal has a higher GI than potato crisps, it doesn't mean that the latter is a healthier choice: it is not, since crisps are high in processed fat that contains unhealthy by-products of processing. Chocolate has a lower GI than cooked carrots but it is certainly not healthier.

What is high glycaemic and what is low glycaemic?

As yet, there is no consensus on this matter. I would say that anything above 55 is high, 35 to 55 is medium, and everything below 35 constitutes a low GI. It is important to note that you should not get hung up on the exact GI number. It is much better to instead think of carbohydrates as high, medium or low-glycaemic. As a rule, foods with a low GI are a good choice, but there are always exceptions, especially foods that are high in saturated fat. You should think carefully before you eat food with a high GI (ideally none at all if you wish to lose weight) and stick to food with a medium or, better still, low GI. However, this does not mean you need to become a fanatic. Eating small amounts of a favourite high-GI food as part of your daily reward meal once in a while will not pose a major problem and may actually make it easier to stick to a balanced diet in the long run.

The calculation of GI in a meal

You will find a detailed list of foods and their GI and GL (which we will look at next) at the end of this book. OK, so you can find the GI of carrots. But it is not often that you eat carrots on their own. What really counts is the GI of the whole meal. It is possible to calculate the GI of a meal, provided that the GI and carbohydrate content of the individual components is known, but this is a task better suited to an experienced nutritionist than to the average lay-person.

You can assume that if all the ingredients have a low GI, then the whole meal will too. This is the safe way to go if you want to lose weight. However, it is possible to combine ingredients with a low GI with small amounts of high-GI ingredients and end up with a medium-GI meal.

A practical approach

With the simplified list opposite I want to show you how to interpret GI lists and put them into practice. The first column lists various foods. In the second column, you will see how much of each food you need to eat in order to get 50g of carbohydrates. The GI number (in the third column) is calculated from this amount.

If you eat a large (200g/7oz) baked potato, or a large helping (250g/9oz) of boiled potatoes, your blood sugar will increase substantially.

You can eat 714g (1lb 9oz) of watermelon and have almost the same rise in blood sugar as you would from eating 100g ($3^1/_2$ oz) – about 3 slices – of white bread, since both have a GI of around 70.

If you eat 100g ($3^1/_2$ oz) of potato crisps, your blood sugar level will be three and a half times higher than if you ate 556g (20oz) of peanuts. Both of them contain a high proportion of fat, and I'm not suggesting that you eat half a

GI List

The first column of numbers shows the amount of food (in grams) that contains 50 grams of carbohydrates. The right-hand column shows the Glycaemic Index.

		GI			GI
Jasmine rice	179	109	Fresh peas	500	48
Glucose	50	100	Oat bran bread	125	47
Boiled, peeled potato	250	88	Grapes	313	46
Baked potato	200	85	Orange juice	455	46
Cornflakes	59	81	Oranges	556	42
Boiled, unpeeled potato	357	80	Freshly pressed		
White flour	91	75	apple juice	294	40
Chips/French fries	152	75	Spaghetti, al dente	200	39
Watermelon	714	72	Apples	417	38
Cornflour	57	70	Pears	417	38
White bread	100	70	Vanilla ice cream	200	37
Sugar (sucrose)	50	68	Wholewheat spaghetti	294	37
Cantaloupe melon	833	65	Low-fat yogurt	943	33
Mars Bar	83	65	Butter beans	455	32
Raisins	76	64	Dried apricots	79	31
Sweet potato	250	61	Green beans	1667	29
Basmati rice	217	58	Kidney beans	294	28
Boiled carrots	833	58	Chickpeas, boiled	227	28
Cola	455	58	Whole milk	1000	27
Long-grain white rice	217	56	Red lentils	294	26
Frosted cornflakes	63	55	Grapefruit	500	25
Honey	63	55	Dried peas, boiled	278	22
Digestive biscuits	67	55	Dark chocolate		
Brown rice	217	55	(70% cocoa solids)	156	22
Oat bran	109	55	Cherries	294	22
Potato crisps (chips)	102	54	Fructose	50	19
Peaches	556	53	Raw carrots	714	16
Kiwi fruit	417	53	Peanuts	556	14
Sweetcorn	234	53	Onion	1000	10
Banana	250	52	Garlic	1797	10
Pumpernickel bread	111	50			
Wholewheat bread	106	49			

kilo of peanuts – although there are many people who can get through 100g of crisps. But you get the point. Of the two of them, peanuts are the healthier option, eaten in moderation.

You can use these numbers to see which foods to avoid and which are better for you.

Glycaemic Load – taking the GI a step further

It is tempting to take a Glycaemic Index list and say that all food with a high GI is unhealthy and everything with a low GI is good for you. The truth is always more complicated. As you will by now be aware, the GI is not the only health measure. If it were, cheese, with a GI of 0, would be very healthy, but that is not the case. Furthermore, you cannot say that banana and mango are bad for you, even though their GI is relatively high.

If we concentrate solely on what is good or bad for your blood sugar – ignoring vitamins, minerals and fat for the moment – the amount of carbohydrates eaten is clearly important. However, the GI is a measure of how fast the carbohydrate in any given food raises blood sugar; it says nothing about the amount of carbohydrate in the food, i.e. how much of it you would need to eat to elicit the response suggested by its GI. Remember, the amount of insulin produced is based on the *amount* of carbs as well as how fast they are converted to glucose.

Researchers from Harvard University have therefore come up with the Glycaemic Load (GL). Introduced in 1997, it is gaining increasing recognition as a more accurate way of expressing the glycaemic effect of foods. The GL is, in the same way as the GI, an index ranking foods according to their effect on blood sugar. While GI gives us information on how fast blood sugar rises after we eat 50 grams of digestible carbohydrate in various foods, the GL takes into account both the GI and the amount of carbohydrate in 100g of food or a given portion.

For the sake of comparison, the lists at the end of this book are based on the GL of 100g of food. There, you will see that boiled carrot (which has a high

The difference between GI and GL

Looking at the Glycaemic Load per 100g of food allows you to compare foods in a way that is familiar from the nutrition information labels on many foods.

Food	GI	GL/100g	Food	GI	GL/100g
Glucose	100	100	Baked potato	85	17
Cornflakes	81	70	Spaghetti	39	10
Sugar	68	68	Chickpeas	28	6
Baguette	95	48	Boiled carrots	58	4
Sourdough bread	54	25	Watermelon	72	4
Fructose	19	19	Lentils	26	3

GI) only has a GL of 4, and high-GI watermelon also has a GL of 4. So you see, there is no need to avoid boiled carrot and watermelon even though their GI is high.

The GL of the food you eat

It is equally important to consider the amount one normally eats. To calculate GL, you take a food's GI and multiply it by the amount of carbohydrates, then divide by 100 (because GI is measured as a percentage of glucose, with a GI of 100).

For example, a regular 30g slice of white bread contains 14g of carbohydrate (this information can often be found on the nutrition information label). The GI of white bread is 70. The Glycaemic Load of a slice of white bread can be calculated like this: 70 x 14 ÷ 100 = 10.

Spaghetti has a pretty low GI of 39. A normal size serving of cooked spaghetti might be 180g, which has 47g of carbohydrate. The Glycaemic Load of a serving of spaghetti is therefore 39 x 47 ÷ 100 = 18. Rice and potatoes also have a GL of about 20. So although pasta has a lower GL than white bread per 100 grams, the amount you eat makes a great difference. A regular serving of pasta in fact has a GL almost twice as high as a slice of white bread.

An average day on the Greek Doctor's Diet

We have calculated that a day's eating plan based on the Greek Doctor's Diet will supply 2000 calories (Kcal) and an average GL of 35, whereas a typical 2000-calorie eating plan that includes medium- and high-glycaemic foods at every meal gives a GL of 135 – meaning almost four times the blood sugar load.

Since it is ultimately the total Gycaemic Load of the day that counts – which in turn depends on each meal and meal constituent – we can categorize GL per day as follows:

GL 0–50/2000 kcal/day: low
GL 51–100/2000 kcal/day: medium
GL over 100/2000 kcal/day: high

Following the Greek Doctor's Diet AB/C model and the palm-of-hand method, and using the menu suggestions featured at the back of this book, makes it easy to achieve a low-glycaemic, well-balanced diet – without the need to calculate or count anything.

Same calories, different Glycaemic Load

The following two meals, with a similar calorie content, have very different GL. This shows how small changes in the choice of foods affect the blood sugar and health.

Meal 1			Meal 2		
Food	GI	GL	Food	GI	GL
150g beef	0	0	150g beef	0	0
1 (60g) boiled potato with skin	80	5	180g cooked jasmine rice	109	52
300g kidney beans	28	12	1 tomato	20	0
200g watermelon	72	7	Handful of raisins	64	19
Total		24	Total		71

TEN TIPS TO REDUCE GLYCAEMIC LOAD

- Eat at least three servings of salads and/or vegetables a day.
- Cut the amount of bread, potatoes, pasta and rice you eat.
- Squeeze lemon or lime juice over fish dishes, vegetables and tropical fruit, and use lemon or vinegar in sauces.
- Replace white bread with dense wholegrain bread (preferably made with stoneground flour).
- Eat some protein-rich food with every meal and snack.
- Avoid cakes and biscuits, doughnuts, pastries and other foods made from white flour and sugar.
- Eat a raw vegetable salad with an oil and vinegar or lemon juice dressing before your main meals.
- Reduce the amount of high GI foods you eat and increase the amount of low GI foods.
- Eating low-GI foods like lentils at night reduces the GL of your meals the next day.
- Add some olive oil or a teaspoon of flaxseed oil to soups, salads and savoury dishes just before serving.

CHAPTER 5

HORMONAL BALANCE: THE KEY TO GOOD HEALTH

ow often do you think of hormones while you eat? Well, believe it or not, every time you eat, several hormones are put to work. Throughout evolution, our bodies have adapted in order to digest and metabolize the food we eat, and these functions are part of a complicated system in which hormones play a central part. To a great extent, your choice of food can have a positive or negative effect on this system.

The word hormone is derived from the Greek *hormo*, which means to move quickly toward something. Hormones are chemical substances produced by glands, but they often act far away from the gland that produced them. Hormones are transported from the glands to their target organs through the blood. In one way or another, hormones control almost all bodily functions. Often two or more hormones work together in order to ensure a balance that is essential to good health.

Mention hormones and most people think of sex hormones such as testosterone and oestrogen, or the thyroid hormones. The thyroid, which is situated in the front of the neck, produces several hormones, the most widely known being thyroxin, which is responsible for increasing metabolic rate and controlling growth. However, hormones play many more roles in the body: they regulate blood sugar, salt and energy balance, they affect our appetite and they are crucial to our ability to react to stress and danger signals. Hence an imbalance in hormone production often leads to a health disorder.

But how do hormones work? Basically, they see to it that their target organs produce specific substances, which, in turn, work locally. What are these substances – and the hormones themselves – made from? You guessed it: FOOD. These substances are made up mainly of amino acids (from protein), fatty acids (from polyunsaturated fat) and cholesterol.

Eicosanoids: the body's super-hormones

In 1982, the Nobel Prize for medicine and physiology was awarded to Bengt Samuelsson, Sune Bergstrøm and John Vane, for their contribution to research on a fairly recently discovered group of substances, eicosanoids. These substances are produced locally under the influence of other hormones. Their life span is very short compared to hormones, and their effect is quick and powerful.

One might say that eicosanoids govern the details concerning our health. Our cardiovascular system, our brain and nervous system, and our immune system are all run by eicosanoids. In fact, life without them would be impossible. There are 'good' and 'bad' eicosanoids but, as with everything else in nature, it is the balance between the various eicosanoids that counts. That balance depends on the hormonal balance and this, in turn, depends on a well-balanced diet.

Despite the enormous power of eicosanoids, very few people have heard of them, mainly because this is a fairly new and complicated area of science. However, many of the most common forms of medication work by influencing eicosanoids in one way or another. Prostaglandins, for example, are eicosanoids, and many modern anti-inflammatory medications, such as aspirin and ibuprofen, influence the production of prostaglandins. Eicosanoids play an important role in inflammatory illnesses – for more on this see chapter 7.

Eicosanoids are made up of essential fatty acids (omega-3 and omega-6). Consequently, it is essential that we choose the right kind of fat in our diet. And it is equally important that we eat enough – but not too much, either – of this 'good' fat. (In practice this means concentrating on omega-3 fatty acids, because most of us already eat too much omega-6, and a balanced intake is vital.) But what determines whether 'good' or 'bad' eicosanoids are produced by the body? The answer is hormones such as insulin and glucagon.

Insulin and the blood sugar balance

Insulin is the most important hormone in terms of the metabolism of fat and sugar, and our energy balance. Insulin is produced in the pancreas, which is situated in the abdomen, behind the navel.

Insulin is a vital hormone but, as you should by now be aware, too much insulin is bad for us. Not only will it have a negative effect on your metabolism and make you fat but it will also lead to the production of 'bad' eicosanoids, which will result in deteriorating health.

Insulin ensures that the cells take up blood sugar, our most important energy currency. It is then used immediately, transformed into glycogen (which is stored in the liver for future use), or transformed into fat. The higher the blood sugar, the more insulin the body produces in order to deal with it. The body depends on stable blood sugar levels and in order to keep them stable it uses an intricate system of different hormones, including insulin, glucagon, cortisol, adrenalin and growth hormone, to mention but a few.

How insulin makes you fat

Let us suppose that you eat something like a baguette with cheese or a pizza – food that provides you with carbohydrate (starch) from white flour and fat from cheese. The carbohydrates are quickly broken down in the stomach and in the small intestine into lots of glucose molecules, which are readily absorbed and transformed into blood sugar. This signals the pancreas to secrete insulin (generally, the level of insulin during fasting and before meals is low). If you have not recently been physically active, or exercised while you ate (and how many of us do that?), most of the blood sugar will be stored as fat, especially around the waist. And what about the cheese? Fat from cheese is absorbed in the small intestine in the form of triglycerides (which consist of fatty acids and glycerol). These triglycerides will eventually come in contact with fat cells. Do you think that fat cells automatically store fat? Fat tissue is a very complex organ, and a lot 'smarter' than one would think. It is extremely hormonally active. The fat cells themselves produce a hormone called leptin (see page 70). They also produce an enzyme, lipoprotein lipase (LPL), which is important for fat metabolism. This enzyme 'opens the door' of fat cells to take up fat so that it can be stored. The more LPL that is produced, the more fat will be taken up and the more you will gain weight. And what determines how much LPL is available? INSULIN! Not only is starch from the baguette or the pizza dough converted into blood sugar and then to fat, but both this newly formed fat and the fat from cheese will very quickly be stored as body fat because of the elevated level of insulin. This illustrates why it is so important to avoid having too much insulin in your body and why you should stay clear of the combination of high-gly-caemic carbohydrates and fats such as cheese. Eaten separately, the effect is not as detrimental.

Insulin has several other effects, too. Being an anabolic hormone (which means that it is responsible for storing energy), it ensures that the body does not expend too much energy. This means that as long as you have too much insulin in your blood, your body will not burn fat; rather, it will store fat.

Fat cells are also under the influence of another enzyme, hormone-sensitive lipase. The more you have of this enzyme, the more fat will be released from the fat cells for burning and the more weight you will lose. And, of course, the more insulin in your blood, the less hormone-sensitive lipase and the less fat available for burning. If you are obese, or are in the early stage of type II dia-betes (i.e. insulin resistance), your insulin level is constantly too high, even when you have not eaten. This explains why your body becomes a very effi-cient fat-storage machine. If you are caught in this vicious circle of too much insulin – a situation that grows worse every time you eat carbohydrates with a high GI and a lot of fat – you are bound to gain weight, even if you eat less than before. And to make matters worse, fluctuating blood sugar levels will lead to increased appetite, especially sugar cravings. So the bottom line is – too much insulin makes you fat.

Glucagon

Glucagon is another hormone produced in the pancreas, but it has a very dif-ferent effect from insulin. Glucagon's main function is to increase blood sugar if it is falling (between meals for example), thus ensuring an energy supply for the body. Blood sugar is released from the liver's sugar supply (glycogen) and is produced from proteins and fat. When a rise in blood sugar occurs there is a decrease in glucagon, which is the opposite of what happens with insulin. This means that glucagon remains low when we eat carbohydrates. However, it increases dramatically when we eat protein. A lot of glucagon means little insulin, and thus little fat storage and more fat burning.

Furthermore, glucagon has an appetite-reducing effect. You might have noticed how satisfying protein sources such as eggs or meat can be. This is due to the protein increasing glucagon and cholecystokinin (see page 69). Glucagon, unlike insulin, leads to the production of 'good' eicosanoids.

Hormonal balance and improved health with the right diet

It should now be clear how important it is to have the right balance between glucagon and insulin. Too much insulin and the wrong kind of fats (too much omega-6 and trans fats) leads to the creation of 'bad' eicosanoids, while glucagon and the right kind of fat (an adequate intake of omega-3) promotes the creation of 'good' eicosanoids. Finding the right balance between these eicosanoids is of vital importance to good health.

By eating a balanced diet, you can make this happen. You can ensure a balance between the right amount of carbohydrates, to avoid excessive insulin levels, and enough protein, which will increase glucagon and growth hormones and thus promote muscle growth and fat burning. It is equally important that you eat the proper amount and type of fat – essential polyunsaturated fats, from plants, nuts and oily fish – to ensure you get enough building bricks for the 'good'

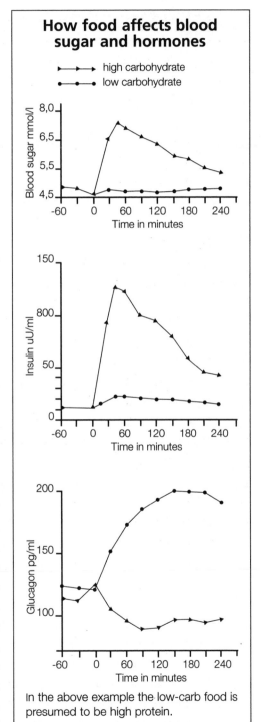

How food affects blood sugar and hormones

▶——▶ high carbohydrate
●——● low carbohydrate

In the above example the low-carb food is presumed to be high protein.

Food controls your hormones; hormones control your metabolism and health

Insulin	Glucagon
Lowers blood sugar	Increases low blood sugar
Promotes fat storage	Mobilizes stored fat
Stimulated mostly by carbohydrates	Stimulated by protein
Leads to the production of 'bad' eicosanoids	Leads to the production of 'good' eicosanoids

eicosanoids. Only a balanced diet, which provides you with all the vitamins and the trace minerals you need, can guarantee weight reduction and good health.

Other important hormones

Thyroxin

This hormone is produced in the thyroid gland, which looks like a butterfly and is situated in the lower front of the neck. Thyroxin influences the metabolism of all body cells, but this does not mean it is central to fat burning. A lot of people with a weight problem, or a tendency to gain weight, think that they have a slow thyroid function. Some might have too little thyroxin (an illness called hypothyroidism), but obesity caused by too little thyroxin is very rare. In general, no more than 2 per cent of people have low thyroid function, but at least 10 per cent suffer from obesity (and many more are overweight). Your doctor can administer the necessary blood tests to assess your thyroid function. If you suffer from low thyroid function, your doctor will usually prescribe thyroxin in tablet form, which will take care of the problem.

Adrenalin

Adrenalin is produced in the adrenal glands and in the sympathetic nervous system. The adrenal glands are small glands located above the kidneys. Adrenalin is a stress hormone. It is of vital importance and is our most significant survival hormone. If we are being threatened, feel stressed or are scared, we will secrete adrenalin, which puts us on the alert. Our blood sugar levels will rise, as well as our pulse rate and blood pressure, preparing us to fight or flee. Naturally, such a hormone has an impact on metabolism and blood sugar. Adrenalin stimulates the release of blood sugar from glycogen in the liver, as well as the production of blood glucose from proteins and from glycerol found in fat. The purpose of this is to ensure that the brain and the rest of the body have the necessary 'fuel' to react to a stressful situation. Chapter 7 looks at the effects of stress and adrenalin.

There are a number of substances that either increase the secretion of adrenalin, or function in the same way. The most common one is caffeine, which is found in coffee and cola. But do not kid yourself that you can lose much weight by drinking a lot of coffee. Only a balanced diet, along with proper exercise and successful stress management, will work in the long run.

Cortisol

You have probably heard of the hormone cortisol. In its synthetic medicinal form (cortisone) it has a similar, although stronger, effect to the natural cortisol produced in the adrenal glands. Cortisone is often prescribed to suppress the immune system when someone suffers from an autoimmune disorder, a rheumatic disorder or asthma. It is also prescribed to reduce inflammation, as it suppresses the immune system and some eicosanoids (prostaglandins) in particular.

Like adrenalin, cortisol is a stress hormone. Its production is increased when physical and emotional stress occur and when blood sugar is low. Have you ever experienced low blood sugar, when you haven't eaten for several hours? Too much cortisol and adrenalin cause the reaction that you probably experienced: hunger, irritability and poor concentration. So you can see how unwise it is to expose your body to unnecessary stress by skipping meals or eating the wrong kind of food. Doing these things also makes us more susceptible to infections and other illnesses. Have you ever noticed that you are more apt to become ill after periods of stress or if you are exhausted?

Increased cortisol levels over a prolonged period of time due to chronic stress also lead to more fat around the waist and neck, in addition to increased growth of body hair. Because cortisol increases blood sugar, it aggravates insulin resistance and may eventually lead to diabetes. But too little cortisol is not good, either. In fact, we cannot live without cortisol – our salt and sugar balance depends on it. So yet again, balance is the key word! See chapter 7 for more on the effects of cortisol.

Cholecystokinin

This hormone does not directly affect metabolic rate, but it does affect our appetite. It is produced in the small intestine after food is digested. The amount produced depends on how much protein and fat you have eaten. The more cholecystokinin, the fuller you get. Carbohydrates do not cause an increase of cholecystokinin. This means that they must be digested and raise the blood sugar before a signal is sent to the brain that food has been taken in, thereby causing satiety. Proteins and fats, on the other hand, cause satiety immediately upon entering the stomach and small intestine.

Leptin

This hormone, discovered in the mid-1990s, was a medical sensation. Leptin is produced by fat cells when fat is stored and the cells increase in volume, its purpose being to signal the brain to lower food intake. When body fat mass is low, leptin levels are low, stimulating appetite – and it is this effect that seems to be more important.

It was discovered that when rats were bred so that they would not be able to produce leptin, they ate without restraint and gained excess weight. But when given leptin injections, they stopped bingeing and regained their natural weight. Aha, the scientists thought, we've discovered the solution to the world's obesity problem – give obese people leptin and the extra pounds will simply disappear! Unfortunately, this was too good to be true. As it turns out, obese people have too much leptin, which is only natural, considering the amount of fat they have in their fat cells. It seems that obese people become desensitized to leptin, either because it does not send the right signals to the brain or there is a defect with the leptin receptors in the brain. This is referred to as leptin resistance.

It is interesting to note that people with high leptin levels also have high insulin levels and insulin resistance. It appears that these two hormones, leptin and insulin, are closely linked – a normal level of insulin means a normal level of leptin, and vice versa. This is yet another reason to eat a balanced diet of low-glycaemic foods.

Testosterone

Both men and women produce testosterone, though men do produce more. In men, testosterone is produced in the testicles, while in women, it is produced in the adrenal glands. This hormone is the reason why men have more body and facial hair and a deeper voice than women; it also increases their libido. Testosterone prevents osteoporosis (brittle bone disease), which is probably the main reason why so few men have this problem compared to women. This hormone is anabolic, which means that it builds muscle and bones and increases fat burning. It is interesting that polyunsaturated fat and cholesterol in food increase testosterone, which reminds us that some fat is essential for good health. It is important to have just enough testosterone – not too much, and not too little. Too little testosterone means less muscle mass and less fat burning. And too much can increase the risk of prostate cancer. An excess of testosterone in women can lead to infertility, irregular menstruation and increased growth of body hair.

How much testosterone circulates in the blood (so-called free testosterone) is indirectly affected by insulin and therefore by carbohydrate intake. High levels of insulin can cause an increase in free testosterone, and this imbalance can have severe consequences for women, causing reduced fertility and a condition known as PCOS (polycystic ovarian syndrome), which as many as 10 per cent of women in industrialized countries suffer from.

Oestrogen

Oestrogen is a female sex hormone produced in the ovaries. Men, too, produce small amounts of oestrogen, both in the adrenal glands and from testosterone conversion in fat tissue. Oestrogen promotes fat burning, but it can also increase fat storage around the hips and thighs, producing the pear shape common in many women. After menopause, when women produce less oestrogen, there is a tendency toward increased fat around the abdomen, and the apple shape that is typical of overweight men. Oestrogen prevents osteoporosis and increases a woman's libido. Too much oestrogen (from long-term use of certain types of contraceptive pill or HRT) may increase the risk of breast and uterine cancer and may even increase the risk of heart disease.

CHAPTER 6

MAKING THE MOST OF YOUR METABOLISM

Man has two fantastic doctors, his left leg and his right leg.
Anon

ou've probably heard this before or said it yourself: 'there must be something wrong with my metabolism or with my appetite; I gain weight even though I eat little or the same as others in my family.' Well, I am sorry, but it is very unlikely that there is anything wrong with your metabolism or your appetite. Your problem is that you make the wrong food choices, which causes hormonal chaos and results in a high level of insulin and therefore increased fat storage. You may, however, belong to a group of people who produce more insulin than others (even those who make the same wrong food choices) and have a tendency towards insulin resistance. But your metabolism and appetite regulation will function properly as soon as you adjust your lifestyle.

Metabolic biorhythm

Metabolism is a term that covers all the chemical processes that occur in the body, resulting in growth and repair of cells, and energy production. Your body uses energy all the time, even when you're asleep, for heartbeat, breathing, maintenance of body temperature and a myriad of intercellular processes. Your 'basal metabolic rate' (BMR) is the energy you would use if you were lying completely still, doing no physical activity and not eating.

Like almost everything else in nature, our metabolism has a biorhythm. This means that it changes during the course of the day, with the seasons, and with the years. The study of the biology of time is called chronobiology and is extremely important. Ignore it, and you will make life a lot harder for yourself – but in this chapter I shall look at some of the ways in which you can use it to your advantage.

While we are asleep, the brain (which is our most metabolically active organ) and most of our other organs move in slow motion, and the BMR is low. If we do not eat or exercise very soon after we wake up, it will take a while before the BMR increases. This is shown in the first graph on page 75. If we keep lying still after we wake up, our basal metabolic rate will gradually increase until it peaks at night, around 8 to 11 pm.

Our basal metabolic rate decreases with age – which is why many people put on weight as they get older, even though they eat much the same as they've always done. As we get older, we tend to lose lean body mass (muscle), and this slows the BMR. An increase in fatty tissue on the body will also lower the BMR. We can use this knowledge to increase our metabolic rate by exercising, both to lose fat and gain muscle.

Your BMR also decreases when you suddenly eat less (diet) or, even worse, when you fast. Your body will try to maintain its weight, which results in your metabolism slowing down. Why is this? Because our genes are still in the Stone Age! Your body does not know whether you are fasting or eating less because you are trying to lose weight, or because food is scarce.

The thermogenic effect of food

Believe it or not, our metabolism increases every time we eat. And this is actually pretty important in keeping our weight stable from day to day. The word thermogenesis means the production of heat, and derives from the Greek: *thermos* means 'warm' and *genesis* means 'formation' or 'production'. Like that of other mammals, the human body maintains a stable temperature regardless of the temperature of its environment. Over millions of years of evolution, man has adapted to a body temperature of 37°C/98.6°F, and that is when the body functions at its best.

But what produces the necessary heat? We do. All the chemical reactions in the body that keep us alive and active (in other words, our metabolism) release energy, partly as heat. During a meal, we burn the food that we have eaten, and thus produce extra heat. This food-related heat is referred to as the food's thermogenic effect – it is energy that we 'donate' to our surroundings and therefore is not stored as fat. The greater the thermogenesis, the less fat is stored. The biggest production of heat derives from proteins. As much as 25 to 30 per cent of all the energy they contain is expended to produce heat. Carbohydrates also lead to considerable energy production, but to a lesser extent than proteins. They have approximately a 12 per cent thermogenic effect. Saturated fat, on the other hand, generates a minimal production of heat, only 3 per cent, and requires little energy in order to be metabolized. In that respect, saturated fat is the least desirable nutrient, but it would be wrong to focus only on its thermogenic effect and forget, for example, its satiating effect and the fact that it is the type of fat that is least prone to oxidation in the body. Different types of fat act slightly differently: polyunsaturated fat – for example, the type found in fish oil – actually has a higher thermogenic effect than saturated fat.

As regards heat production, alcohol tops the list. Almost half of the energy in alcohol is changed into heat when metabolized in the liver. Consequently, alcohol contributes much less than the 7 calories per gram (or 199 calories per ounce) that its calorie model suggests. But alcohol is not food, and it contributes little to our overall health (for more about alcohol, see page 48). Alcohol and fat consumed together is a particularly bad combination: your body will prefer to burn alcohol rather than fat, so fat will be stored.

Tea, especially green tea, boosts the metabolism. And with its high antioxidant content, it can also help to protect you against cancer and cardiovascular disorders.

Guess what else can increase your production of heat and therefore your metabolism? Spices! Many spices, especially those that make food taste 'hot', increase metabolism – for example, ginger, chilli/cayenne pepper, paprika, mustard, pepper and horseradish/wasabi. Garlic increases metabolism, too, in addition to all its other beneficial properties. So be my guest: use as many spices as you like. Not only will you prepare tasty dishes, but you will also receive the bonus of increased fat burning.

Breakfast – your most important meal

Let's return to the subject of biorhythm. A hearty breakfast will increase the metabolism. The third graph on page 75 shows what the metabolic curve looks like after a good breakfast and some morning exercise. It is also better to have

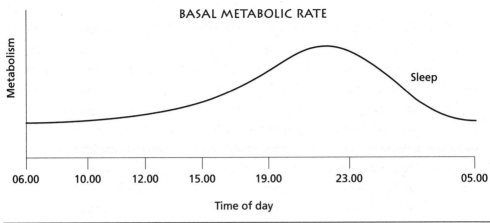

BASAL METABOLIC RATE

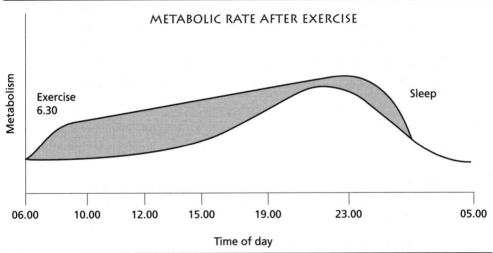

METABOLIC RATE AFTER EXERCISE

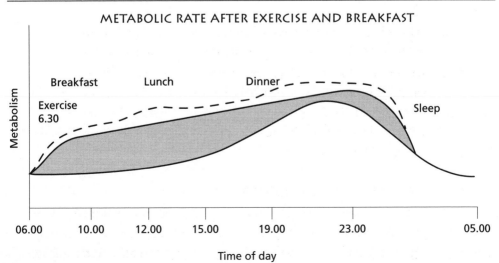

METABOLIC RATE AFTER EXERCISE AND BREAKFAST

a bigger lunch (maybe a hot meal) and a slightly smaller dinner than most of us are used to. You should avoid eating for two or three hours before you go to bed. The reason for this is that during sleep metabolism is slower, and it will not increase much even if you do eat.

A HEALTHY BREAKFAST

- Scrambled eggs or an omelette made from one egg and two egg whites or 2 whole eggs
- Chopped spinach and mushrooms, fried with 1 teaspoon of olive oil in a non-stick frying pan
- Two rye crispbreads or one thin slice of pumpernickel, very dark rye bread or stoneground wholemeal bread
- Herbal, green or regular tea or filtered decaffeinated coffee – no sugar, a little skimmed milk is optional – and one or two glasses of water.

Exercise and your metabolism

Another thing that increases your basal metabolic rate considerably is proper exercise. Knowing that the BMR is lowest when you wake up and during the morning, when do you think that exercising will be the most beneficial? Correct: early in the day, preferably shortly after you wake up (see the second graph on page 75). Research shows that the effect of morning exercise increases the metabolic rate for about 10 to 12 hours afterwards – and that is important. If you exercise in the evening, your metabolism will increase for no more than four or five hours, then it will slow down when you go to bed.

After a night's sleep (during which you have not eaten), your body will have used quite a lot of glycogen (stored carbohydrate) from the liver; blood sugar is at its lowest level and so is insulin. Your body will have to burn fat in order to move. But remember, exercise has to last more than 20 minutes.

Ideally, you should drink a large glass of water, and have some low-glycaemic fruit immediately after you get up if you wish, and then exercise for 20 to 30 minutes (a brisk walk is splendid exercise and can be done almost anywhere). To maximize the effect of this morning exercise, you can have some protein (for instance natural, unsweetened yogurt, cottage cheese, or a protein powder drink based on soya or dairy protein) shortly before starting to exercise or not later than 1–1½ hours afterwards. This increases the production of glucagon and growth hormone, thereby enhancing muscle tissue and promoting fat burning. After exercising, you should eat a healthy, well-balanced breakfast. The great lesson we can learn here is that every day is a new day for your body.

Exercising early in the day every day is simply the best gift you can give yourself and your metabolism. That said, any exercise during the day is clearly better than not exercising at all. Investing 30 minutes a day in exercise is something you will never regret.

Use your body and improve your health

Our bodies have the amazing ability to improve the more we use them. That ties in with the fact that our genes are still the same as they were in the Stone Age. Back then, you had to be pretty physically active to get food; those who could not get food did not survive. This means that our genes reward us when we exercise. Our health improves, and we get a more efficient metabolism, too.

Many people believe that rigorous and prolonged exercise is necessary if you want to lose weight and be in good health. Neither is correct. Without a change in diet, the weight loss from exercise alone is small; most studies suggest 3–4kg (6–9lb). It is only when you improve your diet that you will see a considerable effect from exercise on your weight, and even more importantly, on your body composition and figure. Moreover, it is not necessary to train very hard to gain positive health benefits: you do not have to sweat in a gym or 'spin' yourself to death on an exercise bike. The biggest problem for many people is that they set their goals too high and then give up after a short while. The crucial thing is to turn a form of exercise that you enjoy into a part of your everyday life.

Exercise does wonders for your health, regardless of your weight. You can be 'fit fat' and reduce the risk of most diseases by exercising on a regular basis. To be physically inactive is in fact a much greater health hazard than being overweight. Unfortunately, the combination of physical inactivity and overweight is not uncommon, and this increases the health risk even more. This brings us to the key point: you should exercise moderately, but daily.

The evolution of exercise

If we want to find out what kind of physical activity is most suited to us humans, we have to consider what life was like in the Stone Age, which lasted some 3 million years, when humans lived a 'natural' life, as many animals still do. Humans and animals needed to move about (exercise) to get food. Consequently, it goes without saying that we are made to exercise on an empty stomach. A lion that has just finished off a zebra will not bother to go hunting that night. In fact all animals (including humans) prefer to rest after a meal, partly in order to assist digestion, and partly because it makes no sense to use energy when it is not strictly necessary. It is only natural that the sofa is a tempting place after a large meal. After all, a lion is not guaranteed a successful hunt every day, so it is imperative to save as much energy as possible. This explains why all humans are 'lazy' by nature: our genes are still in the Stone Age – they do not 'know' that we can get food at any time of the day just by walking to the fridge, or taking the car to to the nearest shop. Going to the gym on the way home from work in the evening or, even worse, after a meal, when we should be digesting and saving energy, does not make sense. No animal would eat a meal and then start chasing around while digesting the food they have worked for hours to catch.

So when *should* we exercise? Man's daily activities in the Stone Age were determined by the daylight. Because we do not see very well in the dark, we had to go under cover at night to rest and protect ourselves against other animals. At the break of dawn we were pretty hungry after nine or ten hours of fasting. Then we had to go hunting or gather plants, which was not always easy. Stone Age man would have had to walk an average of 30km (19 miles) a day in search of food, and sometimes in vain. If he got something to eat, the important thing was to stay put until he got hungry and had to start searching for food again. This is the reason why it makes sense to exercise early in the day and on an empty stomach: it works with our hormones and biorhythm. When we get up in the morning, the carbohydrate store in the liver is nearly empty, blood pressure is relatively low and the insulin level is at its lowest. Low insulin means that the body is better able to burn stored fat as fuel. Remember that a high level of insulin means fat storage, whereas low insulin means that fat can be burnt efficiently.

It is therefore a good idea to exercise in the morning. No, that's impossible, you might say, I don't have time, I have so many chores to do before leaving for work. Maybe you only have 20 minutes from the time you get out of bed until you have to leave for school or work? But you can start the day with exercise if you put your own health and well-being high enough on your priority list. You might have to go to bed a bit earlier, perhaps even skip your favourite TV series, and rise 30–45 minutes earlier than you are used to. You can prepare everything you need – exercise clothes, breakfast – the night before. Maybe you can find ways of exercising on your way to work: perhaps you could walk or cycle to work, or get off the bus a couple of stops earlier so that you get a brisk 20–30 minute walk. Like everything else in life, this just takes some prioritizing and planning. Nonetheless, it is important to remember that you will get more return for your sweat and exercise early in the day.

What is the ideal form of physical exercise? Humans are not particularly good at running fast. Other animals are. What humans do best is walking, as well as performing short bouts of activity requiring strength. Even the laziest person in the world, with all kinds of health problems, would manage to walk quite far, if they were hungry enough. However, we no longer need to do that, and that is the great challenge we are facing. Why should we exercise when it is not necessary in order to get food? Well, it is important to realize that, if you wish to live a long and healthy life, it is absolutely vital to be physically active. I know it is not easy to break away from the agreeable life on the sofa in front of the TV or at the computer and actually start exercising. We have all made futile attempts at a rigorous exercise regime, paid our membership fee to a gym, or suffered on long painful runs. We often fail because our ambitions are too high. Any kind of physical activity is good for you. There is no need to spend a lot of money on gyms or pound along the road, dripping with sweat. It is far better to choose an activity that you enjoy, preferably something you can do with a friend. Walking for at least 20–30 minutes every day and strength training for the major muscle groups two or three times a week could be enough, especially if you improve your diet at the same time, and reduce stress.

The right fuel for your engine

Think of a famous athlete, say a marathon runner. Do you think this person was born like that? There are no supernatural human beings. Top athletes are individuals who have achieved success by setting specific goals, using their knowledge and working hard. They can be compared to Formula 1 cars, for they have optimized their metabolism in order to achieve maximum perform-ance. Athletes train for many, many years. Most of them receive help from experienced coaches, people who know a lot about appropriate nutrition and effective training techniques. Training to run a marathon is quite different from preparing to run a 100-metre race. The dietary requirements before and after training are different for each, too.

At the opposite end of the metabolic efficiency range, we find those who are overweight. Owing to genetic factors and a less focused lifestyle, these peo-ple have a less efficient metabolic engine – more like that of a tractor. Top ath-letes get results by eating sensibly and exercising. For overweight individuals to optimize their metabolism and lose weight, they have to be equally goal-ori-ented as those athletes. Maybe your family and friends, or your doctor, have told you: 'Eat less, exercise more, and you will lose weight!' But you need to know what kind of food and exercise. Eating the right foods is important if you are to get the best-possible results from your exercise. You cannot use diesel in a petrol engine, even if the car is a Porsche.

Aerobic exercise versus anaerobic exercise

Most overweight people will have been given the following advice at some time in their lives: 'Take the stairs, walk the dog, walk to the next bus stop, and you will lose weight.' While any physical activity is better than none, can you expect to lose weight from this kind of activity? An obese person can be compared to a person of normal weight carrying a bag of, say, 30kg (67lb). For a normal person, walking and taking the stairs is an aerobic activity. Aerobic means an activity that uses a lot of oxygen and that, to a large extent, burns fat to pro-vide fuel. The longer the activity lasts, the more fat one will burn. However, the same activity will put a considerable strain on the obese person, or on a normal person carrying a heavy load. Try to imagine walking up the stairs with a 30kg (67lb) bag on your back. That makes for a considerable workout, a real challenge to the muscles in your thighs and back. Weightlifting is an anaero-bic exercise. If you do it frequently, it can lead to increased muscle mass, but little fat is burned during the exercise session. On the contrary, you burn glyco-gen – the form in which carbohydrates are stored in your muscles. And if your muscles are not well trained, you will quickly start to run out of glycogen. The body starts producing lactic acid, and you will feel tired and stiff. So what can we conclude from this? If you are significantly overweight, you should start exercising at a lower impact level than people of normal weight when performing aerobic exercise such as walking, running, or cycling, and increase the intensity as you lose weight and become fit. You should also include resistance training two or three times a week to stimulate muscle growth.

One of my patients, who was obese, went to the gym twice a week. One day she would exercise hard by running on the treadmill for 50 minutes. As might be expected, she became exhausted and was stiff the next day. She had actually been doing anaerobic exercise (strengthening the muscles in her thighs and in her back) instead of aerobic training. The other day she would work out with weight machines. This was her workout pattern for years, but she did not lose weight. Anaerobic exercise performed optimally builds muscle mass, hence it increases fat burning, but only indirectly. Instead of working out so hard and for such a long time, my patient ought to have exercised more frequently, at a low-impact level, for 30 minutes or more each day, in addition to her resistance exercise routine.

How to burn fat by exercising

If you are overweight and wish to work out properly, you should exercise four or five times a week, or every day if you can. A brisk walk is excellent. Any exercise lasting more than 20 minutes will help you burn more fat. As mentioned earlier, it is best to work out early in the day because of your metabolic biorhythm, and preferably shortly after you get up in the morning. Start by warming up and then take a brisk 10-minute walk. Gradually extend the exercise period to approximately 40 minutes. Avoid working out so hard that you get out of breath. After a brisk 10-minute walk, you should be only slightly out of breath – you should be able to have a conversation without panting. If you find it difficult to say a few words, you are probably working anaerobically.

You can monitor your exercise intensity more effectively by assessing your heart rate, using a heart rate monitor. Ten to fifteen minutes into the walk, you should reach 50 to 60 per cent of your maximum heart rate (this is in the beginning, when you are not fit). Gradually increase this to 75 to 85 per cent as you become more fit. The simplest way to work out your maximum heart rate (MHR) is to subtract your age from 220. You can then work out the target heart rate zone by multiplying your MHR by the appropriate lower and upper cardiorespiratory levels. A 45-year-old, for instance, would have an approximate MHR of 175 (220 – 45 = 175); 60 per cent of their MHR would be 105 (175 x

.60 = 105); and 85 per cent of their MHR would be 149 (175 x .85 = 148.75). Remember, however, that any figures you derive from using this formula should be used as a guideline only, as people differ in their response to exercise.

Resistance training and fat burning

Resistance training, such as weightlifting, is mainly an anaerobic form of exercise, and it affects your metabolism only indirectly. During anaerobic exercise, it is the glycogen in your muscles that you will use for energy, not fat. However, after you finish your workout, fat burning will increase, as you will have emptied your carbohydrate stores (glycogen) and your body will have to turn to stored fat as its energy source. But most importantly, your muscles will gradually develop and burn more energy all day long (because your resting BMR will rise). Provided that you eat correctly and avoid high insulin levels, this energy will come from your body's stored fat.

What should I eat before and after exercising?

Your insulin level drops both during aerobic exercise (a brisk walk, for instance) and for several hours afterwards. This is a useful piece of information, especially if you have already developed a high level of fasting insulin – that is, insulin resistance. A lower insulin level makes it possible to burn fat, and you will also store less fat after a meal.

If you have type II diabetes, aerobic exercise is a fantastic way to obtain better control of your blood sugar, because exercise increases your insulin sensitivity. If you also eat low-glycaemic carbohydrates and choose the right kind of fat, you are likely to achieve very good results. You might manage without insulin, or with less medicine. At the same time, you will gradually lose weight.

The mistake many people make is to eat a lot of carbohydrates, especially in the form of bananas, pasta or bread, before exercising. This increases the levels of blood sugar and insulin, and decreases fat burning. And because your body cannot burn fat efficiently as fuel when you are exercising, it has to burn carbohydrates, of which only a small amount are stored in the body. The blood sugar level drops and we feel tired and hungry. Consequently we have to fill up with more carbohydrates, even during exercise.

Avoid carbohydrates, especially high-glycaemic carbs, before you exercise. After *intense* exercise, eating high-glycaemic food will help you recover more quickly. This is a time when you can eat this kind of food with a better conscience, knowing that it will have fewer unwanted health effects.

Another thing to remember is that you will make the most of exercise if you give your body enough protein. Exercise stimulates the production of growth hormones, which build muscle, but only if there are enough bricks, i.e. proteins. Therefore you should eat food containing some protein shortly before starting to exercise or not later than 1–1½ hours after working out, especially after weight training.

Fat loss versus weight loss

Are we striving for weight loss or fat loss? If you lose weight primarily because of loss of muscle mass, your basal metabolic rate will slow down and after a while you will gain more weight than you started with. On the other hand, if you gain weight because of increased muscle mass, your metabolism will increase: a positive result. Therefore, it is not what you weigh that matters, but what that weight is made up of.

Your body consists of water, bones, various organs, muscles and fat. The amount of body fat varies quite a lot within a so-called normal range. Ideally for men, that means about 16 to 18 per cent fat. Normally, only top athletes have a lower percentage of fat. For women, 20 to 22 per cent body fat is considered ideal. Looking at your percentage of body fat, rather than at your body weight, is a much better way to judge good health. The simplest way to determine whether you have lost body fat is to take into account both your BMI (see page 85) and your waistline measurement, especially if you have a lot of abdominal fat. That said, I will continue to refer to fat loss as weight loss, as it is a term we all are familiar with, but I hope that you will understand and remember the important difference.

CHAPTER 7

LIFESTYLE DISEASES OF MODERN SOCIETY

*If more of us valued food and cheer and song above
hoarded gold, it would be a merrier world.*
JRR Tolkien, 1892–1973

The number of people with so-called lifestyle diseases is exploding – even in developing countries. The World Health Organization (WHO) claims that, globally, obesity is a much bigger problem than malnourishment. Along with obesity comes an increasing number of people with type II diabetes – so many, in fact, that we can justifiably call it an epidemic.

Most of the western world follows trends in the United States, which has more overweight people than any other country. However, this development affects not only industrial countries but also countries that until recently have had a more traditional lifestyle. For instance, around 44 per cent of black women in South Africa are overweight. In Norway, studies in 1986 and 1997 show that from the mid 1980s to the mid 1990s obesity in individuals in their twenties increased by 7.5 to 14 per cent in men and 13 to 17.8 per cent in women. About 10 per cent of all Norwegians are obese.

Childhood obesity is even more disturbing. About 75 per cent of all children between the ages of ten and eleven with a body mass index (BMI) over 23 will end up having a serious weight problem when they reach adulthood. And as many studies indicate, overweight children have an increased risk of developing diabetes and coronary heart disease as adults.

Body Mass Index (BMI)

BMI (Body Mass Index) is a general indicator of your body weight status. BMI takes height into account, but does not take into account the make-up of body weight. Someone with a lot of muscle – a bodybuilder, for instance – may have a BMI within the overweight range, but this does not mean that he needs to lose weight.

This is how to calculate your BMI:

Your weight in kilograms, divided by your height in metres squared
So someone who weighs 100kg (15½st) and is 1.8 m (5ft 11in) tall would have a BMI of 31 (1.8 m x 1.8 m = 3.24: 100kg ÷ 3.24 = 30.86)

Definition of overweight and obesity:

BMI 19–25: normal weight
BMI 25–30: overweight
BMI 30–35: stage 1 obesity
BMI 35–40: stage 2 obesity
BMI over 40: stage 3 obesity

Obesity – a greater problem than malnourishment

Obesity is linked to:
Type II diabetes
Coronary heart disease
High blood pressure
High cholesterol/blood fat (triglycerides)
Gallbladder disease
Joint problems (e.g. arthritis)
Certain forms of cancer

Diabetes and excess weight

The explanation for the correlation between obesity and type II diabetes is simple: both are caused by the same hormonal disturbance – insulin resistance. Most people who develop high blood pressure, elevated blood lipids and coronary heart disease belong to the group of people who are predisposed to diabetes and obesity. Diabetes is the illness that costs the most per patient treated, because treatment lasts so long and leads to so many complications and to frequent use of expensive high-tech health services. Worldwide, diabetes and coronary heart disease are predicted to be the most widespread illnesses by 2020. In 2000, there were 130 million diabetics worldwide. By 2025, the number is expected to reach a staggering 300 million! The increase is especially significant in developing countries, where the number is likely to have tripled in the period from 1997 to 2010. In the United States, close to 50 per cent of the population has health problems due to excess weight and obesity. But diabetes, obesity and coronary heart disease can be prevented! It is alarming to see how little money goes into preventing these diseases, as opposed to the staggering sums of money that are being spent on treating them. Research shows that a weight loss of 5 to 15 per cent in overweight people results in substantial benefits, such as reduced blood lipids, blood sugar levels and blood pressure.

I generally recommend that those who need to lose more than 10kg (22lb) of body weight do so under the supervision of a doctor, preferably one who is knowledgeable in the areas of nutrition and metabolism. It is important that your doctor is genuinely interested in your problem, particularly if you are very overweight or obese (i.e. if you have a BMI over 30) or if you have an additional medical condition, such as diabetes, cardiovascular disease, sleep apnoea, etc. In these cases, it is often necessary to involve other specialists in addition to a doctor. A clinical nutritionist (dietician), a psychologist, a behavioural therapist, as well as an exercise physiologist or trainer, may be a great help.

Diabetes and better control of blood sugar

While weight loss is an important aim for those who are overweight and have type II diabetes, control over blood sugar is vital – and in this context, use of the Glycaemic Index (see chapter 4) has shown remarkable results, with both type I and type II diabetes.

Type I diabetes is caused by reduced insulin production, and type I diabetics are dependent on insulin shots. It is usually diagnosed in children or teenagers, but the disorder may also appear in adults. Type I diabetics are often slim, but they may also be genetically disposed to insulin resistance. In that case, the individual requires a much higher insulin dosage to keep blood sugar within acceptable limits, they may gain excess weight around the abdomen and may develop all the other problems related to insulin resistance. The Greek Doctor's Diet, with its low Glycaemic Load, ensures a steady blood sugar curve after a meal, and this makes insulin dosage a lot easier to determine and more predictable. This balanced way of eating also prevents great variations in blood sugar levels and thereby avoids large fluctuations in insulin needs and the danger of hypoglycaemia (low blood sugar).

Insulin resistance – that is, when insulin does not work properly – is the main cause of type II diabetes, previously referred to as adult-onset diabetes. The cause is partly genetic and partly linked to an unhealthy lifestyle, one with little exercise and an unbalanced diet. After many years of insulin resistance and insulin overproduction, some people develop diabetes when their pancreas starts to fail. If you have one parent with type II diabetes, the chance of developing the disease yourself is around 40 per cent. This is why a healthy lifestyle with a proper diet, regular exercise and little stress (as well as avoiding smoking and too much alcohol) is so important.

By following the Greek Doctor's Diet, diabetics can gain much better control of their blood sugar, which in turn reduces the need for insulin, whether we are talking about insulin shots or insulin produced by the body itself. This means that many people with type II diabetes are able to do without insulin treatment, even after having used insulin for many years. Others can manage without diabetes medication. They can also avoid developing complications linked to the disease, such as problems with the kidneys, eyes and nerves and cardiovascular disorders.

Syndrome X and insulin resistance

Sixty years ago, a doctor named H P Himsworth wrote an article in *The Lancet* concerning a hormonal disorder that he termed chronic hyperactive hyperinsulinemia (increased production of insulin) and insulin resistance (the body's defence mechanism against increased insulin). According to Himsworth, overproduction of the hormone insulin was the cause of several diseases. Fifty years went by before this theory was confirmed by medical research. In an article published in the medical journal *Diabetes* in 1988, G M Reaven described how increased insulin production and insulin resistance are connected to a number of illnesses. He called the condition 'Syndrome X'. Following this article, there was an explosion of research about the relationship between hyperinsulinemia and insulin resistance – and the illnesses they lead to. In 1983, 300 scientific articles were published connecting insulin to several diseases. By the end of 2004 more than 21,000 articles had been published on the subject! Names other than syndrome X have been used, such as 'metabolic syndrome' and 'insulin resistance syndrome'.

A recent study in England shows surprising results: slightly high blood sugar levels lead to an increased mortality rate even among non-diabetics. An article published in the *British Medical Journal* in January 2001 referred to a study of 4,662 men monitored from 1995 to 1999. The study found a strong correlation between elevated blood sugar levels and coronary heart disease. Many healthy non-diabetics have a slight to moderate increase in their blood sugar, which is still within the normal range. This is caused by a diet with an excess of high-glycaemic carbohydrates. This study demonstrates that there is a stronger link between elevated blood sugar and increased mortality than is the case with high levels of blood cholesterol.

So exactly what does a slightly high blood sugar level do to our bodies? It stimulates insulin production and, over time, increases insulin resistance and accelerates the ageing process. A high production of insulin and insulin resistance are known to influence a number of medical conditions and illnesses, several of which can result in premature death.

Problems associated with insulin resistance

• Obesity (especially excess weight around the abdomen, even if the rest of the body looks normal)
• Type II diabetes and its early stages (reduced glucose tolerance)
• High blood pressure (hypertension)
• High triglycerides (blood fat) and/or low HDL cholesterol (the 'good' cholesterol)
• High uric acid levels (kidney disease and gout)
• Increased risk of thrombosis (heart attack, stroke)
• Infertility in women, ovarian cysts, irregular menstruation and increased production of body hair (PCOS, or polycystic ovary syndrome)

Hyperinsulinemia and insulin resistance are also believed to increase the risk of several forms of cancer (insulin being a so-called growth factor that stimulates cell growth and may lead to the formation of tumours). This is well documented for, among others, breast cancer and colon cancer.

Through an increase in 'bad' eicosanoids (see pages 64–5), insulin contributes to an increase in inflammatory diseases such as asthma, allergies, rheumatic diseases, muscular and skeletal pain, psoriasis, Crohn's disease, ulcerative colitis, migraine and pre-eclampsia. This is worsened if you eat too much of the wrong type of fat (an excess of omega-6 fatty acids and trans fats in relation to omega-3 fatty acids).

Medicines that can trigger insulin resistance

Many common medicines can worsen or even cause insulin resistance and its accompanying problems, including increased weight. These include ordinary, over-the-counter painkillers (anti-inflammatory drugs, sometimes called NSAID) that you take to relieve headaches, fever or joint pain; certain types of high blood pressure medication, beta-blockers and some diuretics; steroids prescribed for inflammatory conditions; female sex hormones during and after the menopause; insulin shots or diabetes medication that increases insulin production (sulfonylurea). Several anti-psychotics can also affect insulin level and increase the appetite. You should never change the dosage or stop using medicines without consulting your doctor. There might be an alternative, but if you need to use these medications, it becomes even more important to eat healthily and to exercise.

What causes the insulin resistance syndrome?

We have come to know a great deal about this syndrome. Among other things, we know that it is a genetic condition, but while a genetic predisposition is an important factor, bad eating habits and lack of physical exercise determine who will develop the condition and how it will affect them.

Insulin resistance – how widespread is it?

Several studies indicate that at least 25 to 30 per cent of Caucasians are genetically predisposed to increased insulin production and insulin resistance. People from the Indian subcontinent, Africa and South America are much more prone to insulin resistance. In some of these populations as many as 80 per cent are predisposed to the syndrome. In a 1998 article in *Diabetes*, E Bonora and his colleagues concluded that the following people (men and women between the ages of 40 and 79) have insulin resistance:

• 65.9 per cent of all individuals with decreased glucose tolerance (the early stage of type II diabetes)
• 83.9 per cent of all individuals with type II diabetes
• 53.5 per cent of people with high cholesterol

- 84.2 per cent of people with high triglycerides
- 88.1 per cent of people with a low HDL cholesterol
- 62.8 per cent of people with high uric acid levels
- 58.0 per cent of people with high blood pressure

As many as 9.6 per cent of all people have insulin resistance without any of the above symptoms. And every year, more than half of the deaths in the United States are related to the insulin resistance syndrome.

Are you insulin-resistant?

There are many ways of measuring hyperinsulinemia/insulin resistance. The easiest way is simply to look at yourself in the mirror. If your belly is bulging even though the rest of your body looks normal, then you are probably pre-disposed to hyperinsulinemia and you may have already developed insulin resistance.

You can also use a measuring tape. Measure your waist, putting the measuring tape over your belly button; write down the measurement. Then measure your hips, placing the measuring tape over the hip joints; write down the measurement. Then divide your waistline measurement by your hip measurement. If the result (WHR: waist/hip ratio) is greater than 0.85 if you are a woman or 1.0 if you are a man, you probably have an increased insulin production/insulin resistance.

If your BMI is over 30 (see page 85), you almost certainly are insulin-resistant. The same is true if you are in the early stages of type II diabetes or have already developed the disease.

Ask your doctor to measure your long-term blood sugar (HBA1C) and fasting C-peptide (which measures insulin production, and should be taken in the morning on an empty stomach: normal levels are 240 to 720 pmol/L) and perhaps your uric acid, which is a metabolic by-product, the level of which increases due to hyperinsulinemia and insulin resistance. These are more relevant than the tests for blood cholesterol. However, if you are having your cholesterol tested, ensure you get your HDL, LDL and triglyceride levels tested (not just your total cholesterol). Insulin resistance is associated with elevated fasting triglycerides and reduced HDL cholesterol (the beneficial type).

Test yourself: are you at risk of syndrome X?

This test can help you find out whether you have high insulin production/insulin resistance or are predisposed to it. Draw a circle around the answer that fits you best and then add up your score.

Part 1: Family and Medical History

One or more of my parents or grandparents have or have had:

High blood pressure	3
Type II diabetes	3
Stroke	3
Heart condition	3
Cancer (ovarian, breast, uterine)	3
Excess abdominal fat	3
Rapid weight gain	3
High cholesterol and/or triglycerides	3

I have or have had:

High blood pressure	4
Type II diabetes	4
Stroke	4
Heart condition	4
Cancer (ovarian, breast, uterine)	4
Excess abdominal fat	4
Rapid weight gain	4
High cholesterol and/or triglycerides	4

I am:

Under 35 years old	0
Between 35 and 49 years old	2
Between 50 and 64 years old	4
65 years or older	6

I am:

Not overweight	0
Overweight by more than 10kg (20lb)	2
Overweight by more than 10–20kg (1½–3 st)	4
Overweight by more than 20kg (3st)	6

I use the following medicines every day:

Hormones	3
Anti-inflammatory medicines that do not contain steroids	3
Diuretics	3
Beta-blocking drugs (heart medication)	3

Part 2: Nutrition Profile

I easily become tired and/or hungry in the middle of the day	3
I often have a midnight snack	3
I often chew gum or eat sweets, either with sugar or artificial sweetener	3
Between meals, I often drink coffee or tea containing milk, sugar, or artificial sweetener	2
I have a soft drink between meals	2
I often feel peckish, and eat snacks like crisps (potato chips), biscuits or sweets	4
I eat fatty food almost every day	2
I normally eat one of the following with every meal: bread, pasta, rice, or another source of starch, fruit or sweets	4
I often eat without being really hungry	2
If I start eating food containing sugar or starch, or snacks, I find it difficult to stop	2

A meal containing just meat and
vegetables does not sustain me   2

Whenever I feel tired, a biscuit
or a piece of cake makes me feel
better   2

I normally will not eat vegetables
or a salad if there are potatoes,
bread, pasta, or dessert on the
table   2

I feel tired, almost sluggish, after
a big meal containing bread,
pasta or potatoes, and dessert,
but I feel more energetic after a
meal of meat or fish and a
green salad   3

If I skip a meal, or if it is delayed,
I get irritable   2

Part 3: Activity Level
(Circle the statement that suits you best)

I am a physically active person   0
I am moderately physically active   2
I am not physically active   6
I often feel tired and physically
weak   3

Part 4: Level of Stress
(Circle only the statements you agree with)

I often experience mental
confusion/tiredness   2

I often experience stressful
situations in my everyday life:
Never/very rarely   0
At work but not at home   2
At home but never at work   3
Both at home and at work   6

I smoke:
Never   0
Less than a pack of cigarettes a day   2
Between one and two packs a day   4
More than two packs a day   8
Cigars or a pipe   2

I drink beer, wine or cocktails:
Rarely   0
Sometimes, and in large quantities   1
Once or twice a week   1
Once a day   2
Twice a day, or more   4

Part 5: The Immune System
(Circle only the conditions that affect you)

Indigestion   4
Chronic sinusitis   3
Hay fever   3
Allergies   3
Infections   3
Sensitivity to chemical substances   3
Eczema or itching, psoriasis, rash   3
Asthma   3

Now add up your points:
The result indicates your chances of
having insulin resistance:

0–16: probably no risk

17–20: low risk

21–25: medium–high risk

over 26: high risk

The American Paradox

Up until 1997, when WHO sounded the alarm and defined obesity as a world-wide epidemic, we tended to think of the United States as the only country where obesity was a significant problem. While it is still a big problem in the US, the rest of the world is rapidly catching up.

At the beginning of the twentieth century, 20 to 25 per cent of the US population was considered overweight. By the 1930s the number of overweight people had reached 35 per cent, and 8 per cent were obese. A study carried out at the National Center for Health Statistics at the Centers for Disease Control and Prevention in the United States showed that from 1960 to 1980 about 25 per cent of adult Americans were considered to be obese. This number increased dramatically to 33 per cent from 1980 to 1991 – an increase of 32 per cent in a matter of ten years. Yet all the while, the consumption of dietary fat has gone down. These findings are shocking, to say the least.

During the last 50 years, low-fat foods have been considered a healthy choice in the United States. Official nutrition guidelines have recommended that energy intakes comes 55 to 60 per cent from carbohydrates, 15 per cent from protein and 25 to 30 per cent from fat, preferably unsaturated fat (from vegetable oils and fish). The focus of attention has been on the amount of calories and fat, rather than on the type of food and its functions. The result is that the food industry (led by the US, and followed by manufacturers around the world) has produced an enormous range of low-calorie products, mainly low-fat/fat-free, products. In many low-calorie products the fat has been replaced with a larger proportion of carbohydrates (starch, different kinds of sugar). The increase in obesity and lifestyle diseases, despite a lower consumption of fat, is referred to as 'the American Paradox'.

The cholesterol connection

Both in Europe and in the United States, fat consumption has gone down since the beginning of the twentieth century, as a result of an increased focus on the risks of high cholesterol. Early studies into cholesterol suggested it increased the risk of heart disease, so people started avoiding foods with a high level of cholesterol, such as egg yolks, meat, poultry and seafood.

A certain amount of cholesterol is necessary and is produced in the body; it forms part of all cell membranes and is used in the formation of hormones, among other functions. But an excess of a type of cholesterol called low-density lipoprotein (LDL) has been linked to increased risk of atherosclerosis (hardening of the arteries), a condition that can result in heart attack. It is when LDL cholesterol oxidizes that it gets involved in the inflammatory process that ultimately forms plaque, a hard deposit that sticks to the walls of the arteries and blocks blood flow. This means that simply having somewhat elevated LDL cholesterol is not synonymous with developing heart disease. If oxidation in the body increases, then oxidized LDL cholesterol becomes a problem.

The cholesterol that is found naturally in food is absorbed and causes a reduction in the amount of cholesterol produced by the liver. Lowering the amount of cholesterol in food therefore has almost no effect on blood cholesterol. The liver just increases its production accordingly. The new, extremely efficient cholesterol-lowering drugs called statins directly influence the cholesterol produced by the body and, more importantly, they are potent antioxidants that reduce the amount of oxidized LDL cholesterol. If the cholesterol in our food had been a decisive factor, it would not have been possible to lower cholesterol using these medicines.

It is when the body produces excess cholesterol that problems arise, and we now know that the hormone insulin stimulates cholesterol production by increasing the activity of the very enzyme that statins inhibit. When we eat the wrong kind of carbohydrates, along with saturated fat and trans fats, we stimulate insulin production, which in turn leads to increased cholesterol production – in particular, the production of small, dense LDL particles that are believed to be especially problematic in terms of heart disease. It is our excessive intake of high-glycaemic carbohydrates, together with junk food and soft drinks, that is behind the explosion of obesity-related problems throughout the world.

The Mediterranean diet

It is a well-known fact that people from most Mediterranean countries have traditionally been slimmer than those in other countries, especially compared to Central European and Nordic countries (though the globalization of the American 'fast-food' diet may soon change this). Mediterranean countries have also had a low incidence of coronary heart disease. The inhabitants of Crete have had the lowest percentage rate of obesity and coronary heart disease. This has led to great interest on the part of physiologists and coronary experts around the world and has resulted in numerous research projects. An extensive study in the 1970s (The Seven Countries Study) concluded that the Mediterranean lifestyle was the reason for the favourable health profiles in these countries.

The diet of Mediterranean peoples is characterized by a low consumption of saturated fat (dairy products and meat), no consumption of trans fats, a low consumption of omega-6 fats and a high consumption of monounsaturated fat (olive oil, nuts) and omega-3 fats (fish). Moreover, they eat a lot of pulses (beans, peas, lentils) and fibrous vegetables. They eat pasta and rice, but fewer potatoes and less bread (which is eaten with a meal, not as a meal).

The low incidence of lifestyle diseases in Mediterranean countries, despite a relatively high consumption of fat (albeit unsaturated), is referred to as 'the Mediterranean Paradox'. It provided further proof that there is more to the world epidemic of obesity and diabetes than a high consumption of fat.

Stress – today's killer

Do you feel stressed now and then? Or most of the time? You are not alone. It is impossible to survive without experiencing stress. That's exactly why stress developed throughout human and animal evolution: as a survival mechanism. Let's suppose you're an antelope grazing quietly on the African savannah, minding your own business, when suddenly you are attacked by a leopard. Now, either you choose to fight the leopard (probably not a wise decision), or you decide to flee, which is your only way to survive. In order to escape, you need to run fast and you need to be extremely alert. This would be impossible if your body wasn't able to react appropriately to stress. You are not an antelope, of course, but all animals, including humans, have the very same stress reaction mechanism.

Faced with a potential danger – or opportunity, seen from the leopard's point of view – your body reacts by releasing a series of hormones, aimed at helping you survive. Almost at the speed of light, a myriad of chemical reactions occurs in your body, which makes up your 'fight-or-flight' reaction. Your heart beats faster, blood pressure goes up, you may start perspiring, you feel very alert. All these are part of the 'alarm' phase of the stress reaction, mediated by a hormone produced in the inner layer (medulla) of the adrenal gland, good old adrenalin (also called epinephrine).

Now, let me see, what else do you need in order to run fast and escape from the leopard, or catch that antelope? You guessed: energy. Energy is required for every chemical reaction in the universe, even those that release energy as a result. Where can you get energy from? Well, since we are not born with an electrical socket attached to our bodies, we must ourselves provide the necessary energy. According to one of the most important laws of physics, energy can neither be created nor disappear. It can only be converted from one form to another. The energy needed by our body to function, fight or flee has to come from somewhere. That somewhere is food, which is why we eat. Faced with a stressful situation, you need a sudden burst of energy in order to cope with the imminent danger or opportunity. But for the antelope (and our ancestors) this is not a good time to eat, so this energy has to come from somewhere else. That is one of the reasons why we store energy. Under stress, your body releases the extra energy required thanks to the effect of another hormone, cortisol, which is produced in the outer layer (cortex) of the adrenal gland. This is our primary stress hormone, without which survival would be impossible in the African savannah.

But wait a minute, what happens when you feel stressed because you are late for work or because you just realized that you cannot meet that deadline you are faced with at work? Or because you're stuck in a traffic jam, outstanding bills have to be paid, your kids are playing up? Well, your body reacts in the very same way it would if you were the antelope facing the leopard. The only trouble is, you cannot run from traffic, your children, bills or problems at work. Running away provided the antelope (and early humans) with the necessary reaction to complete the 'fight-or-flight' response and find relief from the stressor.

After having successfully escaped the danger, our antelope would return to grazing peacefully and the stress reaction would become a thing of the past. The difference with humans living modern lives is that our most common stress reactions rarely provide us with the opportunity to fight or flee, the physical part that should complete a normal stress reaction. This leads to constantly elevated levels of stress hormones, both adrenalin and cortisol. You are gradually caught up in chronic stress. The symptoms come sneaking up on you, extra fat around your waist, waning sex drive, lower energy levels, difficulty in concentrating, and your memory is not what it used to be. You may think that this is simply an inevitable result of ageing. Well, think again: these are the signs of chronic stress. In fact, many children and young people experience the same problems nowadays.

Stress and chronic disease

Chronic stress, with constantly elevated cortisol levels, is one of the major causes of many modern lifestyle disorders. The following is a short, and by no means complete, list of diseases and medical conditions associated with over-production of cortisol levels:

- carbohydrate cravings and increased appetite (obesity)
- increased abdominal fat (type II diabetes, obesity, heart disease, cancer)
- high blood pressure (heart disease)
- high triglycerides, low HDL cholesterol (heart disease)
- reduced muscle mass and metabolism (obesity, osteoporosis)
- anxiety, depression and mood swings
- lower sex drive
- reduced bone mass (osteoporosis)
- learning impairment and poor memory (including Alzheimer's disease)
- impaired immune response and frequent infections
- increased PMS symptoms and menopausal symptoms

How food causes stress

Did you realize that food can actually cause you stress? Each time you eat food that causes a rapid and sharp rise in your blood sugar levels (foods with a high glycaemic load), excess insulin is produced to make sure that blood sugars return to normal, fast. Our brain depends on a steady flow of blood sugar for energy and dislikes both high and low blood sugar levels. Rapidly falling blood sugar levels 45 minutes to 2 hours after eating high-glycaemic foods is a potential hazard for the brain. In fact blood sugar often falls slightly below fasting levels 2 hours after eating high-glycaemic foods, a condition called reactive postprandial hypoglycaemia. Unless something is done to stabilize blood sugar, it could end up in hypoglycaemia and we would faint or suffer from seizures. Our body perceives this as a stressful situation and – you guessed it – our adrenal glands start secreting adrenalin and cortisol, the universal reaction to stress.

Remember what I said earlier about these hormones? They provide the extra energy needed during stress. So how do they do this? In order to stabilize falling blood sugar levels, adrenalin and cortisol break down liver glycogen (stored blood sugar) to release glucose, fat tissue to release fatty acids *and* muscle tissue to release amino acids, which are then converted to blood glucose for energy. If you frequently eat high-glycaemic foods, you will start up a blood sugar roller-coaster and chronic stress, reducing your muscle mass and thus slowing down your metabolism. That sets the stage for weight gain, diabetes, heart disease and cancer.

And that's not all: as adrenalin and cortisol levels increase in response to stress, levels of another adrenal gland hormone, DHEA, and of testosterone decrease, which leads to reduced sex drive as well as to muscle and bone mass loss, lowering your metabolism and increasing your risk of osteoporosis.

By now you are probably thinking, wouldn't I be better off without cortisol and insulin? However, a normal level of these hormones is not a problem; in fact you would not survive without them. Insulin is necessary for blood sugar control and energy storage, and cortisol is needed for the restoration of energy stores as a response to stress. It is chronically excessive levels that cause the trouble.

The important point here is balance, keeping both insulin and cortisol levels from being neither too high or too low. Chronically elevated cortisol and insulin put you in a continuous fat-storing and muscle-depleting mode, gradually lowering your metabolism and inducing insulin resistance. I think we can all agree that it makes no sense to expose your body to stress just by choosing the wrong food.

Comfort eating

Elevated cortisol increases your appetite and cravings for sugar and high-glycaemic foods in combination with fat (ice cream, chocolate and other comfort foods). You may have noticed that you can get through the whole day without eating, only to overindulge in comfort foods when you 'relax' in the evening in front of the TV. This is the result of stress and high cortisol levels during your day at work. Foods that are rich in both carbohydrate and fat are soothing, calming and antidepressant. They increase the levels of serotonin and endorphins in the brain, which drop as a result of high cortisol levels. Interestingly, there is only one natural food for humans that is rich in both carbohydrate and fat: mother's milk. About 50 per cent of the calories in mother's milk come from fat (with a well-balanced proportion of saturated, monounsaturated and polyunsaturated fatty acids), 42 per cent come from a medium-glycaemic carbohydrate (lactose) and 8 per cent from protein. Natural whole foods are either high in carbohydrate and low in fat (fruits, berries, grains, pulses), high in fat and low in carbohydrate (nuts, olives, seeds, avocados) or high in protein and often in fat with almost no carbohydrate (meat, poultry, eggs, fish, seafood). You will only find the combination of high carbohydrate and fat in processed, man-made foods. Just like mother's milk, these foods provide us with a soothing, calming, pleasant sensation, and of course this is something we like to experience often. Stress and high cortisol levels cause you to eat this type of food more frequently, leading to high insulin levels, storage of abdominal fat and a higher risk of diabetes, heart disease and cancer.

Cortisol and your body clock

Cortisol secretion follows a natural circadian rhythm: levels are highest in the early morning around awakening and gradually fall during the day, reaching their lowest levels during the evening and first part of the night. Obese and diabetic individuals do not necessarily have a higher total cortisol production, but may have a disrupted secretion pattern, with one or several peaks during the day and in the evening. This interferes with normal metabolism, and disrupts the production of neurotransmitters like serotonin and the sleep hormone melatonin, resulting in mood disorders and poor sleep, paving the way for increased appetite, obesity and chronic disease.

The stress-inflammation connection

In addition to providing your body with the necessary fuel to 'fight or flee' in an acute stress situation, cortisol also has profound effects on regulating various aspects of your metabolism, your mood, immune system and inflammatory responses, blood pressure, contraction or relaxation of blood vessels, repair and maintenance of muscles, skin, bones and connective tissue. Most of these processes are mediated through eicosanoids, the superhormones secreted by all cells in your body, making up your internal 'biological internet' (read more about this on page 64).

In a normal, healthy body, these processes run smoothly, as long as you do not overproduce cortisol as a result of chronic stress. Cortisol suppresses the production of both 'good' and 'bad' eicosanoids. During periods of increased stress, you are likely to experience an increase in conditions like asthma and allergies, psoriasis and eczema, migraines, rheumatoid arthritis and inflammatory bowel diseases such as Crohn's disease, ulcerative colitis and irritable bowel syndrome. All of these conditions can be alleviated by controlling the balance of

Just how stressed are you?

Try this test to get a rough idea of your current stress level.
Answer every question, scoring 0 for 'no/never'; 1 for 'occasionally'; 2 for 'yes/often

How often do you feel:
anxious or depressed?
aggressive or angry?
confused or overwhelmed?
inadequate?
tired without an obvious reason?

How often do you:
get exposed to stressful situations (at work, home or elsewhere)?
have trouble getting to sleep?
not manage to sleep a full 8 hours?
experience low sex drive?
diet to control your weight?
crave sweets, refined carbohydrates and junk food?

have poor memory and/or concentration?
experience aches and pains in your head, neck or shoulders?
suffer from heartburn, flatulence, bloating, loose stools or constipation?
get infections like flu, colds, sinus problems, skin infections?

Have you been diagnosed with:
high blood sugar?
high blood pressure?
high triglycerides?
high total cholesterol and low HDL cholesterol?

A total score of 0–6 indicates a low/normal stress level.
7–12 points indicates a moderate stress level requiring lifestyle changes.
12 or more points puts you at risk of chronic disease due to a high stress level. You should seek help to manage this problem.

eicosanoids through a balanced, low-glycaemic diet with higher protein levels, no trans fats (from partially hydrogenated vegetable oils found in processed foods), and a balanced intake of omega-3 and omega-6 essential fatty acids.

Coping with stress

So how do you cope with the stress of modern life? It is obvious that reducing exposure to stress is very important. However, none of us is immune to stressful situations, so coping with stress is as important as reducing or avoiding stress. All the negative effects of stress and excessive cortisol and insulin secretion can be avoided through a combination of stress management techniques (such as meditation, yoga, tai chi, prayer) and physical exercise (both endurance and resistance training) together with a healthy, well-balanced, low-glycaemic diet: the Greek Doctor's Diet.

Oxidation and inflammation: the cause of all chronic disease

Oxidation is basically the process by which cell membranes are damaged by oxidative stress. Just as iron eventually becomes rusty due to exposure to oxygen, our bodies go through a similar process. We need oxygen to survive, therefore a certain amount of oxidative stress is unavoidable, and indeed it is what brings about a natural death. However, oxidative stress is also caused by external factors such as smoking, exposure to pollution and consuming highly-processed, chemically altered foods. By eating a lot of foods that oxidize rapidly we age prematurely and become chronically ill. We also increase our need for antioxidant foods like unprocessed nuts, vegetables, berries, herbs and spices – the very foods that are displaced in the modern diet by fast food.

Ageing, diet and antioxidants

Have you ever wondered why we age? There are a few theories, but one of the most important and most likely centres on so-called free radicals. To understand this theory, you have to know how the body produces energy. Each and every cell in the body contains tiny structures called mitochondria. These are our 'energy factories' where food is processed with oxygen to provide energy. Without oxygen and without food, there would be no metabolism. However, in the same way as a car produces waste – i.e. fumes – in the process of utilizing fuel, our body also produces waste when it metabolizes food. During this oxidation process substances are formed that we know as free radicals. When metabolism works perfectly, relatively few waste substances and free radicals are formed, and the body is prepared and capable of rendering them harmless. If, on the other hand, we eat the wrong type of food, with many artificial additives or that lacks the vital vitamins and minerals that counteract free radical damage, we produce more toxic waste and free radicals for the body to get rid of. This is compounded if the body is attacked daily by harmful substances (toxins) such as traffic fumes or chemicals.

What are free radicals? To understand them we need to consider our cells. The cells in the body are made up of molecules, which in turn are made up of atoms. As we know, atoms consist of protons and electrons, which have reverse electrical charges – protons have a positive electrical charge and electrons a negative charge. The two are attracted to each other in the same way as two magnets. When there is a fine balance between the two, the system is externally electrically neutral. However, for life to function, the system needs to be 'disturbed' so that energy is released. Normally electrons are moved from atom to atom in an orderly and controlled way, under the guidance of numerous bodily enzymes, our internal antioxidant system. When the balance is upset and an atom loses an electron, the atom becomes unbalanced and positively charged. It then becomes a free radical. The free radical is very electrically active and tries to get hold of another electron to pair up and regain electrical balance. When the free radical steals an electron from its surroundings, a new free radical is formed, and so the process continues. As long as this process takes place in a controlled way, everything is normal. However, if too many free radicals are formed (due to toxic substances or other sources of oxidative stress), the system loses control. The result can be cell damage, disease, ageing and eventually death, as cells simply corrode more quickly.

What then are antioxidants? Imagine life as a fireplace with a flame that burns for as long as we live. We metabolize food and oxygen in the same way that the fireplace does with wood and oxygen. In this process random sparks occur. The wrong type of wood or too much air, or the addition of oil, may increase the number of sparks. If there is nothing to catch the sparks, a fire could start. That is why we use a fireguard. If we think of the fireplace as our body, the flame is the metabolism, the sparks are free radicals and the fireguard is the antioxidants. The antioxidants catch, or 'quench', superfluous free radicals so that they can be made harmless. Some examples of antioxidants or substances needed for our own antioxidant production are vitamin C, vitamin E, beta-carotene (provitamin A), bioflavanoids, coenzyme Q10 and selenium. Low intake of these through poor diet, or a high level of oxidative stress due to a harmful environment or an unhealthy lifestyle, may result in an inadequate supply of antioxidants, with accompanying premature ageing or illness.

Is the answer then to take some of these antioxidants as dietary supplements? This is not the easy solution it may first appear to be. Various antioxidants are dependent on each other for optimal functioning. Vitamin E, for instance, needs enough vitamin C to do its job properly. That is why it is extremely important to get enough of a wide range of vitamins and minerals, as well as other antioxidants, preferably through a balanced and natural diet rich in vegetables, pulses, fruit, whole grains and nuts, together with high-quality protein like fish, chicken, game and meat. This does not mean that antioxidants in the form of dietary supplements have no value. The trio of vitamin

C, vitamin E and betacarotene (provitamin A), along with selenium, should ensure you are well equipped in the fight against free radicals. In combination with a balanced, natural diet these supplements can prevent diseases like cancer, cardiovascular disease and diabetes, to mention but a few.

Inflammation

We have already seen how stress and an unbalanced diet are linked to both obesity and chronic disease, through the effects of hormones like cortisol and insulin. Now let's look at what happens at the cellular level. You have probably at some point in your life experienced a sprained ankle or a minor burn. You will have noticed that the wounded or burned area gets red, swollen and warm – the classic signs of inflammation. This is caused by hormone-like substances called eicosanoids. The purpose of these biochemicals, which are manufactured within the body from fats, is to fight the assault. This is a natural and necessary reaction, pretty much like the body producing adrenalin and cortisol as a result of acute stress, and ultimately it promotes healing. However, under certain conditions, inflammation can become chronic and exacerbate an existing condition or cause chronic disease.

Due to stressful lives, poor diets and lack of physical activity, as well as exposure to tobacco smoke and other environmental pollutants, many of us suffer from one or several chronic inflammation disorders. These can include gastritis, dermatitis, osteoarthritis, asthmatic bronchitis (asthma) and vasculitis – a general term for a group of diseases characterized by inflammation of the blood vessels, which can affect the heart, brain, kidneys, eyes and other organs (migraine, for example, is a form of vasculitis). Inflammation is in fact involved in every type of chronic disease. The only thing that varies is the organ and type of cell affected. Millions of people in the western world suffer from inflammatory diseases and use some type of anti-inflammatory medication – such as aspirin, ibuprofen or cortisone – every day.

Chronic inflammation means that something has gone very wrong with your health. Instead of repairing your body – which is the purpose of localized, temporary inflammation – chronic inflammation breaks it down, speeds up the ageing process and causes disease. Inflammatory diseases have increased dramatically over the last four or five decades, in tandem with the increased consumption of junk food, trans fats, refined carbohydrates and sugars and a decline in the consumption of natural whole foods such as vegetables and nuts.

Some foods promote inflammation (pro-inflammatory foods) while others reduce inflammation (anti-inflammatory foods). What you eat – proteins, essential fats, vitamins and minerals – directly affects the amount of inflammation in your body. If your intake of pro-inflammatory foods is regularly higher than that of anti-inflammatory foods, you are setting the stage for chronic inflammatory disease. Unfortunately, having one type of chronic inflammation, such as asthma, greatly increases your risk of developing others in the future.

Pro-inflammatory foods

The following foods are known to promote inflammation, by increasing the levels of arachidonic acid, an omega-6 fatty acid (see box), in your body, or by reducing the anti-inflammatory effects of the omega-3 fatty acids.

• Vegetable oils, processed foods and margarines: Excessive amounts of vegetable oils, such as sunflower, soy, corn, safflower, as well as all processed foods

ARACHIDONIC ACID

Arachidonic acid is an omega-6 fatty acid. An excess of arachidonic acid causes the formation of various inflammatory substances (including series-2 prostaglandins) that can lead to high blood pressure, an increased risk of thrombosis, and inflammatory conditions such as asthma, allergies, arthritis and skin problems.

The body can produce arachidonic acid itself from other fatty acids, so there is no need to get even more from food. Note also that too much or the wrong type of carbohydrates (high-glycaemic carbohydrates such as sugar, potatoes, white bread and other flour products) also lead to a higher production of arachidonic acid, because they cause blood sugar and subsequently insulin production to increase. A high level of insulin boosts the production of arachidonic acid and 'bad' eicosanoids (see page 64).

Not everybody is equally sensitive to the harmful effects of arachidonic acid. The major symptoms of sensitivity to, or an elevated level of, arachidonic acid are chronic exhaustion, poor sleep quality, problems getting out of bed in the morning, thin or fine hair, thin nails that break easily, indigestion, dry flaky skin and rashes.

containing these oils (including most types of margarines and fried foods), will have a pro-inflammatory effect. This is due to the fact that they contain too high a level of omega-6 polyunsaturated fatty acids, which increase levels of inflammatory eicosanoids in the body. Omega-6 fatty acids have been promoted as a healthy fat during the past few decades, but while they do lower total cholesterol levels, and are therefore thought to decrease the risk of heart disease, over-consumption can lead to inflammation and exacerbate oxidation. Note also that polyunsaturated fat (for instance, that found in walnuts, soya beans, fatty fish etc) goes stale (oxidizes) much faster than monounsaturated (that found in olive oil, avocados, almonds) or saturated fat.

• Trans fatty acids: These are found in foods containing 'hydrogenated vegetable oils/fats'. Common sources include processed foods like margarine, non-dairy creamers, cookies and biscuits, croissants and Danish pastries, industrially produced breads, salad dressing, soup mixes etc. Trans fatty acids are chemically altered during processing, rendering our body unable to metabolize them properly. They interfere with the metabolism of non trans (also called cis) fatty acids and in particular with the beneficial anti-inflammatory omega-3 fatty acids (found in flaxseed, fatty fish, cod liver oil etc.). Trans fatty acids are associated with a greatly increased risk of heart disease and many other inflammatory and degenerative diseases. Denmark and Canada have introduced new regulations aimed at minimizing the level of industrially-produced trans fatty acids in food.

• Pro-oxidant foods and substances: These are foods that increase oxidation by providing excessive free radicals, increasing the risk of chronic disease and premature ageing. Examples include barbecued food, trans fats, excessive alcohol consumption, smoking and exposure to traffic fumes and toxic substances.

Anti-inflammatory foods

The following foods are some of those known to decrease inflammation, by increasing the levels of anti-inflammatory eicosanoids.

• Omega-3 fatty acids: These are the building blocks of the anti-inflammatory series 3 eicosanoids. In addition, the long chain omega-3 fatty acid EPA (which is either produced in the body from the plant-based alpha-linolenic acid, found in flaxseed or walnuts, or supplied directly in the form of fatty fish, fish oil or cod liver oil) positively interferes with the metabolism of omega-6, ensuring lower production of arachidonic acid and a higher production of the anti-inflammatory series 1 eicosanoids. Omega-3 fatty acids make sure that your body turns off inflammatory reactions when they are no longer needed, thus preventing chronic inflammation. By including 100g of fatty fish daily and 1–2 teaspoons of ground flaxseeds or flax oil, you will get enough omega-3 (alternatively, take a daily supplement of cod liver oil or fish oil with pure omega-3 – see Chapter 10 for more on supplements). If you suffer from a chronic inflammatory condition, you may have to increase substantially the amount of omega-3.

• Omega-6 fatty acids: An adequate intake of omega-6 fatty acids is necessary for the production of the anti-inflammatory series 1 eicosanoids, under the influence of omega-3 EPA. If the diet is biased too much in favour of omega-6 fatty acids, arachidonic acid is produced (see the box on page 104), which increases inflammation. Western diets are generally too high in omega-6 and too low in omega-3, hence the prevalence of chronic inflammation. We should be getting 2–4 times more omega-6 than omega-3 in our diet, but we get as much as 20–30 times more omega-6. By changing from vegetable oils such as soy, corn, sunflower, safflower, cottonseed and margarines and processed foods based on these oils to extra virgin (cold-pressed) olive oil and rapeseed oil and eating a handful of mixed unprocessed nuts and seeds daily, you will get enough, but not too much, omega-6.

• Antioxidant-rich foods: These include whole nuts and seeds, in particular walnuts; berries (for instance, blueberries); spices such cinnamon and cloves; and herbs like oregano, which prevent oxidation and inflammation. Antioxidant supplements (which generally contain vitamins C and E and selenium) are also widely available and particularly valuable if you have a high intake of omega-6 or suffer from chronic inflammation.

Eicosanoids

One of the most important functions of essential fatty acids is that they act as the building blocks for the formation of eicosanoids, molecules with 20 carbon atoms (from the Greek *eicosi*, which means twenty). These are very biologically-active, hormone-like substances that all multicellular living organisms produce. They belong to our paracrine system, a part of our internal 'biological internet'. This is the communication system of our cells, enabling the many trillion cells of our body to function in a coordinated manner. Around 100 different eicosanoids have been identified and they regulate almost all physiological functions, including:

• Inflammatory response
• Blood coagulation
• Immune response
• Contraction of smooth muscle cells (abdominal pain, menstrual cramps, etc.)
• Sexual function (erection)
• Pain and fever, sleep
• Production of stomach acid
• Contraction or relaxation of the bronchi (asthma)
• Contraction or relaxation of the blood vessels (hypertension, migraine)
• Cell growth and division

Eicosanoid balance defines optimal health, and eicosanoid imbalance is involved in one way or another in every disease. The following disorders are among those that are due to eicosanoid imbalance:

• Blood clots
• Asthma and allergies
• High blood pressure
• Rheumatism and joint problems
• Inflammatory bowel disease
• Eczema and psoriasis

Eicosanoids are made of omega-3 and omega-6 fatty acids and their production is influenced by the balance of these fatty acids in the diet, the intake of other fats that interfere with the production of eicosanoids, and the effect of hormones like insulin, glucagon and cortisol. Other factors that can adversely affect eicosanoid balance include ageing, virus infections, stress and toxins. It is therefore important to:

• Ensure adequate intake of omega-3 and omega-6 fatty acids: omega-3 to omega-6 ratio should be 1:2–4 (usually a fish oil supplement is needed)
• Reduce any excess intake of saturated fat and omega-6 and most importantly ban trans fats
• Reduce insulin production by reducing intake of sugar and high-glycaemic carbohydrates
• Ensure adequate intake of protein, vitamins and minerals
• Reduce alcohol and stress
• Avoid smoking
• Supplementation with zinc, chromium, magnesium, vitamin B complex, vitamin E and C may also be beneficial (see chapter 10).

THE GREEK DOCTOR'S ANTI-INFLAMMATORY DIET

The Greek Doctor's diet not only helps you maintain healthy blood sugar and insulin levels and avoid food-induced stress, but it is designed to reduce inflammation as well. By following this diet plan, you:

• increase the amount of non-starchy vegetables, pulses, berries, raw nuts, herbs and spices and lean protein, providing powerful antioxidants and healthy blood sugar and insulin/glucagon levels
• reduce sugar and refined grains, pasta, bread, rice and potatoes, avoiding excessive blood sugar, insulin and cortisol
• ban pro-inflammatory trans fat and replace excessive omega-6-rich oils with monounsaturated olive oil and rapeseed oil
• increase your intake of anti-inflammatory omega-3s in flaxseed, nuts, seeds, fatty fish, cod liver oil or fish oil.

CHAPTER 8

SURVIVAL OF THE FATTEST – OUR GENES TAKE REVENGE

here is a lot to be learned by taking a closer look at our Stone Age ancestors. Genetically, man and his predecessors are considered to be about 7 million years old, and our genes are thought to have remained almost unaltered during the last 10,000–40,000 years. Did you know that 98 per cent of our genes are identical to those of a chimpanzee? That is one reason why all vaccines are tested on chimpanzees before their use is approved for humans. We are closely related to all mammals, and if we go far enough back in time, we will find that we are related to other animals and also to plants. In fact, all life has the same origin.

Most animals know instinctively what they should and should not eat. A lion, for instance, does not eat grass just because there is no prey to be had, and a cow does not eat meat if it cannot find grass. Why is it that humans no longer know what they can and should eat and how best to use their bodies?

Until relatively recently in evolutionary terms, food was scarce, and humans had to be physically active to get enough food – by gathering or hunting. Individuals with the ability to digest and store effectively the food that they ate (and who thus had a tendency to become overweight) were at a considerable advantage because they were able to maintain normal weight with less food. The evolution of the species is based on this principle of survival.

Infections, from simple throat infections to diseases like tuberculosis, were the most common causes of death. And it was slim people with a high metabolism who more often died of infections. It was not until the twentieth century, when food became abundant and modern medicine and antibiotics made it possible to treat a long list of infectious diseases effectively, that our genes turned against us. People with a genetically slow metabolism and a tendency to gain weight easily are the ones who have survived throughout human evolution, and it is their genes that have been passed on.

We are what we eat

How is it possible for such a genetic advantage to change, resulting in conditions that are so detrimental to our health, such as obesity, diabetes and other lifestyle diseases?

Our genes have developed over millions of years, and evolution has determined the way we relate to food and our need for certain nutrients. Not only are we what we eat but we are what our forefathers ate during those 7 million years of evolution. In fact, our genes still operate as they did in the Stone Age. The functions of our heart, muscles, immune system, reproductive organs – our entire system – are based on a certain diet. Provided that we supply our body with the nutrients it needs, it will do a good job and we will stay healthy. On the other hand, if we consume unnatural, refined foods or have a badly unbalanced diet, the result is illness and premature ageing. It is ridiculous to believe that we can eat what we like without paying a price for it. Take mad cow disease (BSE), for example. No wonder things like this occur when we feed our cows with beef carcasses. We have to respect nature if we are to stay healthy. But in order for us to do so, we need to know more about what kinds of food are naturally good for us.

Stone Age man

Anthropology and paleontology study human behaviour from a historical perspective. By analysing food and stool remnants found in early human settlements, it is possible to get an idea of what Stone Age man ate and how life was conducted. Other sources of information include the stomach contents of mummies and bodies that have been preserved in peat bogs; ancient cave paintings and tools also provide valuable clues. We can also learn from still-existing aboriginal societies such as those in Australia, parts of Africa and

THE EVOLUTION OF MAN IN A NUTSHELL

- 98 per cent of our genes are identical to those of the chimpanzee (over 7 million years old).
- For 3 million years (100,000 generations), we lived as hunters and gatherers.
- For 10,000 years (300 generations), we lived as farmers.
- For 200 years (less than ten generations), we have lived in the Industrial age.
- For 30 years (one generation), we have lived with junk food and computers.
- Our genes have remained almost unaltered for the last 10,000 years.

South America, whose hunting and gathering lifestyle remains to a certain degree unchanged.

The oldest remains of hominids (human-like creatures), estimated to be around 7 million years old, were found in Chad in 2002. The skeleton of a female hominid, named Lucy by its discoverers, was found in 1974 in Ethiopia; it is believed to be approximately 3 million years old. *Homo erectus*, upright man, appeared around 2 million years ago. These early humans mastered the technique of kindling a fire and were good with simple tools; over the next 100,000 years or so they spread from Africa as far as Indonesia and China. Traces of a Stone Age man known as *Homo heidelbergensis* dating back at least 500,000 years have been found in Europe. He evolved into Neanderthal man, who lived about 200,000 to 300,000 years ago, and died out about 30,000 years ago. Early modern man, *Homo sapiens*, appeared around 40,000 years ago, co-existing with Neanderthal man and, according to many evolution biologists, even causing his extinction.

Man originated in Africa, where the tropical climate was rich in fruit, berries, vegetables and roots; early humans also hunted for meat and fish and followed big animal herds on the savannahs. The availability of food varied with the seasons. If we take a look at the chimpanzee, our closest relative, we get a good picture of what Stone Age man ate. Chimpanzees are not entirely vegetarian. For the most part, they have a vegetarian diet, but from time to time they gather and go hunting for meat. They also get a certain amount of animal protein from eating insects that are found among the leaves, fruit and vegetables that they regularly eat.

Homo sapiens (modern man) has shown a remarkable adaptability. It is only 10,000 years since the last ice age in Europe. At that time our 'European' ancestors were forced to adapt themselves to a life with fewer fruits and vegetables and more protein, in the form of fish, fowl and meat. If you look at the hunter-gatherer societies of today, you will find a wide spectrum of dietary composition. Ninety-five per cent of the Eskimos' diet comes from animals (fish, seals, whales), whereas the Australian Aborigines' diet consists mainly of plant foods and only 10 to 15 per cent meat. We are one of the few species that can be found all over the world, from the Arctic regions to the great deserts, with little variation in our genetic make-up. Our genes are still in the Stone Age, while we live in the Internet age.

The Stone Age diet

There is a big difference between the Stone Age diet and what we eat today. The Stone Age diet was characterized by low-energy density, which means it was high in fibre and water and low in energy-providing nutrients. The result was that our forefathers, who were very active, had to eat relatively large amounts of food in order to obtain enough nourishment. Carbohydrates were mainly found in fruit and roots, not in vegetables, which contain only low amounts of carbohydrates. Starch in the form of cereals and potatoes was not available. Carbohydrates made up, on average, around 40–45 per cent of their diet; today's diet contains around 52–55 per cent carbohydrates – but it is a very different type of carbohydrate.

The average Stone Age diet and the modern diet

Our diet is becoming increasingly less healthy.

	Stone Age	Today
Protein	34%	13%
Fat	21%	35%
Carbohydrates	45%	52%
Fibre	46g/day	20g/day
Sugar (added)	0%	14%
Salt (added)	0g/day	approximately 10g/day

About 30–35 per cent of the energy in the Stone Age diet came from protein. Protein was mainly found in meat, fish and eggs. Game (wild animals and birds) is fairly lean, and people in the Stone Age did not keep animals. High-fat foods are not abundant in nature: egg yolks, nuts and oily fish, as well as game, were the main source of fat for Stone Age man, who got 25 – 30 per cent of his energy from fat – mostly unsaturated fat from nuts and fish. It was not until about 10,000 years ago that man started growing grain and keeping animals (fattening them by feeding them on grain and restricting their ability to roam). It was at this time that people (mainly in Europe and colder climates) started drinking milk from goats, sheep and cows. Today, the majority of the earth's population (approximately 80 per cent) cannot drink milk without discomfort (due to lactose intolerance).

Stone Age people also consumed about six times less salt (sodium) than we do. In fact, no other land-based creature has such a high salt intake as modern man. We only need about 1g of salt a day, yet the average intake is far higher. A chronically high salt intake from a young age might explain the problem a lot of people are having with high blood pressure.

The consumption of fibre from fruit and vegetables was considerably higher in earlier times, at least 45g (1½ oz) a day rather than the 10–20g we eat today. Before preservatives, food had to be eaten fresh. Fruit and vegetables were eaten straight from the tree or plant, bursting with vitamins and antioxidants. Moreover, man was constantly on the move and walked approximately 30km (19 miles) a day searching for food.

The Mediterranean diet

Diets vary with each country, and many different factors play a role in the development of food traditions. Most important is the availability of different foods. The first humans came to Europe from Africa and the Middle East more than 500,000 years ago. In the beginning, they populated southern Europe, but gradually some of them moved north in search of food.

The Mediterranean and North African climate is much more hospitable than that of the Northern countries. Man is genetically equipped to live in latitudes with a warmer climate, with temperatures around 25 to 35 degrees Celsius. This includes the countries around the Mediterranean, northern parts of Africa, South Africa, parts of the southern United States, Central America and the northern parts of South America – and, on the other side of the world, the northern parts of Australia. In such climates, man can live without clothes and an artificial heat supply, and the food found in these areas is the food that we are genetically programmed to eat. The Mediterranean diet that has recently been proved to be so favourable to health is characterized by a great variety of vegetables and pulses, olive oil, nuts and fruit, and fish.

Why does sweet food and fat taste so good?

Our brain needs blood sugar. Natural sugar is found in fruit and honey, and breast milk, the first food we encounter, also contains a sugar, lactose. It would be strange if this taste did not appeal to us. We are, in fact, programmed to like this sweet taste and to look for sweet foods. (Most natural poisons taste quite bitter, something that has made it possible for us to survive.)

Similarly, fat is a rich source of energy. By eating as much as possible of it, one could store energy for use later on. And since fat is relatively seldom found in nature, it was important for Stone Age man and his chances of survival that he was good at recognizing fatty foods.

The agricultural revolution

About 10,000 years ago, a gigantic experiment in the history of man began. The need for more reliable sources of food led man to start keeping animals and growing grain and pulses. As farming became widespread, man gradually gave up his nomadic lifestyle and began to establish larger and more stable social units. Knowledge and culture developed rapidly. The transition from hunting and gathering to a life based on farming revolutionized the world. Eventually, trade led to closer contact between groups of societies, and advanced civilizations such as those of China, Egypt and Greece began to develop.

The cultivation of cereal products made it possible for man to settle all over the world. Unlike fruit and vegetables, grain is a dense carbohydrate, packed with energy. Increased consumption of cereal products soon led to a dramatic increase in man's carbohydrate intake, at the expense of other energy sources such as protein and unsaturated fat. Farm-raised animals were also fed with grain, thus the fat content of meat and poultry increased. Along with milk, this led to an increase in the amount of saturated fat in people's diet. Since the need to hunt and the search for fruit, roots and vegetables diminished, man also became less physically active.

The industrial revolution – from natural to refined

Diet-wise, little changed between the time man started farming and the eighteenth century. Farming became more specialized, but people ate more or less the same type of food. As the industrial revolution got under way, people became even less physically active as heavy chores were taken over by machines. At around the same time, three ingredients began to find their way into our diet in unprecedented quantities: sugar, potatoes and white flour – between them, they are the cause of much of today's obesity and other lifestyle-related illness. In many ways, sugar and white flour are antinutrients. In order for the body to burn them, they feed on vitamins, minerals and antioxidants, while they themselves contribute very little (in the case of white flour) or nothing at all (in the case of sugar).

Sugar – sweet but dangerous

Historically speaking, honey was the only sweet additive that was available to us. Fruits and dates satisfied man's need for sweetness. Honey was not available everywhere, and certainly not in large quantities. A cave painting dating back to 10,000 BC in Valencia in Spain shows two women gathering honey. Honey is high in fructose and glucose and has a varying GI, depending on its composition. Fruit contains mostly fructose, which has a low GI.

Sugar (sucrose) as we now know it, is extracted from sugar cane or sugar beet. Sugar cane has been grown in India for about 3000 years. In the past, it was eaten as a fruit and chewed raw (providing fibre, vitamins and minerals), but basic ways of refining sugar to form syrups and crystals made it more easily transportable. Sugar made its way to the Mediterranean countries between the seventh and eleventh centuries, and the sugar trade developed throughout Europe, though sugar remained a luxury commodity. Columbus took sugar cane to the Americas and the West Indies at the end of the fifteenth century, and Spanish, Portuguese, English, French and Dutch colonists soon began a massive expansion of the sugar trade, hand-in-hand with the slave trade. At the beginning of the eighteenth century sugar was still a luxury: Arthritis urica, popularly referred to as gout, was an illness that affected mainly the wealthy – it is linked to a high consumption of sugar. During the eighteenth century, as imports of sugar from the colonies increased, so did its consumption among the bourgeoisie. After Napoleon's defeat at Trafalgar in 1805, a trade embargo forced him to find a new way to produce sugar. A French man named Benjamin

Delessert developed the first factory to extract sugar from sugar beets in 1812; the rest is history, and today 30 per cent of the world's sucrose comes from sugar beet. In 1789, the average consumption of sugar per person in France was less than 1kg (2lb) a year. By 1880, consumption had reached 8.5kg (19lb) per person. During the nineteenth century, factories also began to churn out sweets and sugary soft drinks.

In the United States (which all western countries resemble more and more), sugar consumption has reached a staggering 65kg (130lb) per person per year, much of it 'hidden' in soft drinks and processed foods.

The link between sugar (sucrose) and illness was described in the book *Sugar Blues* by William Dufty in 1976. The funny thing is that this has been known for more than 150 years. In the middle of the 1850s, the first cases of cardiovascular disease were reported on the island of Saint Helena, after the English started importing sugar. Eskimo people had not experienced either tooth decay (caries) or any coronary disease until they were introduced to foods rich in sugar, white flour and processed fat. It took less than one generation before they developed modern lifestyle diseases.

Too many potatoes?

Potatoes, indigenous to South America, were introduced to Europe and parts of Asia in the sixteenth century. It took more than 150 years before they became really popular, but now they are an almost indispensable accompaniment to meals and a major snack food. The potato is a robust plant that can survive a relatively harsh climate, and it is easy to understand why such an efficient source of energy became so popular. A large part of the potato crop is also used to feed pigs. In fact, potatoes and grain are some of the most efficient and tasty foodstuffs for fattening domestic animals. Raw potatoes are indigestible to humans, but when a potato is cooked, its starch is altered and it becomes easily digestible. When eaten, cooked potato leads to a quick rise in blood sugar and insulin level.

Our daily bread

Until the middle of the nineteenth century, and the invention of high-speed steel roller mills, it was not technically possible to grind grains very finely. Instead they were ground between stones, which retained the outer part (bran and germ) of cereal grains – the part that contains the most protein, fibre, vitamins and minerals. Industrial-scale flour-refining resulted in the loss of the most nour-ishing parts of the grain. White flour consists almost solely of easily digestible starch, which leads to a quick rise in blood sugar levels. Bread and other prod-ucts based on white flour are therefore not healthy food choices.

Really coarse bread is seldom found in supermarkets. Many of the darker breads actually contain a high proportion of white flour and are coloured with malt, so don't be misled by the colour. The best bread is made of very coarse grains, such as rye, barley and oats, with perhaps small quantities of whole-meal wheat flour with wheat bran added. Look for heavy bread, since the same volume of wholegrain bread will weigh more than white bread. Certain types of ancient wheat, such as spelt, emmer and giant durum wheat (kamut), have a higher nutritional quality, are most often organically grown, and cause fewer allergic reactions or intolerances than ordinary wheat. These products can increasingly be found in health-food shops and larger supermarkets. Pumpernickel bread is healthier than many other breads and has a medium GI. Remember that bread hardly ever has a really low GI. However, it is now possible to pro-duce bread with a reduced GL – by using very coarse grains and selecting those with a lower GL, by using a sourdough starter and by replacing some of the flour (carbs) with 'functional' protein and fibre.

The junk food generation

Throughout the twentieth century, and especially after World War II, we expe-rienced a lifestyle revolution. We are less physically active than at any time in history and everyday life is dominated by automated appliances. We drive around in cars and our work is often sedentary. The food industry produces refined, energy-packed products with a lot of high-glycaemic carbohydrates and a relatively large proportion of highly processed oils and fats, including trans fat. Junk food is easily accessible. The nutritional value of fruit and veget-ables is diminished because of refrigerated transport, mass production and the use of chemical fertilizers. (Organically produced fruit and vegetables have a much higher nutritional quality. Remember that all farming was once 'organic'.) We have become victims of our own progress. The more time we spend at work, or on the Internet, or in front of the TV, the less time we have left to spend on healthy cooking and exercise – or to nurture our relationships with other people.

Committing suicide with knife and fork

The theory of evolution was introduced by Charles Darwin in 1859 in his book *The Origin of Species*. Darwin claimed that all species compete for limited natural resources, and it is the law of nature that creatures will develop variations that allow them to better adapt and thus procreate more successfully. As this evolutionary process unfolds, the strongest survive and the weakest perish – the survival of the fittest. But what happens when one species, such as man, changes nature and the natural balance of resources? What happens when those who were supposed to be the fittest and the strongest become the weakest? Today, it seems to be those individuals with what used to be the most advantageous genes who become ill and die from lifestyle diseases.

Has man reached his evolutionary end? In around 10,000 years, we have gone from hunting and gathering to an agricultural and industrial existence, and then to a way of life that is physically passive. We have moved from ignorance to nuclear power and the Internet, from superstition and herbal medicines to antibiotics and modern heart surgery. These and many other strides in our evolution have changed our lives forever, but they did not happen through natural selection, nor did they alter our genetic make-up. We defy evolution and change our surroundings, all the while remaining biologically the same.

We can thank modern medicine for the survival of millions of people despite the laws of evolution. When we choose to disregard evolution in this manner, there is only one way left to go: we constantly have to increase our knowledge and use it properly in order to outsmart evolution and survive as a species. Among other things, we need to understand what we are meant to eat and we have to try to adjust our way of life accordingly. Today's diet is in conflict with our genes. Our digestive system is designed to process large quantities of natural food, but now it has become virtually unemployed. Even worse, our diet has produced a hormonal nightmare: elevated insulin production and insulin resistance.

CHAPTER 9

WHY DIETING FAILS

I've been on a diet for two weeks: all I've lost is two weeks.
Anon

Dieting usually means changing the way you eat for a limited period of time in order to lose weight. But this type of dieting does not work in the long run. As many as 95 per cent of dieters return, within a year, to their original weight or a higher weight than when they started dieting. Only an appropriate and permanent change of lifestyle can help control weight and blood sugar – at the same as it brings better health. Interestingly, the word diet originates from the ancient Greek word *diaita*, which means 'way of living'. As you have already guessed, this book is not about 'dieting', but about finding the key to why you gain weight or why you have a weight-related illness.

Why we eat

Food supplies us with the necessary nutrients to ensure good health. This applies to all animals. We have evolved as a species along with our food, and we depend on it to function properly and to survive.

Unlike other animals, however, humans eat for many reasons other than survival. There is an important connection between eating and emotions, and one influences the other. Our first contact with food is mother's milk. It warms us, feeds us, provides a sense of security and ensures contact with our mother. It is a pleasing experience, and one that we carry with us for the rest of our lives. To most of us, food and eating subconsciously represent warmth and security.

Most of us will agree that chocolate tastes particularly good. The same goes for the combination of sugar and fat found in cakes, or the starch and fat found in potato crisps and chips. Interestingly, mother's milk is the only nat-ural food that is rich in both carbohydrate and fat. Natural whole foods are either high in carbohydrate and low in fat (fruits, berries, grains, pulses), high in fat and low in carbohydrate (nuts, olives, seeds, avocados) or high in pro-tein and often in fat with almost no carbohydrate (meat, poultry, eggs, fish, seafood). You will only find the combination of high carbohydrate and fat in processed, man-made foods. Such foods cause chemical changes in our brain that produce a feeling of comfort, and sometimes this can lead to addiction. Sugar and chocolate increase the serotonin level in the brain, which creates a sense of well-being and acts as an antidepressant. Stress may cause you to eat this type of food more often, which in turn will lead to high insulin levels, stor-age of abdominal fat and a higher risk of diabetes, heart disease and cancer.

Very often, we eat because we are stressed, or because we are at a social func-tion, even though we are not necessarily hungry. At other times, food can be a substitute for something we lack, supplying a sense of comfort or replacing lack of love or closeness. Or we may use food to battle anxiety and depression.

For overweight people, frequent diets and yo-yo dieting, with defeat after defeat, can make the situation worse. It is therefore important to become aware of when and why you eat and what triggers your eating behaviour. Are you really hungry, or are you upset, bored or stressed? There is a huge difference between actual hunger and an emotional craving for food. If you are physically hungry, you will ask yourself, 'Is there something I can eat?' But if it is an emotional craving, the question is, 'What do I want to eat?' The process of developing an awareness of why you eat may be too demanding for you to handle by your-self and you might need help and support from a professional therapist.

Do you need to lose weight?

The process of going on a diet might be a bad idea for some people, especially if poor food choices are not the only cause of their excess weight. Low self-esteem, stress or depression can and should be tackled in other ways. Being slightly overweight (a BMI between 25 and 27 – see page 85) is probably no threat to your health, unless the excess weight is concentrated around your waist and you do not exercise. It is important to accept yourself the way you are and not to become obsessed with dieting. After all, being physically active coun-teracts many – but not all – of the negative health effects of overweight.

We come in all shapes and sizes, and overweight people should be spared social stigma and discrimination. Obesity has nothing to do with lack of intelligence or willpower. And who is to say that all your problems will disappear when you reach a 'normal' weight? You can be very happy and be overweight at the same time, just as some people are slim and unhappy. The more you learn to accept yourself, the less of a psychological problem your weight will become.

On the other hand, being seriously overweight (a BMI over 30, or weighing about 30kg/2st too much for a person who is 1.7m tall) is likely to have consequences in terms of your health. You may feel healthy at twenty, thirty or forty years old, but most weight-related disorders increase with age. So if you want to remain in good health, you must treat your body with love and respect. Obesity and weight-related disorders are self-inflicted but not deserved – at least this is the case as long as you do not know why you gain weight. As soon as you figure out the reason why, you are responsible for making the necessary changes to your lifestyle. If you do nothing, you will suffer the consequences.

In search of a quick fix

If there existed such a thing as an easy, effective and permanent way to lose weight and to metabolize fat efficiently, why are there so many different diets? If someone had figured out exactly which 'cure' was the best, wouldn't everyone have followed that particular diet? The truth, however, is that there is no quick and easy solution that will have a long-term effect. If you want to stay in good health, you have to learn about the subject, and be willing to put effort into changing your lifestyle. If you are to succeed, you have to develop a good relationship with yourself, with your body and, last but not least, with food.

The calorie model

Let us take a look at the most common weight-loss theory, the one that many nutrition experts worldwide seem to accept. A calorie equals the amount of energy necessary to increase the temperature of 1 gram of water from 14 to 15 degrees Celsius. Strictly speaking, a calorie is not an energy measure limited to food – it is a universal energy currency. All things in nature contain energy and thus calories. But when it comes to nutrition, calories have been the common way of measuring a food's energy content since the beginning of the twentieth century. Nutritionists have started using a more modern unit called a joule (kilojoule), but to many of us the calorie (to be precise, this should be called a kilocalorie) remains the unit that we understand.

The calorie model is based on the principle of energy balance. Energy cannot simply disappear. The calorie model thus indicates that energy balance is attained when energy intake equals energy expenditure – that is, energy consumption. Each individual has a certain intake of energy (calories), which should equal that person's energy consumption. This, in turn, depends on the body's basal metabolic rate, level of physical activity and the thermogenic (heat-producing) effect of different foods. During childhood and pregnancy, and during physical exercise, the body's metabolic rate increases. One of the flaws in the calorie model lies in the fact that it does not take account of the way our metabolism increases when we eat – and increases more rapidly when we eat spicy foods, for example – and slows down when we don't eat. Nor does it consider the fact that our metabolism changes according to the seasons and the time of day (see chapter 6).

To find out how much energy various nutrients contain, one has to think of them as fuel and measure how much energy is produced as heat when they are burned. Thus we know that 1 gram of protein or carbohydrate contains approximately 4 calories, alcohol 7 calories and fat 9 calories. The theory here is that all food is available for oxidation (burning) in the body, but we must also consider the properties of any given food. For instance, we know that dietary fibre, which is carbohydrate (and therefore has the same number of calories as, say, sugar), cannot be metabolized by humans in the same way as sugar and therefore does not actually contribute calories.

Digestion makes a difference

The degree of digestion and absorption from the small intestine are thus important elements to consider. How easily a food is digested is not based solely on its energy content and its composition. What you eat along with any given food (and we normally eat meals composed of more than one food) determines how much is absorbed by your body and how it is handled. The more fibre and fat, the lower and slower the absorption capacity of the small intestine.

In some instances, it makes a big difference whether the food you eat is raw or cooked. For example, humans have a problem digesting raw potatoes. That means that raw potatoes do not give us many calories, while boiled, fried or baked potatoes are easier to digest and therefore contribute more energy. Even cooked and cooled down potatoes contribute less calories and have approximately a 30 per cent lower glycaemic load, because some of the starch turns into resistant starch during the cooling process, and this behaves much like soluble fibre.

What kind of calories is more important than how many

The type of calories – for example, the kind of fat – determines what happens in the body later on. Saturated fat is easily stored, whereas polyunsaturated fat can be used as building bricks for hormones and eicosanoids(see page 64).

Glucose and fructose are both carbohydrates, and they are both simple sugars. They both taste sweet and contain an equal number of calories per gram. They are, however, metabolized quite differently. While glucose is quickly absorbed into the bloodstream and can be used as energy immediately, or stored as glycogen or fat, fructose is converted partly into glucose in the liver – a process that requires energy. Thus fructose does not provide the same 'efficient' calories as glucose. Furthermore, fructose is 30 to 50 per cent sweeter than sugar, so you need to use less to start with to achieve the same degree of sweetness. See page 29 for more on fructose.

Eat frequently

How often we eat is also important. It would appear that our metabolism becomes more efficient the more frequently we eat. This is also true for other animals. Chimpanzees, for example, snack all day long while they move around (and 98 per cent of our genes are identical to those of a chimpanzee). We were never meant to eat three big meals a day with long periods between mealtimes, and we were certainly not meant to skip food deliberately. The calorie model does not take this into consideration.

Don't fall for this diet myth

If you have ever been overweight, chances are you'll have been told that a common cause of weight gain is eating when you're not hungry. All the diets based on calorie counting implicitly back this theory: if excess weight is a simple matter of too many calories going in, surely the obvious answer is to cut back on your calorie intake – and one easy way to do this is to skip a meal, thus 'saving' calories for another time. Not only is this wrong, it has caused untold damage to our health. When you skip a meal, your blood sugar level dips. In order to stabilize blood sugar, your body goes into stress mode (see page 95) and your brain tells you to grab some high-carb, high-fat food. Just eating less food causes your metabolism to slow down, which, in evolutionary terms, is crucial for survival. The Greek Doctor's Diet works because you eat *before* you get hungry: your blood sugar remains more stable so you do not overeat at mealtimes or binge between meals. It works also because it provides you with more food but less energy-dense food, and food that promotes hormonal balance after meals.

Fasting (and low-calorie diets) can make you fat

When you suddenly eat less (diet) or, even worse, when you fast, your body will try to defend its weight, which results in your metabolism slowing down. Why is this? Because our genes still belong in the Stone Age! Your body does not know whether you are fasting or eating less because you are trying to lose weight, or because food is scarce.

Dieting by fasting or drastically reducing the amount you eat is an absurd idea. No other animal with respect for itself would do this. When you are tired of dieting and give up, your weight will skyrocket. Stop eating less, and never ever skip a meal to lose weight! Healthy, regular and frequent meals are your best weapon against weight gain.

What happens when we fast?

When you are fasting, you do not eat even after all circulating blood sugar is gone. Your body will then start producing blood sugar by itself, drawing from the glucose stored in the liver (as glycogen) – around 50–80g ($1^3/4$ –$2^3/4$ oz) of glucose, providing 200–320 calories. Our muscles also contain glycogen – approximately 200–400g (7–14oz), though a bodybuilder may have as much as 800g (28oz), about 800 to 1600 calories. Muscle glycogen, however, is not available as energy during rest, even if we are fasting, but can only be used by working muscles (i.e. during exercise). Knowing that a person who weighs 70kg (11st) consumes nearly 2000 calories a day without being physically active, it goes without saying that you will not survive for long on glycogen alone. Actually, it takes no more than 10 to 12 hours before this energy source is completely depleted. The only way to fully replenish this glycogen store is to eat carbohydrates. So what can your body use when both blood sugar and glycogen are gone? The answer is protein and fat. The body can convert protein (certain amino acids) and glycerol from fat into blood sugar in the liver, a process that is called gluconeogenesis (the remaking of blood sugar). This process is not very efficient, and a lot of energy is lost along the way. Crucially, though, the breakdown of protein, which all our bodies' cells are made of, is tantamount to suicide in the long run. It is therefore very important to eat enough protein every day. Then you can be sure that the only alternative energy source for the body is burning stored fat.

The low-carb/ketogenic diet

Knowing that the body needs protein, you might very well say, 'I will simply avoid carbohydrates altogether, eat enough protein, and thus increase fat burning.' Well, this is only partially correct. Although many diets are now based on this principle, you have to look at what happens when you go on such a diet, and why it would not be wise in the long term – although it will work in the short term. When the body has to burn fat as an energy source because there is not a sufficient supply of glucose, it triggers a condition known as ketosis. This starts around 24 hours after fasting has begun or after no carbohydrates have been eaten. Breaking down body fat leads to the release of energy, as well as the formation of substances called ketones, which even the brain can use as energy instead of blood sugar to a certain extent. Ketones are acidic substances that smell of acetone (like nail polish remover), and when your body is in ketosis your breath may smell a bit like acetone (or like overripe apples). Your body disposes of excess ketone bodies through exhaling and increased urination; you can check whether you are in ketosis by using special urine-testing strips. Apart from bad breath, a major disadvantage of this diet is that you lose fluids and important minerals through increased urination. It is possible to replace these by taking supplements, but in my opinion ketogenic diets should only be followed under medical supervision and should never be tried by type I diabetics and pregnant women.

A variation of the popular do-it-yourself low carb diet is the protein-sparing modified fast, which is a very low calorie diet with a high protein percentage (not a high absolute amount of protein). This method of dieting, which consists of eating enough protein and only a very limited amount of carbohydrates (or avoiding carbohydrates completely), in addition to small amounts of saturated fat, is used by many clinics that specialize in weight reduction. This kind of diet is usually for only a short period of time, followed by a gradual increase in carbohydrate fat and energy intake. The advantage is that you lose weight quickly. Another advantage is that when you are in ketosis, you do not have much of an appetite, because of the appetite-suppressing effect of ketones.

Foods that contain protein also increase the feeling of fullness because of the effect of the hormones glucagon and cholecystokinin (see page 69). There are situations where going on a ketogenic diet may be beneficial, but it should be undertaken only with the guidance of a doctor or nutritionist. It is of vital importance that you eat enough protein and get enough fluid, and you will probably need to take extra potassium and maybe other vitamins and minerals. Without proper medical guidance and follow-up, you risk a rapid weight gain after ending such a diet, as well as mineral disturbances. And bear in mind that food without carbohydrates becomes pretty boring in the long run. The more radical a diet is the less probable it is that you will adhere to it long term.

The high-carb, low-fat diet

Most people in the western world today eat a high-carb diet, often based on highly processed white bread, breakfast cereals, and other products made from refined grains, flours, sugar and potatoes. Those wishing to lose weight will cut down the amount of fat they eat, because they know that fat has twice as many calories as carbohydrates – but they will then eat even more high-carb foods to fill themselves up. Many of the fat-free products in our shops today have simply had their fat replaced by sugar, flour or a chemically altered form of carbohydrate.

Contrary to popular belief, in most developed countries we eat less fat now than we did at the beginning of the twentieth century and even 25 years ago. Yet as we moved into the latter end of the century, we experienced a huge increase in obesity and lifestyle diseases.

If you eat a lot of high-carb food, your glycogen supply (glucose stored in the liver and muscles) will always be complete. Since most of us do not fast for more than eight hours at a time (during sleep), we never completely run out of glycogen. If our food intake were spread out in smaller meals over several hours (a more natural eating pattern for humans), and we were continually moving around, this would not be a problem. Instead, we tend to eat large meals and avoid eating between meals; often, we are not physically active. Considering each of us has five to six litres of blood, intended by nature to contain only a teaspoon of blood sugar at any given time, we can easily understand where most of the excessive carbohydrates that we eat end up – as fat, particularly around our waists. The glycogen store is full, it is not used for physical activity, and so most of the incoming carbohydrates are transformed into body fat.

Hormones play an important part here. The body produces the hormone insulin (which regulates blood sugar levels) as soon as we smell, see or taste carbohydrates. Many of the high-carb foods that we eat create rapid rises in blood sugar, which can lead to overproduction of insulin. The more often your body experiences a high level of insulin, the more difficult it becomes for insulin to lower blood sugar; this is referred to as insulin resistance. The more insulin you have in your blood, the more fat will be stored around the body, consequently you will burn less fat. Rapid changes in blood sugar levels also increase our appetite and provoke sugar cravings.

Besides weight gain, insulin resistance has also been linked with a number of life-threatening conditions, including type II diabetes, high blood pressure and cardiovascular disorders. It is absurd to eat foods that disturb one's hormonal balance. Animals instinctively know what to eat. Why don't we?

If you get most of your carbohydrates from pulses, vegetables and fruit, your blood sugar will remain relatively stable. This is *not* a high-carb diet, but a more natural way of eating, and is the basis of the Greek Doctor's Diet.

Dissociation diets

You have probably heard of dissociation diets, even if you have not tried them yourself. For instance, you might eat only pineapple for a limited number of days, or only eggs, or only tomatoes for breakfast, potatoes for lunch and celery for dinner.

Unfortunately, all these dissociation diets have one thing in common: they do not work and can be dangerous. Such diets are unbalanced; they do not supply your body with the macro- and micronutrients that it needs – and I am sure that you do not want to live on pineapple alone. When you return to your normal eating habits you will not have achieved much at all.

Meal-replacement diets

There is nothing intrinsically wrong with meal replacements, such as shakes and bars, except that they do not taste as good as proper food and they do not contain as many different micronutrients. They are far from natural, and if you are to stay slim in the long term it is important to have a positive attitude towards food.

There are various kinds of meal-replacement diets. The most common ones are low-calorie and low-fat. Some are low-carb (ketogenic), others are protein-rich. But most of them are designed to provide the body with all the vitamins and minerals it needs. They work best if you have a considerable weight problem to begin with, and may be safer than going on a diet of your own devising. However, before you start on such a diet, you must consult your doctor. I would advise against any meal-replacement diet that is used for every meal unless this is undertaken at the advice of your doctor and is monitored carefully.

The way to successful weight loss

If you focus only on how much you eat, you will never be able to lose weight over the long term. If you make the wrong food choices, you will not be able to compensate by eating less of those foods. If you drastically reduce the calories you eat, you are almost certain to end up hungry, and likely to 'cheat' by snacking. First, you have to concentrate on choosing the right foods, which will get your body in balance. Choosing the right types of food will also regulate your appetite after a while. The Greek Doctor's Diet gives you an average intake of 2000 calories a day – most people find that this satisfies their hunger. Once you get into the habit of avoiding over-refined sugary and starchy foods, your appetite and sense of fullness will function as nature intended, and you will be able to eat as much as you want – because you will want less.

Awareness

If you are to succeed with a permanent change in lifestyle, you have to find out what your body really needs. It is important not to work against your body, as many low-calorie and low-fat diets do. You need to know how different types of food affect your metabolism and health in order to compose a balanced diet.

But how easy is it to change your diet? You might think that once you know what your body needs, all your problems will be solved. Unfortunately it is not that simple. Everybody knows that smoking is harmful, yet around 30 per cent of the population still smoke daily. Knowledge is essential, but it is not enough. You also need motivation.

Motivation

Most people have wishes and dreams about how they and their lives should have been. We would love to change, but we hate the process of change. There is always a price to pay to achieve results. Most people would like to be attractive, slim, healthy and rich. Relatively few, however, really work hard to reach their goals. Of course, these goals do not guarantee happiness. Personally, I think the only goal that is really important is to be healthy.

During consultations many patients tell me that they have decided to change their lifestyle, eat better and lose weight, but... their work or their family take so much time and energy, but... it is hard to exercise because of a painful knee... When I hear these 'buts' three or four times during a consultation, I start doubting whether this person is truly motivated and able to take the necessary steps to change his or her lifestyle at this stage. Perhaps there are actual practical obstacles, or maybe the obstacles are mental or psychological. It is important to discuss them and to look at the situation objectively. Is the change you want and plan truly feasible? Is there anything you can do to remove some of the obstacles? Do you need help with this? You can be very successful in your professional life, hold considerable responsibility both at work and in the family, but still not master every aspect of your life, like having a healthy diet, exercising appropriately, quitting smoking or managing stress. Asking for help must not be considered to be a defeat – it could be your first step to success.

CHAPTER 10

DO YOU NEED DIETARY SUPPLEMENTS?

itamins and minerals are found in small amounts in various foods. Their job is not to provide the body with energy, but to make possible the numerous chemical reactions that keep us healthy. You can compare them to the cement that holds the bricks of a building together. You need both the right type and quantity of bricks and the right type and quantity of cement.

Vitamins and minerals are not magic bullets that can make you well if your lifestyle is unhealthy. Cement without bricks will not get far. The proper choice and the right combination of proteins, carbohydrates and fat is vital (see chapter 2). And do not believe, even for a second, that life's elixir can be found in a bottle or in a capsule. People put too much faith in vitamin and mineral supplements, when in fact they need to put a little effort into eating properly. Knowing what substances in a tomato or a carrot are beneficial to our health and then getting them from capsules is not the same as actually eating tomatoes and carrots. The supplement industry naturally prefers that people buy pills, but having a well-balanced and varied diet is the best thing you can do to achieve good health.

Think before you swallow a supplement

The use of food supplements is a much-debated issue. Some people will always be the first to try the latest craze in vitamins and dietary supplements. On the other hand, there are the sworn sceptics, who will accept that a supplement is necessary only if a blood test shows they have a serious deficiency in particular vitamins or minerals. As with everything else in life, the truth lies somewhere in between. If most people eat too few fruits and vegetables, which is often the case, the average level of vitamins and minerals in the blood will, for a representative part of the population, be low. And it is this kind of average that forms the basis for what is considered a 'normal' range. The difference between 'normal' and 'optimal' or 'health beneficial' can thus be quite great.

The same applies to dietary supplements. Some people, especially those who generally have a higher risk of developing certain diseases, probably need a larger dosage of some vitamins and minerals than others. Although nothing can replace a varied, well-balanced diet and a healthy lifestyle, a food supplement or multivitamin pill may be considered an inexpensive health insurance premium. The problem is knowing what to take. There is so much to choose from – multivitamins, specific vitamins and minerals, herbal remedies and other 'natural extracts' – and every producer claims that their products are exactly what we need.

Unfortunately, you cannot always be sure that the bottle contains precisely what the label states. Producers of medicines have to prove that a new medicine is both effective and safe, but producers of food supplements are not bound by the same rules at present. Research on dietary supplements often does not adhere to the same high standards as research on medicine. Also, since many dietary supplements come from natural resources, they cannot be patented unless they are mixed in a certain way or their chemical structure is changed. If they are not protected by a patent, manufacturers are not very eager to finance research from which other manufacturers might profit. Thus, most of this research is publicly funded, and we all know that very little money goes into publicly-funded research. This is why it is so important to obtain reliable information, based on well-documented research, about which food supplement will provide the desired effect, and to buy dietary supplements only from reputable manufacturers and distributors.

In this chapter I will look at several dietary supplements that might be of special interest to you if you wish to increase your metabolism and perhaps lose weight, or to prevent or improve insulin resistance. If you are diabetic, these supplements may help you gain better control of your blood sugar and improve blood lipids. Just remember that these supplements must be in addition to a well-balanced diet, not instead of it. Also note that dietary supplements are chemical substances, just like medicines. Simply because they appear in nature does not mean that they are always good for you, or that the more you take the better. If used incorrectly, there may be side effects. Not everyone can or should take food supplements. Talk to your doctor before you take a food supplement, because some of them are contra-indicated if you are taking medication for another condition. Remember: the key to good health does not come in the shape of a pill.

Who needs supplements?

Is there a point in taking dietary supplements? First of all, many of us are likely to encounter situations in which we need to take special supplements, either because of an illness or for other reasons, such as pregnancy and breastfeeding. Vegetarians should take a vitamin B12 supplement, as this vitamin is only found in animal food sources. Secondly, in the modern world we are all subject to environmental pollutants and unresolved stress situations, which can increase our bodies' needs for additional vitamins and minerals. Thirdly, much of the food we eat today no longer has the same nutritional quality it once did. In order to give people the cheap food that they demand, we dictate the diets of farmed animals – cattle, battery-farmed poultry and pigs do not eat the variety of foods they would in natural circumstances – and we give them antibiotics to control diseases. Even the simple egg is often no longer as nutritious as it should be.

Vitamins: lost and found

If you have ever eaten an orange fresh from the tree or a tomato ripened naturally in the sun, you will have noticed how much better they taste; what you can't tell from eating them is that they also contain their full complement of vitamins. The fruit and vegetables in our shops and supermarkets have often travelled across the world. In many instances they have been picked before they are ripe and stored in refrigerated containers en route to the store where they will be sold. After we buy them, we often keep them for several days before eating them. This process is hardly natural, and it leads to a far greater loss of vitamins and minerals than if you had bought fresh produce and eaten it immediately. Fruits and vegetables that grow naturally where you live are usually the best choice.

What about frozen vegetables and fruit? They are picked, cleaned and frozen – and they remain in peak condition until you eat them. Have you ever found spoiled fruits or vegetables in a bag of frozen produce? Freezing is far better than the refrigerated transport of fresh produce, and it keeps the vitamins and minerals intact. But no matter how and where fruits and vegetables have been grown, eating a lot of them is very important for good health.

Antioxidants: natural is best

Antioxidants are vitamins, minerals and other phytochemicals (substances found in plants, from the Greek *phyton*, meaning plant) that protect the plants, and indirectly the human body, against oxidative damage – also referred to as oxidative stress or free radical damage. Are free radicals dangerous, then, since we need to be protected from them? Well, not exactly. The body needs oxygen for energy and all cellular reactions: without oxygen, life is impossible. When the body burns oxygen, it creates unstable oxygen molecules called free radicals; it is designed to cope with a certain amount of these, but not with an excess of free radicals, or free radicals that stay in the body too long.

Free radicals are also created when the body is exposed to traffic fumes, everyday chemicals, cigarette smoke and excessive sunlight, among other things. You know the effect that air – that is, oxygen – has on iron: it causes it to rust. And you will have noticed how fat, especially the sort found in nuts and oils, turns rancid after a while. Rust is oxidized iron and rancid fats can also be described as oxidized. Oxygen has a similar damaging effect on the body, especially on the unsaturated fatty acids that are part of the structure of cells throughout our bodies. This oxidation is the ageing process. Besides premature ageing, a surplus of free radicals can lead to cancers, cataracts and macular degeneration, arteriosclerosis (hardening of the arteries), heart disorders, arthritis and many other illnesses. Antioxidants protect the body against this oxidation process by removing free radicals before they can stay around too long.

Vitamin C, vitamin E and beta-carotene (also called provitamin A) are the best-known and most researched antioxidants – others include the red pigment, lycopene, that colours tomatoes; the flavonoids found in onions and many other foods; and various compounds found in nuts, berries, vegetables, herbs and spices. It is important to get antioxidants from food, as natural foods contain myriad substances that work together, and research indicates that micronutrients in their natural form are absorbed better than synthetic forms.

It is the balance between free radicals (also called pro-oxidants) and antioxidants that determines our health. Too many antioxidants, however, particularly high concentrations of one or two types, can disturb this balance – another good reason to eat a wide variety of fruits and vegetables.

Note that beta-carotene and vitamin E are much more efficient when taken together with an adequate amount of vitamin C. It appears that 6000 micrograms (mcg) of beta-carotene, 500 milligrams (mg) of vitamin C and 100mg of vitamin E provide good protection. These amounts are a good deal higher than the officially recommended dosage, but they are justifiable. Food containing beta-carotene is usually dark green, orange or yellow: spinach, watercress, kale, green cabbage and other dark green leafy vegetables, mangetout, carrots, orange-fleshed melons, mangoes and apricots. Good sources of vitamin C include broccoli and kohlrabi, cabbage and cauliflower, spinach and watercress, red and green peppers, tomatoes, kiwi fruit, melons, citrus fruits, blueberries, strawberries, raspberries and blackcurrants. Eating plenty of fruits and vegetables will generally meet your need for vitamins A and C, although perhaps not for vitamin E. Vitamin E is fat-soluble: good sources are extra virgin olive oil, nuts, especially almonds and hazelnuts, sunflower seeds, avocados and whole grains. It is also found in some fruits and vegetables, but if you are on a diet based on a moderate or low fat intake, it can be hard to get 100mg of vitamin E every day, so a food supplement might be a good idea. Vitamin E can improve the action of insulin in healthy people and people with type II diabetes.

Today we have a greater need for antioxidants than ever before, yet, as we have seen, our food is likely to have greatly reduced levels of vitamin C and other useful phytochemicals by the time we eat it. We need to replenish our antioxidant levels continuously, through our diet and, if necessary, by taking dietary supplements.

Omega-3 fatty acids

Cod liver oil is a traditional food supplement in many countries; it has been taken to prevent vitamin D deficiency, ward off colds and ease joint pain caused by arthritis. Cod liver oil contains vitamin A and vitamin D, and in recent times it has been proven that cod liver oil is very beneficial to good health because it contains large amounts of omega-3 fatty acids.

Omega-3 fatty acids are essential fatty acids: we cannot make them in our bodies, but they are essential to the healthy functioning of the brain, the nervous system and the immune system; they also contribute to healthy joints, improved insulin action and softer skin. Depression and many disorders of the nervous system – for example, multiple sclerosis (MS) – are linked to a low intake of omega-3 fatty acids. A study from the University of Bergen found that an increased intake of omega-3 fatty acids along with a diet rich in fruits and vegetables can be more effective in relieving symptoms in MS patients than medications such as interferon. It is also known that omega-3 fatty acids are transformed by the body into 'good' eicosanoids – substances that have an anti-inflammatory effect – that can reduce the risk of artery damage, stroke and heart disease, as well as some cancers (for more on eicosanoids and inflammation, see chapter 7).

In an ideal world, we would all eat at least 100g of oily fish, such as salmon, mackerel, herring, sardines, trout or tuna, every day. Unfortunately, the world is not ideal, and there is growing concern about environmental toxins in fish, to the extent that we are now being advised to limit our intake of oily fish to three times a week. Farmed fish are fed artificial feeds and live in a far from natural environment, and wild fish may be exposed to toxins at any point in their life cycle. Bigger fish such as salmon and tuna eat smaller fish and live longer, so they are more likely to accumulate toxins such as mercury and PCBs in their flesh; smaller fish such as sardines and mackerel are less likely to be contaminated to the same extent.

Pregnant women have a particular need for omega-3 fatty acids, which are vital for the development of the brain, eyes and central nervous system of the growing foetus. However, because of the potentially high levels of toxins I advise expectant mothers to avoid oily fish, but to eat plenty of white fish and to get their omega-3 fatty acids from high-quality supplements.

To everyone else, I recommend that you eat both oily and white fish; variety is important – don't overdose on salmon! Even if you eat fish every day you ought to take an omega-3 supplement: 5–10ml (1–2 teaspoons) of cod liver oil, supplying 1.2–2.4g of omega-3, or, if you choose a refined fish oil (60 per cent omega-3 content), 4 teaspoons of liquid, or capsules of at least 2000 milligrams. If you suffer from inflammatory diseases or have high triglycerides (blood lipids), you may need to take a much higher dose, but only after consulting your doctor or nutritionist. Omega-3s from plant sources are not as readily used by the body as fish oils, but good sources of omega-3 fatty acids are flaxseeds and flaxseed oil (1–2 teaspoons a day), and walnuts (10 walnut halves) and walnut oil (use for salad dressings).

When increasing your intake of omega-3 fatty acids, remember to limit – but not omit – omega-6 fatty acids. The average diet today has an excess of omega-6 fats, which are found in sunflower oil, corn oil, soya oil and other polyunsaturated oils used in margarines and spreads and in many ready-made foods. When eaten in excess, omega-6 fats can increase inflammatory reactions within the body, giving the opposite effects to the beneficial omega-3s.

Vitamin D

Vitamin D is a fat-soluble vitamin that many overweight people have too little of in their blood, especially those in northern latitudes. It is produced in our skin upon exposure to sunlight: overweight people tend to get less exposure to the sun than others. Vitamin D is found in very few foods, but you can get it by taking cod liver oil or by eating oily fish (salmon, mackerel, sardines, herring and tuna), butter and egg yolks. Vegetables are generally low in vitamin D.

Vitamin D – together with calcium and magnesium – is vital to healthy bone structure, so a lack of it predisposes one to osteoporosis, among other things. There is also a link between vitamin D and insulin resistance: the lower the level of vitamin D, the higher the degree of insulin resistance. I would say, then, that sunshine is good for you: it can help prevent diabetes, high blood pressure and heart disease.

Folic acid/folate

Folic acid has been proven to protect the foetus against neural tube damage, and it is recommended that all women of childbearing age take a daily supplement of 400 micrograms of folic acid.

Does this mean it is less important for men and older women? Far from it! Folic acid (along with vitamins B6 and B12) reduces blood levels of homocysteine (a by-product of our protein metabolism). Elevated homocysteine levels can damage blood vessels, and appear to be an important risk factor in the development of cardiovascular disorders. It is suggested that testing homocysteine levels in the blood might be more relevant than testing blood cholesterol levels in assessing the risk of heart problems. High homocysteine levels have also been linked with Alzheimer's disease.

Folic acid is found (in its natural form, folate) in most green vegetables, particularly in asparagus, spinach, broccoli, Brussels sprouts, kale and lettuce. It is greatly reduced by the action of heat, so don't overcook your vegetables. Aim to get at least 200 micrograms a day; three or more servings of vegetables and salads should do it.

Nicotinic acid (niacin, vitamin B3), pyridoxine (vitamin B6) and vitamin B12

These vitamins are very important in the production of the 'good', anti-inflammatory eicosanoids (see chapter 7). It is also thought that they work together with folic acid to lower homocysteine levels in the blood.

The body can produce nicotinic acid from an amino acid (tryptophan) that is found in almost all protein sources. If you eat enough protein-rich food, it is very unlikely that you will lack nicotinic acid. Vitamins B6 and B12 should also be available in adequate quantities from the food we eat. Vitamin B6 is found in pulses, nuts, eggs, meat, fish, whole grains and fortified breads and cereals. Vegetarians should be aware, however, that vitamin B12 is found only in animal sources such as eggs, meat, poultry, shellfish, milk and dairy products. Some research suggests that supplementation with vitamin B12 may reduce the symptoms of Alzheimer's disease.

Chromium

Chromium stimulates fatty acid and cholesterol synthesis, which are important for brain function and other body processes. It activates several enzymes that are needed to drive numerous chemical reactions necessary to life.

If you suffer from insulin resistance, the mineral chromium is very important to you. We get it through the foods we eat, but many people need more chromium than they get in their diets. Chromium is part of the so-called glucose tolerance factor, or GTF. This makes it easier for insulin to get blood sugar into the muscle cells; it improves the action of insulin and thus decreases insulin resistance. The more chromium you have, the less insulin your body needs to produce, and vice versa. The more carbohydrates you eat, especially the processed, high-glycaemic kind, the more chromium you will need; these foods lower the chromium level in the blood. So does physical and emotional stress, as well as hard exercise. Moderate exercise, however, can help to stabilize insulin and chromium levels. Also, the older we get, the less chromium we have and the more insulin our bodies produce – we therefore need more chromium as we get older. If you get enough chromium you will also have fewer sugar cravings. The best source of chromium is brewer's yeast, but many people avoid this because it can cause feelings of bloatedness and nausea. Other good sources of chromium include beef, liver, eggs, chicken, oysters, wheatgerm, green peppers, apples, bananas and spinach. Black pepper, butter and molasses are also good sources of chromium, but they are normally consumed only in small amounts.

How much chromium is enough? Anything between 200 and 400 micrograms daily would be appropriate. If you decide to take a chromium supplement, note that chromium should be taken only with water and not together with food or with other medications or dietary supplements, especially zinc, which may inhibit absorption.

Magnesium

Magnesium is used in the metabolism of blood sugar, among other things, and it influences both the production and action of insulin. Too little magnesium in the cells leads to reduced insulin action and thus higher insulin resistance. This is seen in individuals with high blood pressure and those with type II diabetes. Magnesium has a stabilizing effect on heart rhythm and on blood pressure. It is also necessary for healthy bones and to prevent fatigue.

In developed countries, up to 75 per cent of people with a typical diet get too little magnesium. Most dietary magnesium comes from vegetables, particularly dark green, leafy vegetables. Other foods that are good sources of magnesium are soya products, such as soya flour and tofu; pulses and seeds; nuts such as almonds and cashews; whole grains such as brown rice and millet; fruit such as bananas, dried apricots and avocados; meat and poultry; and fish and shellfish. The best way to get enough magnesium is to eat nuts such as almonds and cashews every day. The recommended minimum intake of magnesium for adults is 300–400mg a day, but a blood test can reveal if you need a higher dose.

Selenium

Selenium is an essential mineral, necessary as a building block for glutathione peroxidase, one of the most important internal antioxidant enzymes in the body and one that is thought to be very important in the prevention of cancer and cardiovascular disorders. Selenium also seems to stimulate antibody formation in response to vaccines. It also may provide protection from the toxic effects of heavy metals and other substances. Selenium may assist in the synthesis of protein, in growth and development, and in fertility, especially in men, as it has been shown to improve the production of sperm and sperm mobility.

Few people in Europe, America, Australia, New Zealand and South Africa get enough selenium in their diet. This is because selenium in plant and animal foods depends on the selenium content of the soil; never high in Europe, it is now lower than ever because of intensive overfarming. Fish, shellfish, red meat, grains, eggs, chicken, liver and garlic are all good sources of selenium. Brewer's yeast and wheatgerm, both considered 'health foods', are also good sources of selenium. Brazil nuts are particularly high in selenium and two Brazil nuts a day should cover your needs. Taken as a supplement, 100–200mcg is recommended.

Zinc

Zinc is needed for the healthy functioning of the immune system and the production of eicosanoids (see page 64). It is also important in the functioning of a number of hormones, such as insulin, growth hormone and sex hormones. The body's reserves of zinc are depleted by stress and smoking. You will find zinc in oatmeal, eggs, nuts, beef, chicken, fish, and especially in oysters and other shellfish, but it may be difficult to obtain the recommended 15mg a day without a supplement.

5-HTP

This is an interesting substance in relation to obesity and weight reduction, as 5-HTP (5-hydroxytryptophan) has been proven to suppress appetite, especially the craving for sweets and starches. The effect is probably due to the fact that 5-HTP increases the level of serotonin, an important signalling substance in the brain that produces a soothing, calming effect. Several foods, including sugar and chocolate, are known to increase the level of serotonin in the brain.

Research has shown that, taken as a food supplement, 5-HTP decreased food intake by approximately 20 per cent in people who had free access to food. The result was a weight reduction of about 2kg (4lb) in two weeks. There have been no reports of serious side effects, although drowsiness may occur if taken during the day, and it is not suitable for pregnant or lactating women. If you decide to try 5-HTP to suppress your appetite, start by taking 25 to 50 milligrams approximately one hour before bedtime a couple of times a week. Then gradually increase the number of nights you take it, until you take it every night. It is important not to buy a food supplement that contains other substances in addition to 5-HTP. Some of these supplements may contain other substances promoted as aids to weight loss, for example, ephedra. Ephedra has been linked to serious side effects and should not be used.

5-HTP is produced in the body from tryptophan, an amino acid found in most protein foods. A well-balanced diet that includes sufficient protein in all meals will ensure an adequate intake of 5-HTP under normal circumstances.

Functional foods and nutraceuticals

The concept of functional foods is big news in nutrition and food technology. A functional food is one that has extra health benefits, in addition to its nutritional content. Examples include low-fat spreads that contain plant sterols, ingredients that lower cholesterol, and yogurts in which sugar has been replaced with the soluble fibre inulin or oligofructose. The term nutraceutical derives from the words nutritional and pharmaceutical, and denotes a combination of food and medicine. It usually means that a specific beneficial nutrient – vitamin, mineral or other chemical compound – normally found in food is put into a capsule.

Although one should always be sceptical about new trends, I have to admit that I feel positive about this field of research. We have already tampered so much with nature and our food that we might as well try to develop new products that may correct some faults and imbalances. Take, for example, milk in which the saturated fat has been replaced with omega-3 fatty acids and monounsaturated fat. Or bread or pasta with more protein and fibre and a reduced amount of carbohydrates. Soya beans, which are high in protein and fibre, are very interesting in this context, and you are likely to find soya protein in an increasingly wide range of products that can benefit your health.

CHAPTER 11

THE GREEK DOCTOR'S DIET

Let me reiterate that this is not a quick fix intended for a short period of time. It is a nutritional concept designed to keep you naturally slim, that you should follow for the rest of your life. You will probably eat differently from the way you do now, but you will not eat less. You will eat great-tasting food and more meals per day.

Be warned, however: changing habits is not always easy. Routines and habits govern our everyday life. You may find yourself resisting any deviation from the status quo. Often, you will not even be aware that you are sabotaging yourself. My advice is this: plan ahead, be aware of why you do things, and try to gain control over your choices. If you stumble, accept that changing your lifestyle is a process that does not happen overnight. Faltering is not the same as failing. We should learn from our mistakes. Think about why you made a mistake and then move on.

What is the Greek Doctor's Diet?

Technically I call this the isoglycaemic diet (*isos* is the Greek word for 'equal'): it is all about balance. You will restore a more natural balance of the types of carbohydrates, proteins and fats you eat, which will lead to more stable blood sugar and better hormonal balance in your body. Improved hormonal balance leads to a better immune system, less joint pain, better skin, fewer allergies or asthmatic conditions, plus improved mental and physical performance. You will avoid yo-yo dieting and lose fat, not just weight.

You will be eating a greater range of natural foods and fewer refined and processed foods – food that suits you genetically and that will improve your metabolism. The food choices ensure you get plenty of vitamins, minerals, antioxidants and fibre. Nothing is banned (I'm just being realistic), but if you eat less favourable carbs and fats, do so in moderation and balance their effect with a greater intake of healthy carbs and proteins.

Approximately one-third of your total energy intake (by which I mean calories, not amount of food) should come from low- and medium-glycaemic carbohydrates: these are carbohydrates that don't make your blood sugar rise rapidly. Less than one-third should come from high-quality animal and plant proteins, and the rest from minimally processed natural fat, primarily monounsaturated and polyunsaturated fats, but also, to a lesser degree, saturated fats. Sounds too much like science? Don't worry, you will not need to count grams, percentages or calories. Naturally slim people do not count the calories they eat, and neither need you. Every person is different, and you will eventually find the mix that is best for you. In this chapter, I will show you how to put the nutritional principles into practice.

You will not need to count or weigh anything at all; the palm of your hand is all you need to judge the amount of food you should eat, as I'll explain on page 144.

Here's what I call the ABC of the Greek Doctor's Diet (see 'plate model' opposite). Most of your meals will consist of approximately one-third protein foods and two-thirds low-glycaemic carbohydrates. One meal a day – your 'reward' meal – may consist of one-third protein, half low-glycaemic carbohydrates and one-sixth medium- or high-glycaemic carbohydrates. You can choose whether to have this for your breakfast, lunch or dinner. To be in tune with human metabolic biorhythm, it is probably best to have your reward meal as your breakfast or lunch, but many people will choose dinner, for practical and social reasons.

The right type of fat will come from cold-pressed, or virgin, olive oil or rapeseed (canola) oil used to prepare your food, as well as from nuts, cold-pressed nut oils, avocados, oily fish and flaxseed oil. Fat from food should be mainly unsaturated; limit your intake of saturated fat, although there is no need to become fanatical about it. The point is that saturated fat from animal sources should not displace the other fat sources mentioned above. A glass or two of wine with your lunch or dinner is fine in terms of health – but if you are trying to lose weight I would recommend that you avoid alcohol or that you use it as the C part of your reward meal.

You may eat almost as much as you want until you feel comfortably full (remember not to eat too quickly and that it takes 10–15 minutes for satiety signals to reach the brain), but you must always balance what you eat. If you want a second helping, that's perfectly OK, but don't just eat more carbohydrates (such as rice, pasta, potatoes or bread). You should eat a corresponding (smaller) amount of protein (such as chicken, fish, meat, cottage cheese or yogurt). No meal or snack should be without protein.

Exercise is essential for good health. The same goes for abstinence from smoking and mastering stress. A combination of the Greek Doctor's Diet, appropriate exercise and a healthier lifestyle in general will give you the best results, whether you want to lose weight or simply stay as healthy as you possibly can.

What to expect from this diet

• If you are overweight, you will gradually lose body fat and weight, in a safe and healthy way. How much and how fast depends on each individual, and on how closely you follow the principles of this method, how much you

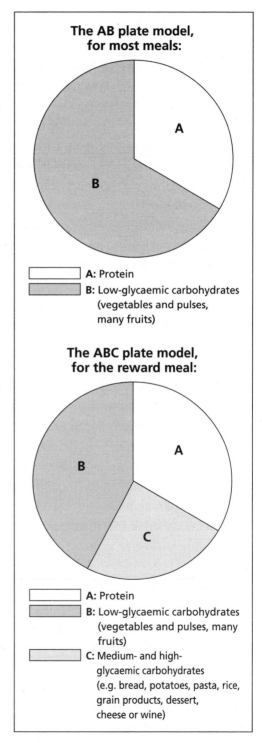

The AB plate model, for most meals:

A

B

A: Protein
B: Low-glycaemic carbohydrates (vegetables and pulses, many fruits)

The ABC plate model, for the reward meal:

A

B

C

A: Protein
B: Low-glycaemic carbohydrates (vegetables and pulses, many fruits)
C: Medium- and high-glycaemic carbohydrates (e.g. bread, potatoes, pasta, rice, grain products, dessert, cheese or wine)

exercise and, last but not least, on your genes. It is, however, important to be aware that the rate of reduction in body fat per week cannot exceed 0.5 to 1 kg (1–2lb) – or up to 1.5kg (3lb) of body weight if you are very overweight – without losing fat-free mass (body muscle).

- If you are very overweight when you start on this dietary regime, you may experience a weight loss of up to 2 to 3.5 kg (4–8 lb) during the first week, partly due to loss of fluids, which are bound to excess glycogen and fat. This is what happens when you reduce the total amount of high-glycaemic carbohydrates in your diet – and hence the levels of insulin in your blood. You may experience a drop in blood pressure. If you are on blood pressure medications, you may have to consult your doctor to have the dosage adjusted. After the first week, if you lose more than 1.5 kg (3 lb) per week you may be dehydrated or not consuming enough protein. Remember that your goal is not another short-term solution, but a safe, healthy and permanent reduction of body fat.

- If you feel hungry or lack energy on this new regime, it is likely that you are not eating enough. Increase the amount of food per meal or eat an extra meal, but always take great care to balance your meals correctly.

- If your body weight is normal, you will not gain body fat by following this diet. You may, however, experience a slight weight gain after a while, especially if you combine your improved diet with resistance training, owing to increased fat-free mass – body muscle – which is good news. This is due to the metabolic and hormonal effects of protein, and the muscle-building effect of exercise. You will have a healthier diet, feel alert and full of vitality, and will avoid gaining body fat.

- If you are underweight, this regime will help you reach a normal weight and increase your fat-free mass.

How much should I eat?

Without weighing and measuring, the diagrams opposite will help you to envisage what your meals will look like. For an adult, the amount of protein food (meat, fish, chicken, eggs, cottage cheese) should be about as big and thick as the palm of your hand. Palm size varies from one person to another and is proportionate with the rest of the body. This is the amount of protein-based food (cooked and ready to eat) that you need, and it constitutes the A part of each of your three main meals.

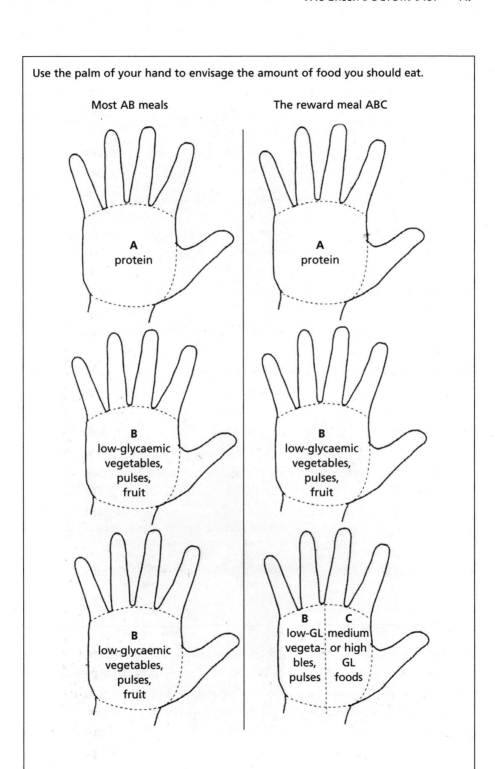

Use the palm of your hand to envisage the amount of food you should eat.

Most AB meals

The reward meal ABC

A
protein

A
protein

B
low-glycaemic
vegetables,
pulses,
fruit

B
low-glycaemic
vegetables,
pulses,
fruit

B
low-glycaemic
vegetables,
pulses,
fruit

B
low-GL
vegeta-
bles,
pulses

C
medium
or high
GL
foods

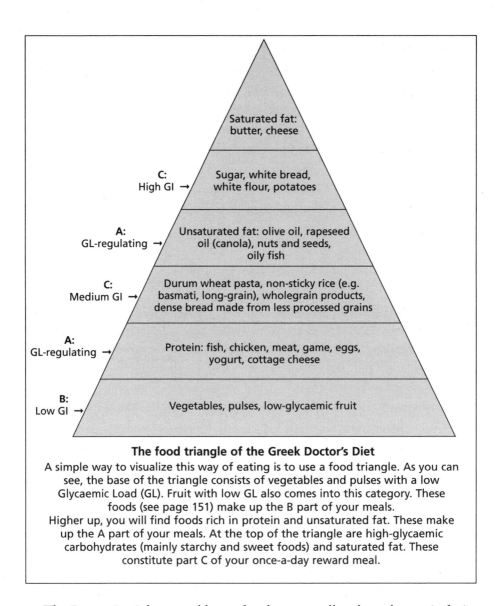

Saturated fat:
butter, cheese

C:
High GI → Sugar, white bread, white flour, potatoes

A:
GL-regulating → Unsaturated fat: olive oil, rapeseed oil (canola), nuts and seeds, oily fish

C:
Medium GI → Durum wheat pasta, non-sticky rice (e.g. basmati, long-grain), wholegrain products, dense bread made from less processed grains

A:
GL-regulating → Protein: fish, chicken, meat, game, eggs, yogurt, cottage cheese

B:
Low GI → Vegetables, pulses, low-glycaemic fruit

The food triangle of the Greek Doctor's Diet
A simple way to visualize this way of eating is to use a food triangle. As you can see, the base of the triangle consists of vegetables and pulses with a low Glycaemic Load (GL). Fruit with low GL also comes into this category. These foods (see page 151) make up the B part of your meals.
Higher up, you will find foods rich in protein and unsaturated fat. These make up the A part of your meals. At the top of the triangle are high-glycaemic carbohydrates (mainly starchy and sweet foods) and saturated fat. These constitute part C of your once-a-day reward meal.

The B part (mainly vegetables and pulses, as well as low glycaemic fruits and berries) should be twice as big as the protein part: two palms.

As for the C part of the reward meal, it should not be bigger than half a palm, and the B part should not be reduced to less than one and a half palms. Part C also includes dessert and cheese or wine/alcohol.

Snacks should be about half to one-third the size of main meals, keeping otherwise to the proportions.

Eat enough protein

As I explained in Chapter 2, it is absolutely essential that you eat enough protein. The palm of your hand acts as a good guideline for most people, but you may need to adjust the amount according to certain factors in your life, especially according to how physically active you are.

If you are not particularly physically active, this is how to calculate your minimum daily protein requirement: your body height in metres multiplied by your body height in metres multiplied by 23 equals your protein need in grams. For example, if you are 1.83m (6 feet) tall, the calculation will look like this:

$$1.83 \times 1.83 \times 23 = 77g \text{ of protein.}$$

Note that we are talking about pure protein here, not the amount of food. Chicken breast, for example, grilled without skin, contains 32 per cent protein. Depending on its size, one chicken breast will contain approximately 30 to 45g of protein.

Depending on how active you are, you may increase your protein intake:
• By 10 per cent if you take limited exercise, for example a 20- to 40-minute walk twice a week
• By 20 per cent if you do moderate aerobic exercise (brisk walking, cycling, rowing) three times a week
• By 30 per cent if you do aerobic exercise or light weight training /anaerobic exercise every day
• By 40 per cent if you exercise hard, including weight training/anaerobic exercise five times a week for 2 hours a day
• By 50 per cent if you exercise extremely hard, including weight training two or three times a day for 2 hours a day

Furthermore, you will have to add 10 per cent for the following:
• An extra 10 per cent for every hour of hard exercise exceeding 2 hours a day
• An extra 10 per cent if you are breastfeeding, and 20 per cent if you are pregnant
• An extra 10 per cent if you have to stand a lot in your work, or 15 to 20 per cent if your job is physically demanding

NB: If you suffer from a chronic kidney disorder (such as kidney failure or nephrotic syndrome), you should consult your doctor. You may need to limit the amount of protein you eat. The same applies if you suffer from a serious liver disorder, such as liver failure or chronic hepatitis (inflammation of the liver). If you are diabetic, it is important that you do not get too much protein, but that will not happen if you follow the principles of this diet.

Let me emphasize that this is *not* a high-protein diet. The amount of protein is somewhat higher than most of us are used to (at the expense of carbohydrates), but the total amount that I recommend is not high. You just eat enough protein.

Good sources of protein

For the average person, the amounts given in the table opposite constitute one palm; this is the amount of protein for each meal. The best choices are those that are lean, not processed (sausages etc.) and not exposed to very high temperatures (e.g. direct grilling or deep frying).

Fish and shellfish

All fish and shellfish (usual portion size 90–125g/3–4 ½ oz) are excellent sources of protein, with 15 to 20g of protein in a 100g serving. Oily fish, which you should aim to eat at least two to four times a week, are rich in omega-3 fatty acids (see chapter 2): sardines, herring, mackerel, salmon, tuna, trout. White fish and shellfish are usually very low in fat.

Eggs

One portion of protein corresponds to six egg whites or three whole eggs, but for most people this will be too many eggs. You could therefore combine, for example, two eggs with a smaller amount of another protein source. Egg yolks contain arachidonic acid, a fatty acid that can cause health problems if the blood level gets too high or for those who are sensitive to it (see page 104). If you eat two eggs a day, this should not be a problem. If you wish to err on the side of caution, mix two egg whites with one egg yolk to reduce the amount of arachidonic acid in your meal. The cholesterol in eggs has no bearing on your blood cholesterol level, a fact that has been established by several large studies.

Meat and poultry
All of the amounts denote cooked and prepared food.

Best choice

Lean beef - 90g/3 oz
Turkey breast or leg, skinless - 90g/3oz
Chicken breast or leg, skinless - 90g/3oz

Venison - 90g/3oz
Rabbit - 90g/3oz

Medium-good choice

Minced beef, less than 10% fat - 90g/3oz
Duck breast, skinless - 90g/3oz
Lamb, lean - 90g/3oz

Lean pork - 90g/3oz
Veal, lean - 90g/3oz
Ham, lean - 90g/3oz

Least-good choice

Bacon - 2 rashers, 75g/2^1/$_2$oz
Beef with fat - 90g/3oz
Minced beef, more than 10% fat - 90g/3oz
Frankfurter (hot dog)- 2 sausages,
   100g/3^1/$_2$oz

Lambs' liver - 90g/3oz
Chicken liver - 90g/3oz
Salami - 60g/2oz
Pork sausage - 2 large, 75g/2^1/$_2$oz

Note: liver is quite nutritious, but it is the 'detox' organ of the body, so this meat is likely to contain toxins. If you like liver, I suggest that you serve calves' liver as a very occasional treat; the younger the animal, the fewer toxins should be in its liver.

Dairy products

Best choice

Cottage cheese - 90g/3oz

Protein powder - 30g/1oz

Medium-good choice

Low-fat cheese, less than 10 % fat - 90g/3oz   Ricotta - 90g/3oz

Note: cheese such as cheddar, Brie, goat's cheese and Stilton may be eaten in small amounts as a snack, but always together with low-glycaemic vegetables or low-gly-caemic fruit – *not* with medium- or high-glycaemic carbohydrates such as bread or crackers. A matchbox-sized piece of cheese weighs about 30–45g/1–1^1/$_2$oz and pro-vides 6 to 8g of protein, but also lots of saturated fat.

Mixed protein and carbohydrate sources

Best choice

Skimmed milk - 250ml/8fl oz
Beans, lentils, chickpeas, tofu -150g/5oz

Buttermilk - 250ml/8fl oz
Yogurt, natural - 125g/4oz

Medium-good choice

Semi-skimmed milk, soya milk - 250ml/8fl oz

Note: all unsweetened yogurt with live cultures is good, as it replenishes healthy bacte-ria in your intestines. If you're trying to lose weight, choose fat-free or low-fat yogurt.

Beans, lentils and tofu

Beans and pulses (for example kidney, cannellini and borlotti beans; red, green and brown lentils; chickpeas, and fresh or frozen broad beans) are a source of both protein and healthy carbohydrate. When cooked, they contain about 12g of protein in a 150g serving.

Soya beans are higher in protein and fat and lower in carbohydrates than other beans, but we don't often eat them on their own. Tofu (soya bean curd) has approximately 8 to 12g of protein in a 100g serving.

Types of carbohydrates

By now, you have learned that not all carbohydrates are the same. 'Slow' carbohydrates, which are those with a low Glycaemic Index (GI) or glycaemic load (GL), are considered more healthy (see Chapter 4 for more information about the concepts of GI and GL, and the tables at the back of the book for a detailed list of food items). 'Fast' carbohydrates, which have a medium or high GI/GL, are less healthy.

When you are looking at a GI or GL list, it is important to remember that both protein and fat regulate the GI and GL. Milk chocolate, for example, has a medium GI (43), but is high in fat and also has a high GL (24/100g). Watermelon has a high GI, but a low GL (4/100g) and is also a good source of the antioxidant beta-carotene (provitamin A) – so no prizes for guessing which I'd recommend for your dessert, although dark chocolate with 70 per cent cocoa solids or more is a healthy food, when eaten in moderation.

Healthy carbohydrates

Some foods lead to a gentle, low rise in blood sugar. They contain relatively few carbohydrates and a lot of fibre and water. These carbohydrates are slowly transformed into blood sugar in the body, and they do not particularly stimulate the production of insulin. This results in less fat storage and other undesirable consequences of a high blood sugar and insulin level. These foods should constitute the B part of the AB/C plate model, and they should always be combined with sufficient protein and unsaturated fat. The table on the opposite page gives a range of examples. Using the palm measurement, this will mean two palms of this kind of food when putting together an AB meal and about one and a half palms with the ABC reward meal.

Examples of low-glycaemic carbohydrates

Raw vegetables	Boiled vegetables	Fruit
Alfalfa sprouts	Artichokes (globe,	Apples
Bamboo shoots	Jerusalem)	Apricots
Broccoli	Asparagus	Blackberries
Cabbage	Aubergine (eggplant)	Blackcurrants
Carrots	Beans (fresh, dried,	Blueberries
Cauliflower	canned)	Cherries
Celeriac	Beetroot	Grapefruit
Celery	Broccoli	Grapes
Chicory	Brussels sprouts	Kiwi fruit
Cucumber	Cabbage	Lemons, limes
Endive	Carrots	Melons
Fennel	Cauliflower	Nectarines
Lettuce, all kinds	Celeriac	Oranges
Mushrooms, all kinds	Chickpeas	Peaches
Onions, spring onions,	Courgettes (zucchini)	Pears
leeks	Fennel	Pineapple (fresh)
Pak choi (bok choy)	Green beans	Plums
Peas and mangetouts	Hummus (chickpea puree)	Redcurrants
Peppers (capsicums)	Lentils (red, yellow,	Strawberries
Radishes	brown)	Tangerines
Rocket	Mushrooms	Watermelon
Spinach	Okra	
Tomatoes	Onions, spring onions,	
Water chestnuts	leeks	
Watercress	Peas	
	Pumpkin	
	Spinach	
	Swiss chard	

Less favourable carbohydrates

Some carbohydrates cause a quick rise in blood sugar and stimulate the pancreas to produce a lot of insulin. If you eat this type of carbohydrate often, or in large amounts, the pancreas will have to produce a lot of insulin in response to the high levels of blood sugar. This can cause all the health problems related to a high insulin level and insulin resistance and can ultimately lead to exhaustion of the pancreas and thus to diabetes. Unfortunately, many of our favourite foods fall into this category. By reducing the intake (both the amount and the frequency) of such foods, and by combining them with the right amount of protein and healthy, predominantly unsaturated fat and dietary fibre, we can avoid negative consequences to our health. Check the Glycaemic Load tables at the back of the book for details on individual items.

You can allow yourself one meal a day that includes these foods – your reward meal. That will constitute the C part of the ABC plate model. If you

Examples of medium- and high-glycaemic carbohydrates

Vegetables	Cereal products
Butternut squash	Bagels, brioches
Parsnips	Barley
Potatoes (baked, boiled, mashed, fried)	Biscuits, crackers
	Bread crumbs
Swede (boiled, mashed)	White bread, baguette, ciabatta, wholemeal bread
Sweet potatoes	Bulgur wheat, couscous
Sweetcorn	Cornflakes
	Cornflour
Fruit	Croissants, Danish pastries
Banana	Doughnuts
Dates	Egg noodles
Figs	Muesli, crunchy oat cereals
Guava	Muffins
Mango	Pancakes, waffles
Prunes	Pasta
Raisins	Pastry, tarts, pies
Papayas	Pitta bread, nan bread
	Popcorn
Dried fruit	Pretzels
All fruit nectars	Rice
	Rice cakes
	Tacos, tortilla chips

use the palm measurement, that means half a palm of these foods a day. Choose the bread and cereal products with the lowest Glycaemic Load (GL). The higher the glycaemic load, the less you should eat. For example, a 30g serving of cornflakes has a GL of 21, whereas a 30g serving of All-Bran has a GL of 4.5.

DON'T GO BANANAS

High- and medium-glycaemic fruits and vegetables are not necessarily unhealthy: the glycaemic index just tells you something about their effect on blood sugar. Prunes, for example, are a better choice for a sweet treat than cakes or popcorn. But don't go bananas: you should limit your intake of these fruits to one serving a day.

Drinks and little extras to avoid

The following foods and drinks contain a high proportion of unhealthy carbohydrates and little or no nutritional benefits, therefore they should be used rarely and in small amounts.

Beverages: Most beer and lager, even non-alcoholic beer, especially dark malt beer (low-carb beer is becoming more widely available, and is the best choice), liqueurs, sweet wines, all canned and bottled drinks containing sugar, fruit nectars (fruit juices are preferable, but all sweet drinks should be limited).

Taste enhancers and snacks: Bottled sauces and salad dressings, sweet pickled cucumbers, cakes and biscuits, ice cream, honey, jam sweetened with regular sugar, molasses, golden syrup, chocolate syrup, maple syrup, sugar (both white and brown).

Eat the right fats

Unsaturated fat from oily fish, cold-pressed (virgin) vegetable oils and nuts is a very important part of this concept. Not only does healthy fat result in a meal with a lower glycaemic load (which means a lower rise in blood sugar), it also creates a better nutritional balance. The essential fatty acids are crucial to good health and an efficient metabolism and they aid in burning fat.

Contrary to what you might have heard, all fat is not unhealthy. But you do have to choose the right sort of fat: mostly unsaturated and, equally important, minimally processed. Trans fatty acids, found in hydrogenated vegetable oil (used in many margarines and in numerous prepared foods), are definitely hazardous and should be avoided completely. Saturated fat is non essential and thus not desirable in large quantities, because it displaces the healthier and essential unsaturated fat, so your intake should be limited. Saturated fat need not be eliminated from a healthy diet, in fact it is impossible to do so, since all natural sources of fat contain varying amounts of saturated fat. We all know that a delicious cake or a good cheese can contribute to our sense of well-being. If you keep to a healthy diet the rest of the time, you can allow yourself an occasional treat without feeling guilty.

Oily fish, such as salmon, trout, herring, mackerel, tuna and sardines, are important sources of healthy fat. They provide you with the essential omega-3 fatty acids (for further information, see chapter 10, in which I discuss dietary supplements).

Fats and oils

The amounts given can be included in every meal.
Athletes and people with physically demanding jobs should increase their intake of fat, mainly unsaturated fat. This has been proved to increase performance.

Best choice

Almonds, chopped - 4 tsp
Almonds, cashew nuts, hazelnuts - 10–12
Avocado - 3 tbs or ¼–½ of an avocado
Olive oil, extra virgin - 1 tsp
Rapeseed (canola) oil, avocado oil, cold-pressed - 1 tsp
Macadamia nuts - 3–5
Vinaigrette - 1 tsp olive oil and 2 tsp vinegar
Olives - 9
Natural peanut butter (without added sugar or vegetable oil) - 2 tsp
Peanuts, pistachios - 18
Sesame paste (tahini) - 2 tsp
Walnuts - 6–8 halves
Ground flaxseeds/linseeds - 3–4 tsp
Brazil nuts - 2
Pine nuts, pumpkin seeds, sunflower seeds - 2 tbs

Medium-good choice

Mayonnaise - 1 tsp (preferably made with cold-pressed rapeseed or olive oil)
Sesame oil - 1.5 tsp (preferably cold-pressed)
Butter, butter ghee, goose fat - 1 tsp
Sunflower oil - 1 tsp (preferably cold-pressed)
Single cream - 3 tbs

Poorer choice

(a lot of saturated fat or too much omega-6 fat)
Double cream - 2 tbs
Sour cream - 1 tbs
Low-fat sour cream - 2 tbs
Cream cheese - 3 tsp
Low-fat cream cheese - 6 tsp
Margarine - 1 tsp (but preferably do not use at all)
Corn oil - 1 tsp (not suitable for frying)
Soya bean oil - 1 tsp (not suitable for frying)

Choosing fats and oils

The table above shows the total amount of fat that you should eat with every meal to balance proteins and carbohydrates (when using the palm measurement). The healthiest types of oil are cold-pressed olive oil (extra virgin olive oil), cold-pressed rapeseed oil (canola oil) and cold-pressed avocado oil. Such oils should be added towards the end of the cooking process – though they do tolerate medium-high temperatures for short periods – or used in salads.

Most of the refined vegetable oils in the shops and used in the catering industry are inexpensive, and have been produced by 'warm pressing'. They have been subjected to high temperatures and chemicals, and they may suffer from peroxidation, which is detrimental to health. Frying, especially deep-frying, destroys the healthy unsaturated fatty acids in these oils and causes the formation of toxic by-products, including unhealthy trans fatty acids. This is particularly the case with sunflower oil, corn oil and soya oil. By eating ready-made and processed foods, we get too many omega-6 fatty acids and trans fatty acids in our diet as it is (see chapter 2, page 35). If you have to fry at high temperatures, try to avoid plant oils high in polyunsaturated fat and margarines that may contain trans fatty acids. Use butter ghee (clarified butter) instead, for instance, together with olive oil or rapeseed (canola) oil or pure coconut oil. Butter ghee – not the cheaper ghee made from vegetable oils – tolerates higher temperatures and thus produces fewer trans fatty acids.

There are great differences between margarines; usually, the softer they are, the better. In general, limit the use of margarines, and avoid them altogether unless they are declared 'free of trans fats'.

Nuts and seeds

Nuts and seeds contain the energy and nutrients a plant needs to develop its first leaf and its first root until the plant is established and can get energy itself from soil, sun and water. Protein and fat are vital, and nuts and seeds contain quite a lot of both. As a rule, a high percentage of the fat is unsaturated, because unsaturated fat contains more active energy than saturated fat. The amount of fat in different types of nuts and seeds ranges from 5 to nearly 75 per cent; even within a single type of nut or seed the amount of various nutrients will vary from place to place and from one year to another. Whole nuts and seeds contain important vitamins, minerals, antioxidants such as vitamin E, as well as fibre and healthy fat. Choose fresh, raw nuts and seeds, not roasted and salted.

The main drawback is that a high content of polyunsaturated fat (omega-3 or omega-6) in some nuts or seeds (e.g. walnuts or sunflower seeds) means that nuts and seeds turn rancid quickly. Ideally they should be stored in the freezer, where they will keep for several months.

What may I eat?

Pulses (legumes):
1 to 3 servings per day
(1 serving = 150g)
Beans
Chickpeas
Dried peas
Lentils

Vegetables:
Unlimited amount
Artichokes
Asparagus
Aubergines (eggplants)
Bamboo shoots
Bean sprouts
Broccoli
Brussels sprouts
Cabbage, all kinds
Cauliflower
Celery
Courgettes (zucchini)
Cucumber
Green beans
Green peas
Onions, garlic, leeks, spring onions
Pak choi (bok choy)
Peppers (capsicums)
Radishes
Salad leaves
  (e.g. lettuce, chicory, rocket)
Spinach
Tomatoes
Watercress

Fruit:
2 servings per day (1 serving =
  1 whole fruit or 100g berries or
  grapes)
Apple
Pear
Apricot
Berries, all kinds
Grapefruit
Grapes
Melon
Nectarine, peach
Orange
Plum
Watermelon (up to 200g serving)

Root vegetables:
1 to 2 servings per day (1 serving =
  100g boiled, 200g raw)
Beetroot
Carrots (preferably raw)
Celeriac
Jerusalem artichokes
Sweet potato

Protein sources:
3 to 5 servings per day, of which
  at least 1 serving is fish (1 serving
  = 90 to 200g prepared; approximately 120 to 180g raw)
Eggs (1 serving = 4 egg whites and
  2 egg yolks)
Fish (preferably oily fish), shellfish
Chicken breast, turkey breast
Game (venison, rabbit, pheasant,
  etc)
Lean meat from lamb, beef or
  pork
Cottage cheese (150g serving)
Tofu (100g serving)

Fat sources:

1 to 3 tbs per day, divided among
all meals (see also page 154)
Cold-pressed olive oil or rapeseed
(canola) oil
Sesame oil
Homemade mayonnaise made
with rapeseed (canola) oil
Half an avocado

Nuts and seeds:

1 to 3 servings per day (1 serving =
15g)
10–12 almonds, cashew nuts or
hazelnuts
6–8 walnut halves
2 tbs sesame, sunflower, pumpkin
or flax seeds

Coarse grain products:

1 serving per day (1 serving = 100g
boiled grains, or 1 slice of whole-
grain bread, or 3 rye crispbreads)
Basmati rice
Brown rice
Wild rice
Oats
Barley
Pasta made from durum wheat
(preferably protein-enriched/
low-carb)
Wholegrain rye crispbread
Very dark wholegrain bread (such
as pumpernickel)

Dairy products:

1 serving per day
125g fat-free or low-fat natural
(unsweetened) yogurt
250ml skimmed milk
250ml soya milk

Taste enhancers

Unlimited amount
Dijon mustard
Vinegar (all kinds)
Herbs
Spices
Chillies
Tabasco and other hot-pepper
sauces
Lemon and lime juice
Grated fresh horseradish

Beverages:

Unlimited amount
Water (as much as possible, at
least 8 glasses a day)
Decaffeinated coffee or decaffeinated tea (if desired, use a
non-caloric sweetener)
Green tea

Guidelines for the Greek Doctor's Diet

- If you both wish and need to lose weight, you should set yourself specific goals. Many overweight people avoid doing that. Generally speaking, the more overweight you are, the greater the resentment you will feel about setting specific long-term goals to lose weight. Instead, you say that you will try to lose some weight or that you will continue the diet until you feel better or until you look better. The problem with such general goals is that it is almost impossible to know if and when you have succeeded. Be honest with yourself: set yourself a realistic goal for your long-term weight reduction and do not give up until you have succeeded. You set goals in other areas of life, so why not in the important matter of your health?

  Everyone is bound to take a different amount of time in achieving their goals, and this certainly applies to weight reduction. But remember this: it is not possible to lose more than 1 to 1.5 kg (2 to 3lb) a week without the loss of lean body mass (muscle). Furthermore, a weight loss of more than 15 per cent within the first year is not recommended. A faster weight loss may have a bad effect on your health. After all, it has probably taken you a considerable period of time to gain weight. Take your time in achieving your goal!

- Avoid getting on the scales every day. Instead, try once a week or every ten days. You should weigh yourself in the morning, before you have had anything to eat or drink, and after you have urinated. That will make the comparison easier. For women, it is preferable to weigh yourself at the same time in your menstrual cycle, as your weight will naturally vary during your cycle.

- Eat three larger meals (breakfast, lunch and dinner) and two snacks in-between. Never skip a meal! That will only lead to a slower metabolism and your energy levels will deteriorate. Your muscle mass will gradually be reduced and you will store more fat the next time you eat. Aim to eat every three or four hours. Plan ahead so that you have the things you need to prepare a well-balanced meal. You plan meetings or decorating your home ahead of time, so why not your meals? If there is one thing that is for certain, it is that you are going to need food several times every day. Your success or failure will depend on how carefully and systematically you plan your diet.

- You may eat quite a lot of food if you stick to low-glycaemic carbohydrates balanced with protein and moderate amounts of healthy fat. Nevertheless, you should try to avoid meals that are too large; it would be better to have an extra meal a little while later if you still need it. Your body is not equipped

A TYPICAL DAY WITH THE GREEK DOCTOR'S DIET

Breakfast
- Scrambled eggs or an omelette made from 1 whole egg and 2 egg whites, chopped spinach and mushrooms fried with 1 teaspoon olive oil

Snack
- 125g fat-free or low-fat natural yogurt with 100g fresh berries (optional: 1 teaspoon fructose or artificial sweetener)

Lunch
- 100–200g grilled chicken breast or salmon (with herbs, spices, lemon, vinegar, or mustard)
- mixed salad (e.g. 200g salad leaves, tomato, red cabbage, cucumber, red onion, radish, 150g cooked beans or lentils)
- salad dressing: 3 teaspoons olive oil with 1 to 3 teaspoons balsamic vinegar or lemon juice, ½ teaspoon Dijon mustard or herbs (optional)

Snack (could be eaten after dinner, if dinner is early)
- 1 pear
- 10 whole almonds

Dinner
- 200ml pea soup or lentil soup
- 120–150g grilled or steamed salmon (with herbs, spices)
- 200g steamed broccoli with 1 teaspoon olive oil
- 100g boiled basmati rice or spaghetti

to handle large amounts of food at any one time without starting to store fat. You should never feel stuffed when you leave the table, only pleasantly full.

If you do decide to have a second helping, make sure that you choose both protein and low-glycaemic carbohydrates.

- No meal or snack should be without protein. That is the only way to ensure a diet that maintains the hormonal balance between insulin and glucagon (see chapter 5) and thus ensures a more effective metabolism and the burning of fat. If you choose an apple for your snack, for instance, try to have some yogurt, cottage cheese, almonds or other nuts with it.

- As far as possible, avoid food with a high glycaemic load (if possible, even in your reward meal), and look for medium-glycaemic foods. For your reward meal, choose small amounts of pasta or non-sticky rice rather than potatoes, white bread, or foods with a white-flour base. Above all, avoid combining high-glycaemic foods with saturated fat. That is the worst combination possible!

- The glycaemic load of your last meal will influence what you eat the next time. A low-glycaemic breakfast will give you a lower rise in blood sugar, even after lunch three or four hours later. Research on obese children, carried out at Boston Children's Hospital, a department of Harvard University, found that if they eat a high-glycaemic breakfast and lunch, they are likely to eat 80 per cent more food (calories) during the rest of the day than if they have a low-glycaemic breakfast and lunch.

- Vinegar and lemon lower the glycaemic load of mixed meals. Use them in salads, salad dressings, sauces, and on grilled food.

- Use a lot of spices and herbs, too. Garlic and 'hot' spices (chilli peppers, mustard, pepper, horseradish) increase metabolism and the burning of fat.

- Avoid using too much salt, which is bad for your health (among other things, it can cause water retention and, in some cases, high blood pressure). Try to gradually reduce your salt intake, and if you really want the taste of salt, use low-sodium or sodium-reduced salt (most supermarkets stock this).

  Try to use homemade stock for cooking. The second-best option is the ready-made fresh stocks and organic bouillon powders that can be found in some supermarkets. Another option is to use a smaller amount of each stock cube than the packet suggests (half or one-third of a cube will do). The food will taste ten times better and you will consume less salt.

- Avoid bread-based meals. Cut thin slices and eat a little bread along with your reward meal, but don't make it an entire meal in itself. If you have bread for lunch, it should be eaten with a lot of protein-rich food (tuna, mackerel, salmon, sardines, chicken, turkey, cottage cheese) – a little bread to go with the protein, not the other way round. In addition, you should eat low-glycaemic vegetables or fruit with your meal.

- Always choose the darkest and densest bread, such as wholegrain rye, stone-ground wholemeal or pumpernickel bread. Better yet, bake it yourself (see recipes 47 and 48).

- When at a restaurant, never eat bread before the meal. This greatly stimulates insulin production and causes you to eat more than you intended to. The restaurant business is well aware that bread stimulates the appetite. Why else would they be serving it? Ask if they have some vegetables, such as celery or raw carrots (or, alternatively, almonds or peanuts), for you to nibble on while you are waiting.
- Eat something rich in protein before you go out to dinner, such as low-fat unsweetened yogurt (with fructose or calorie-free sweetener if you like) or some cottage cheese. Two to three tablespoons will satisfy your appetite and stimulate glucagon production, thus increasing the burning of fat.
- Eat oily fish (sardines, tuna, mackerel, salmon, trout, herring) for lunch or dinner at least two to four times a week. Avoid processed fish products such as pâtés and pastes, which often contain starch or processed fat, and also tinned fish with a sugary tomato sauce. Read the label!
- Saturated fat (whole/full-fat milk, butter, most cheese, cream and sour cream, visible fat from meat) should not exceed more than 10–15 per cent of your total energy intake. Avoid drinking full-fat milk; if you want to drink milk at all, choose skimmed milk. Choose the leanest meat products, fat-free or low-fat yogurt and low-fat cheese, or eat smaller quantities of the regular types.

    Think of rich dairy products (cream, sour cream, cheese) as festive food to be enjoyed only on Saturdays or Sundays, for instance. If you love cheese, eat it with vegetables and fruit and not with bread or crackers.
- If you are going to use mayonnaise, choose the regular type and not the low-fat kind, which usually contains quite a lot of carbohydrates instead of fat. You can reduce the fat content of regular mayonnaise by beating in a small amount of water. The mayonnaise will be just as thick, but will have a lower percentage of fat.
- Hydrogenated or partially hydrogenated vegetable oil or fat is found in all sorts of ready-made food, from biscuits, doughnuts, pies and pastries to peanut butter and some breakfast cereals. It is also in many margarines and low-fat spreads, even some of the polyunsaturated ones that claim to be heart-healthy. Read the label: unless it specifically states a product is free of trans fats (trans fatty acids), it is likely to contain a lot of these very unhealthy fats, which increase the risk of coronary heart disease.

    Hydrogenated oils are also widely used (and re-used) by fast-food outlets for deep-fat frying.

- Choose olive oil (extra virgin oil is the best) or cold-pressed rapeseed (canola), walnut or flaxseed oil for your salad dressings or to drizzle over vegetables, or whenever you need some fat in your cooking. It's better if you can add the oil at the end of the cooking process, since all of these oils lose their best qualities when exposed to high temperatures.
- Avoid deep frying and frying with a lot of fat. Use a good-quality non-stick frying pan and you will be able to 'fry' without fat or at least with very little. Starch absorbs fat, so don't coat foods with flour or breadcrumbs before frying.
- For stir-frying, use coconut oil or butter ghee, which can withstand higher temperatures than sunflower, soya or corn oil. Rapeseed (canola) oil, avocado oil or macadamia oils may also be used.
- If you have to fry at high temperatures, ghee (clarified butter – but not vegetable ghee) and goose fat remain stable at higher temperatures and produce fewer toxic by-products, including trans fatty acids.
- An alternative to frying vegetables is to blanch them in boiling water or stock and then finish cooking them in a small amount of fat for a short time at a low temperature.
- If a particular dish really needs the flavour of butter, use just a small amount or melt it with some rapeseed (canola) oil.
- Steaming, boiling, grilling and roasting in the oven are always preferable to frying. Try cooking meat and fish at low temperatures (approximately 100 to 120°C/200°F) for a longer period of time. Use a meat thermometer (which measures the core temperature of the food). Your food will be so succulent that there will be no need for fatty gravy or rich sauces. Less fatty meats really benefit from this cooking method.
- Avoid fatty sauces based on cream or butter, and those made from flour or cornflour. Try making a sauce by adding stock or white or red wine to the hot pan in which you have just cooked the food; let it boil until it thickens; then add a wine or fruit vinegar, or herbs and spices, and olive oil.

   A tablespoon of pesto on your meat, chicken or fish is a tasty alternative. Buy ready-made pesto or make it yourself (see recipe 14).
- Avoid eating ready-made cakes. They usually contain a lot of processed and/or trans fat, sugar and refined flour – an unhealthy combination and one that can have an extremely negative effect on your metabolism. Instead, choose desserts based on fruit, milk or cream, yogurt or cottage cheese, and fructose

or a calorie-free sweetener – or on eggs and/or gelatine (for example panna-cotta, cheesecake with a nut crust). See the recipe section at the back of the book for some ideas.

- Drink a lot of water – at least eight glasses a day. If you live in a warm climate or do physical exercise, you need to drink even more. The same applies if you are pregnant or breastfeeding. Almost 70 per cent of the body consists of water, and this fluid has to be replenished all the time! Some carbonated mineral waters contain a great deal of salt (sodium). Look for bottled low-sodium mineral water or drink tap water (if your local water is not heavily chlorinated).

- Avoid too much coffee. Even though the caffeine in coffee temporarily increases your metabolism, large or frequent amounts may have a negative effect. A moderate coffee intake has been shown to have positive effects, due to its antioxidant content (this also applies to decaffeinated coffee).

    Coffee, by the way, is a diuretic, which means you will have to compensate for your coffee drinking by consuming extra water. Note that no beverage can or should replace water!

- Avoid bottled and canned drinks (and ready-made iced tea): they contain a lot of sugar and thus stimulate insulin production. Cola is also high in caffeine and acids, which are thought to damage the teeth and promote osteoporisis (the latter also applies to sugar-free drinks). Homemade iced tea, on the other hand, is an excellent alternative and is rich in antioxidants.

- You should include moderate physical activity in your everyday life; this is not just for those who want to get in better shape, but is absolutely essential for overall long-term health. A brisk walk for more than 20 to 30 minutes is most effective, preferably early in the day, shortly after you get up. If you can also fit in some anaerobic exercise such as weight training, two to three times a week will do. Focus primarily on large muscles (those in the thighs and legs), because those are the ones that burn the most fat.

REMEMBER

- Eat three main meals and two snacks every day.
- Eat enough protein with all meals.
- Eat a lot of low-glycaemic foods (especially vegetables and pulses) and few medium- to high-glycaemic foods (especially sugar, white bread and products made from refined flour, potatoes, pasta, rice).
- Eat two servings of fruit and at least three servings of vegetables every day.
- Eat moderate amounts of healthy, unprocessed, predominantly unsaturated fat each day (oily fish, nuts, seeds, olive oil, rapeseed oil).
- Avoid large amounts of saturated fat (full-fat milk, cream and cheeses).
- Stay well away from trans fats (hydrogenated vegetable oil found in margarines and industrially-baked goods) and processed omega-6-rich plant oils.
- Reduce your salt (sodium) intake.
- Do not eat for two or three hours before you go to bed.
- Drink at least eight glasses of water every day.
- Do at least 20 minutes of aerobic exercise a day, five to seven days a week (brisk walk or cycling) and resistance exercise two to three times a week.
- Avoid cigarettes and excess alcohol (limit yourself to one glass of wine or other alcoholic drink with one meal a day for women, or two glasses for men).
- Avoid stress and find methods of mastering stress (e.g. yoga or meditation).

CHAPTER 12

A FOUR-WEEK MENU PLAN

his menu plan should help you get started on a new way of eating. There is no need to follow it strictly; rather, think of it as a guide to help you break away from your current eating habits and choose the path to good health.

It is important that you seek support from those close to you. It can be difficult to change your lifestyle on your own, and when trying to change your food habits it is especially important – if you do not do the shopping or cooking – that the person preparing food at home is willing to help you. Besides, a healthy diet is good for the whole family!

- The suggested amounts are meant only as a guideline. Feel free to increase them if necessary, so that you feel pleasantly full, but make sure that each meal is properly balanced, following the AB or ABC plate model (see page 143). In each meal there should be a certain ratio between protein-rich food and carbohydrate-rich food in order to obtain the best-possible glycaemic effect and balance between insulin and glucagon.

- For main meals, the amount of protein should be approximately the size and thickness of your palm. Most meals follow the AB pattern: one palm of protein-rich food and two palms of low-glycaemic carbohydrates. The reward meal (ABC) has: one palm of protein-rich food, half a palm of medium- to high-glycaemic carbohydrates, and one and a half palms of low-glycaemic carbohydrates.

- The times indicated for each meal are there to make sure that you eat often enough. You may need to adjust them to your own schedule.

- The numbers in parentheses refer to the recipes in this book.
- The letter (C) is a suggestion for the medium- to high-glycaemic carbohydrates that form the C part of your ABC reward meal.
- Drink water or tea with your meals, unless something else is specified, and drink at least eight glasses of water every day. A 150ml glass or two of wine a day is optional – but if you are trying to lose weight I recommend that you avoid alcohol or use it as the C part of your reward meal.
- Variety is vital. Mindlessly eating the same foods day after day is a sure path to weight gain, and diets that restrict your choice of foods are difficult to stick to for very long. But there's more to it than that. Many vitamins and minerals work best in combination with other micronutrients, and eating a variety of foods will ensure you get a good mix of micronutrients. Our Stone Age ancestors had a diet that varied with the seasons, and with the luck of the hunt – they didn't eat pizza every night!
- Make sure that you have some protein-rich food (fish, poultry, egg, milk, cottage cheese, yogurt, tofu) with every meal.
- Two (or even three) eggs would constitute a normal helping, but remember that egg yolks contain arachidonic acid, a fatty acid that can cause health problems for those who are sensitive to it (see page 104). To reduce the amount of arachidonic acid in your diet I recommend that you mix two egg whites with one whole egg when you are making scrambled eggs and omelettes.
- Cottage cheese, fromage frais and quark are all are good, low-fat sources of protein. For variety, add berries, chopped nuts, spices and fresh or dried herbs.
- Plain, natural yogurt is another good source of protein. If you're trying to lose weight, look for fat-free yogurt – it tastes just as good as the regular type. Avoid fruit-flavoured yogurts, as most are loaded with sugar. Opt for sugar-free alternatives, if available.
- The menu plan aims to show that you do not have to have bread with three meals a day. When you buy bread, remember that the denser it is, the better. Wholemeal bread is often highly processed; look for stoneground wholemeal or other wholegrain breads. Home-baked breads made from whole grains are best: try the recipes (47 and 48) in this book.
- Keep a small stock of frozen and canned fish, frozen vegetables and canned beans, so that you always have good healthy food in the house.
- Try to reduce the amount of sugar you eat in all forms. If you have a sweet tooth you may want to do this gradually. Replacing sugar with small amounts

of fructose in desserts and on cereals and yogurt is one way to cut down; fructose is sweeter than sucrose, so you will need less, and fructose has a low glycaemic effect.

- Try to reduce the amount of salt you eat; I recommend low-sodium salt. When you reduce the amount of salt, fat and sugar in your diet, you may at first find that food is less tasty. It is a good idea to experiment with other ingredients to provide flavour. Herbs, garlic, ginger, mustard, vinegar (white wine or balsamic), nuts, extra-virgin olive oil, and ready-made sauces such as soy sauce, chilli sauce and Tabasco, Worcestershire sauce, Oriental oyster sauce and fish sauce can all be added for flavour just before serving. Spices, stock, (preferably homemade, although bouillon powder can be be OK, too) and wine can be used for cooking. Many spices and herbs have health benefits: they can boost the metabolism, they may be high in antioxidants, and their individual essential oils can have specific health benefits.
- A squeeze of fresh lemon juice over cooked vegetables, salads, fish and shellfish, and even some poultry and meat dishes, reduces the glycaemic effect and adds a wonderful fresh taste of the Mediterranean.
- Many meals and snacks benefit from the addition of a teaspoon of flaxseed oil just before you eat them: this gives you all the benefits of omega-3 fats and reduces the glycaemic effect of your meal.

Menu Plan Week 1

	7am Breakfast	10am Snack
Monday	3 tbs All Bran (C) 1 tbs ground flaxseed 100g berries 125g natural yogurt	yogurt and dill dip (1) raw vegetables
Tuesday	1 or 2 poached eggs 1 slice Dr Lindberg's 8-grain bread (47) (C) 250ml skimmed milk 1 orange or 2 satsumas	grated carrots 1 tbs sunflower or sesame seeds 1 tsp olive oil or sesame oil
Wednesday	small bowl of unsweetened muesli (C) 1–2 tsp fructose (optional) 250ml skimmed milk 1 or 2 kiwi fruit	100–150g cottage cheese chopped cucumber and dill
Thursday	omelette (1 egg and 2 egg whites, or 2 eggs) tomato and basil (cooked with 1 tsp olive oil)	125g natural yogurt 100g fresh berries 1 tsp fructose (optional)
Friday	oatmeal and almond porridge (42) (C) 1 orange	100–150g cottage cheese 1 tbs pumpkin seeds
Saturday	1 or 2 fried eggs 2 slices of lean bacon 2 tomatoes 250ml skimmed milk	100–150g cottage cheese 1 nectarine or peach
Sunday	small bowl of porridge (C) 1–2 tsp fructose (optional) 1 kiwi fruit	125g natural yogurt 100g berries

12.30 Lunch	4pm Snack	7pm Dinner
mixed bean salad (7)	1 pear 4 walnut halves 30–40g plain dark chocolate (70% cocoa solids)	rocket salad with olive oil and lemon juice lemon chicken with chick-peas (24)
lentil soup (3) 1 apple	125g natural yogurt 10 almonds	green salad with olive oil and lemon grilled trout grilled tomatoes steamed green beans
canned sardines in olive oil chopped red pepper, celery, onion, radish, 150g chick-peas with lemon juice and 1 tsp olive oil	1 apple 12–18 peanuts	green salad with olive oil and lemon Dr Lindberg's ratatouille (37)
100–200g grilled chicken or turkey breast mixed salad (lettuce, tomato, cucumber, spring onion, 150g kidney beans, fresh herbs)	100g grapes 10 almonds	lentil soup (3) grilled salmon with herbs steamed broccoli 100g boiled basmati rice or baked sweet potato (C)
shellfish and fish platter (5) raw or steamed fennel, carrots, cucumber, cauliflower	125g natural yogurt 3 dried apricots 8 hazelnuts	tomato and onion salad Moroccan chicken (21) steamed courgettes and green beans, with lemon, olive oil and parsley
spinach and avocado soup (4) mixed salad	1 pear 10 almonds	rocket salad grilled sesame salmon with asparagus (18) 100g boiled basmati rice (C) Dr Lindberg's lemon mousse (45)
stuffed mushrooms (39) lamb with rosemary (32) steamed spinach	100–150g cottage cheese 1 tbs ground flaxseed raw carrots, cucumber 10 cashew nuts	Greek salad (6)

Menu Plan Week 2

	7am Breakfast	10am Snack
Monday	1 slice of pumpernickel bread (C) 2 tbs cottage cheese 1 apple, chopped sprinkling of cinnamon 250ml skimmed milk	125g natural yogurt 1 tbs chopped nuts 1 tsp fructose (optional)
Tuesday	3 tbs All Bran (C) 250ml skimmed milk 1–2 tsp fructose (optional) 1 or 2 boiled eggs ½–1 grapefruit	125g natural yogurt 4 walnut halves 30–40g plain dark chocolate (70% cocoa solids)
Wednesday	scrambled egg (1 egg and 2 egg whites, or 2 eggs) 50g smoked salmon 1 slice stoneground whole-meal bread (C)	125g natural yogurt 100g raspberries 1 tbs sliced almonds
Thursday	small bowl of unsweetened muesli (C) 1 tbs sunflower seeds 250ml skimmed milk 100g berries	tzatziki (2) raw carrots, red peppers, fennel
Friday	small bowl of porridge (C) 1 tbs ground flaxseed 1 peach or nectarine 1 or 2 boiled eggs	100–150g cottage cheese fresh or dried oregano or basil 4 cherry tomatoes
Saturday	blueberry pancakes (44) (C) 2 tbs natural yogurt 1 tsp fructose (optional)	100g grapes 2 Brazil nuts
Sunday	3 slices ham with mustard 1 or 2 poached eggs grilled tomato grilled mushrooms	1 apple 10 almonds

12.30 Lunch	4pm Snack	7pm Dinner

canned salmon or tuna
150g cooked chickpeas
spring onions
fresh or sun-dried tomatoes
rocket
	100–150g cottage cheese,
	  fromage frais or quark
	1 tbs ground flaxseed
	100g berries
		green salad with olive oil
		  and lemon juice
		lamb casserole with cab-
		  bage (33)
		red lentil purée (34)

prawn, avocado and feta salad (11)	1 orange 10 almonds	lentil stew (35) large mixed salad

lentil soup (3)
2 plums, 1 satsuma
	100–150g cottage cheese
	red pepper, carrot,
	  courgette
		green salad with olive oil
		  and lemon juice
		grilled mackerel (16)

Spanish omelette without potatoes (36) green salad	100g grapes 10 almonds	chicken fajitas (25) shredded lettuce

90g lean ham
shredded white cabbage,
  carrot and onion, with
  1 tsp mayonnaise and
  1–2 tbs natural yogurt
	1 kiwi fruit
	10 hazelnuts
		rocket salad with olive oil
		  and lemon juice
		fish casserole with pesto
		  (14)
		red lentil purée (34)

fresh tuna salad (8)	100–150g cottage cheese carrots	green salad with olive oil and lemon juice Dr Lindberg's moussaka (30) peach meringue (43)

roast chicken
barley risotto with nuts (41)
steamed broccoli, carrots
	1 slice Dr Lindberg's 8-grain
	  bread (47) (C)
	2–3 tbs cottage cheese
	smoked salmon
		Indian spiced beans and
		  vegetables (38)
		1 orange or 2 satsumas

Menu Plan Week 3

	7am Breakfast	10am Snack
Monday	omelette (1 egg and 2 egg whites, or 2 eggs) spinach and mushroom (cooked with 1 tsp olive oil) 250ml skimmed milk	1 apple 10 hazelnuts
Tuesday	1 slice of Dr Lindberg's sunflower rye bread (C) 2–3 tbs cottage cheese 1–2 slices lean ham 1 kiwi fruit	yogurt and dill dip (1) raw carrots, celery
Wednesday	1 or 2 eggs (cooked in 1 tsp olive oil) 2 slices lean bacon 1–2 tomatoes, grilled	125g natural yogurt 1 kiwi fruit 3–5 Brazil nuts
Thursday	small bowl of porridge (C) 100g berries	125g natural yogurt 1 apple 1–2 tbs sunflower or pumpkin seeds
Friday	3 tbs All Bran (C) 1 tbs ground flaxseed 1 tsp fructose (optional) 250ml skimmed milk ½–1 grapefruit	2 tbs hummus raw cauliflower, carrot, red pepper
Saturday	scrambled egg (1 egg and 2 whites, or 2 eggs) 50g smoked salmon 100g strawberries	100–150g cottage cheese grated carrot 1 tbs ground flaxseed 1 tsp flaxseed oil
Sunday	1 slice of pumpernickel bread (C) 2–3 tbs cottage cheese 150g prawns 1 slice watermelon or ½ small orange-fleshed melon	8 olives 10 almonds

12.30 Lunch	4pm Snack	7pm Dinner
turkey with nut sauce (27) shredded white cabbage, carrot and onion, with 1 tsp mayonnaise and 1–2 tbs natural yogurt	100g berries 125g natural yogurt 1 tbs ground flaxseed or sunflower seeds	green salad with olive oil and lemon juice chilli con carne (29) 100g boiled basmati rice (C)
chilli con carne (leftover from Monday dinner) mixed salad	1 orange 4 macadamia nuts	green salad with olive oil and lemon juice stir-fried salmon (19)
mixed bean salad (7)	100g cherries 10 almonds	colourful chicken and cous-cous (23) (C)
½ avocado 150g prawns 1–2 tbs fromage frais 1 tsp tomato purée (concentrate) lemon juice, paprika	1 carrot 2–3 tsp natural peanut butter	rocket salad with olive oil and lemon juice tomato and onion salad lentil stew (35)
chicken salad (9)	1 pear 4 walnut halves 30–40g plain dark chocolate (70% cocoa solids)	salmon burgers with green tartar sauce (17) tomatoes green salad
asparagus and rocket salad with 1 tbs grated Parmesan cheese	1 slice watermelon or ½ small orange-fleshed melon 125g natural yogurt 10 almonds	green salad with olive oil and lemon juice Chinese stir-fried chicken (20) Dr Lindberg's cheesecake (46) (C)
baked red mullet roasted courgettes, red peppers, aubergines 1 tsp olive oil 1 tsp balsamic vinegar	100g raspberries 125g natural yogurt or 3 tbs single cream	green salad with olive oil and lemon juice Spanish omelette without potatoes (36)

Menu Plan Week 4

	7am Breakfast	10am Snack
Monday	small bowl of unsweetened muesli (C) 1 tbs ground flaxseed 1–2 tsp fructose (optional) 250ml skimmed milk 100g berries	2–3 tbs hummus raw cauliflower, carrot, red pepper
Tuesday	1 or 2 scrambled eggs mushrooms (cooked with 1 tsp olive oil)	125g natural yogurt 1 pear 2 Brazil nuts
Wednesday	3 tbs All Bran (C) 1 tsp fructose (optional) 1 tbs ground flaxseed 250ml skimmed milk ½–1 grapefruit	8 olives 10 almonds
Thursday	oatmeal and almond porridge (42) (C) 100g raspberries	tzatziki (leftover from Wednesday dinner) raw carrot, red pepper, celery
Friday	1 or 2 boiled eggs 1–2 tbs cottage cheese 1 slice wholegrain rye bread (C) 1 peach or nectarine	grated carrots 1 tbs pumpkin or sesame seeds 1 tsp olive oil or sesame oil 1 tsp balsamic vinegar or lemon juice
Saturday	omelette (1 egg and 2 egg whites, or 2 eggs) 75g prawns 3 spring onions 100g grapes	125g natural yogurt 5 hazelnuts 30–40g plain dark chocolate (70% cocoa solids)
Sunday	blueberry pancakes (44) (C) 250ml skimmed milk ½ small orange-fleshed melon	100g grapes 10 almonds

12.30 Lunch	4pm Snack	7pm Dinner
mixed bean salad (7) with canned sardines instead of ham or turkey	1 apple 6–8 walnut halves	rocket salad with 1 tbs pine nuts, 1 tbs grated Parmesan, olive oil and balsamic vinegar chicken with spinach and yogurt sauce (22)
watercress, orange and walnut salad with 1 tsp walnut oil	100–150g cottage cheese or fromage frais 1 tbs ground flaxseed 1 tbs pumpkin seeds	spinach and avocado soup (4) herb-baked fish (13) mixed salad boiled basmati rice (C)
3 tbs cottage cheese 100–150g smoked mackerel tomato cucumber green salad	125g natural yogurt 50g grapes 50g raspberries	keftedes (Greek meatballs) (28) tzatziki (2) Greek salad (6)
tuna salad (8)	100–150g cottage cheese 1 apple or pear sprinkling of cinnamon	vegetable and cashew stir-fry (40)
tomato, avocado, mozzarella, rocket and basil salad 1 tsp olive oil 1 tsp balsamic vinegar	125g natural yogurt 10 almonds 1 kiwi fruit	green salad with olive oil and lemon juice baked fish on a bed of spinach (15) red lentil purée (34)
lentil soup (3)	100–150g cottage cheese 1 tbs ground flaxseed fresh or dried oregano or basil cherry tomatoes	steamed asparagus with olive oil and balsamic vinegar chicken in apricot curry sauce (26) green beans boiled basmati rice (C) peach meringue (43)
boiled globe artichoke, lemon juice, olive oil and parsley dressing roast chicken steamed courgette, cauliflower, broccoli, carrots, fennel, cabbage	100–150g cottage cheese 75g prawns cucumber dill	green salad with olive oil and lemon juice meat sauce (31) with green beans

RECIPES

Tomatoes and oregano make it Italian; wine and tarragon make it French.
Sour cream makes it Russian; lemon and cinnamon make it Greek.
Soy sauce makes it Chinese; garlic makes it good.

Alice May Brock

f you want to cook good food, with or without recipes, you need
to have a basic range of ingredients on hand. How many times have
you come home tired and hungry, thinking it would be nice to have
something good to eat, only to open a cookery book and discover that you lack
most of the ingredients? Having to buy food every day can be a drain on your
energy; why not set aside a little time at the weekend to plan the week's menus?

Plan how much preparation can be done in advance; perhaps you could
prepare the entire meal, so that when you get home all you need to do is heat
it through. Why not prepare food for the next day after you have had your dinner and relaxed for a while? Cooking more food than you need and storing extra
portions in the refrigerator or freezer is also a good idea, and means you don't
have to cook every night.

- You don't need a vast battery of utensils and gadgets, but you will find it easier to prepare great-tasting healthy food if you have a few good-quality
  saucepans, a large non-stick frying pan amd a set of sharp, efficient knives.
  I also recommend a cooking/meat thermometer (many of these have a built-
  in alarm) and an electric blender.
- Always read a recipe carefully before starting to cook. Even if you are not
  using a recipe, you may find it helps to jot down a rough time plan and set
  out all the equipment and ingredients you will need. Start with the most
  time-consuming stages, such as putting meat, poultry or fish in the oven or
  cooking the lentils, beans or rice (remember that brown rice and wild rice

take longer to cook than white rice). Lentils, beans and chickpeas can be soaked and cooked two or three days ahead and stored in the refrigerator.

- Quick cooking methods such as grilling and stir-frying are not your only options. Why not try slow cooking at a low temperature? It is a traditional method not just in Greece but throughout Europe, dating back to the days when few people had ovens at home, so they took food to the local baker to use the residual heat of the bread oven. Roasting at low temperatures requires a longer cooking time (chicken pieces take about 50 minutes and a leg of lamb about 2 hours – see recipe 32), but very little attention once the food is in the oven, giving you time to relax. Preheat the oven to 250°F/120°C/gas ½. Put a roasting pan over low heat, add a couple of teaspoons of olive oil plus herbs or garlic, then place the meat, poultry or fish in the pan and insert a cooking thermometer into the thickest part. The internal temperature of the food will vary depending on what you are cooking, but generally it should be around 125–150°F/55–75°C (150°F/75°C for chicken and turkey). Cooking at low temperatures means the muscle cells in the meat or fish are not destroyed, so the flavour is fantastic and there is less shrinkage than with cooking at high temperatures. The food will be so tender and succulent that you will not need extra salt or rich sauces, and you will have some delicious leftovers for lunch the following day.
- Do not add too much salt; I recommend that you always use low-sodium/sodium-reduced salt.
- Unless the recipe states otherwise, always use virgin or extra virgin olive or rapeseed (canola) oil. 'Virgin' denotes that the oil has been cold-pressed, in other words not subjected to heat or chemicals before bottling.
- Polyunsaturated fat does not tolerate high temperatures well and is not suitable for frying. Olive oil, rapeseed oil, peanut oil and avocado oil contain mainly monounsaturated fat and tolerate frying at low temperatures relatively well, but not deep frying. If you want to fry at high temperatures or deep fry, which you should avoid, use butter ghee (clarified butter) or goose fat. Above all, don't let the oil or fat burn.
- Fructose can be bought as a powder in health food shops and some supermarkets. When adapting your own recipes, you will need about one-third less fructose than sugar. For baking, reduce the oven temperature by around 50 degrees and bake for slightly longer than you would with recipes containing sugar. Fructose caramelizes at a lower temperature than sucrose (table sugar).
- Instead of crushed biscuits, use finely ground nuts for a cheesecake base.

- Instead of white flour, choose wholemeal flour, preferably stoneground. Soya flour, which is very high in protein and has a low GI, can be used to replace about half the white flour in most recipes. You can also grind oats (or buy oat flour) or look in health food shops for flour from ancient wheat types, such as spelt and kamut; the latter contain more fibre, vitamins, minerals and protein than regular wheat flour. Try using them instead of a proportion of white flour in your favourite recipes.
- Glycaemic Load (GL) per serving has been calculated based on the total carbohydrate amount in grams, multiplied by the Glycaemic Index (GI) of the main blood-sugar-influencing ingredient(s) and divided by 100. If the carbohydrate source is solely very low-glycaemic vegetables, the GL is practically zero. Since many of the recipes that follow include significant amounts of protein and/or fat, and also lemon, yogurt or vinegar – all known to reduce the GI and thus the GL – they have a very low GL of less than 6.5 per serving. Following the Greek Doctor's Diet, with an average energy intake of 2000 kcal/day, the average GL for a whole day will be low, around 35. (Anything less than 50 is low.)

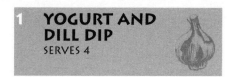

1 YOGURT AND DILL DIP
SERVES 4

The perfect snack or first course: plenty of raw vegetables with a tasty, protein-rich dip.

200g (7oz) cottage cheese
1 tablespoon natural yogurt
1 clove garlic, chopped
1 tablespoon chopped fresh dill
salt and pepper

To serve:
raw carrot
celery
cucumber
red, green or yellow peppers
    (capsicums)
cauliflower florets

In a bowl or, better still, a food processor, mix together the cottage cheese, yogurt, garlic and dill; season to taste.

Cut the vegetables into sticks, arrange on a plate and serve with the dip.

PER SERVING: GLYCAEMIC LOAD 1; PROTEIN 8G; CARBOHYDRATE 2G; FAT 2G (OF WHICH 1.5G SATURATES); FIBRE 0G

2 TZATZIKI
SERVES 4

This dip contains a useful amount of protein and calcium to serve with raw vegetables as a snack or first course. It also makes a fresh-tasting accompaniment to Greek meatballs (recipe 28).

1kg (2lb) natural yogurt
1/2 cucumber, peeled
1 tablespoon extra virgin olive oil
4 cloves garlic, crushed
1/2 teaspoon fructose (optional)
1/2 tablespoon white wine vinegar
salt and white pepper

Line a strainer or sieve with a double layer of cheesecloth and place over a bowl. Pour in the yogurt and leave in the refrigerator to drain for a few hours. You will be left with about 500g (1lb 2oz) of thick yogurt.

Grate the cucumber roughly and squeeze with your hands to remove as much liquid as possible. Add it to the yogurt, together with the olive oil, garlic and fructose, if using – this balances the acidity of the yogurt and vinegar. Add vinegar, salt and pepper to taste. Mix well and leave in the refrigerator for a couple of hours before serving.

Tzatziki keeps very well in the refrigerator for at least a week. The longer it is stored, the stronger the taste of garlic.
Note: if you are able to obtain strained Greek yogurt, buy 500g (1lb 2oz) and omit the first stage.

PER SERVING: GLYCAEMIC LOAD 7; PROTEIN 15G; CARBOHYDRATE 22G; FAT 5G (OF WHICH 1.5G SATURATES); FIBRE 1G

3 LENTIL SOUP
SERVES 6

4 SPINACH AND AVOCADO SOUP
SERVES 4

There are many varieties of lentil: brown, green, Puy, yellow, red, even black – or Beluga, because they resemble caviar. Very nutritious, lentils are high in protein, fibre, folic acid, iron and magnesium. Like other pulses, lentils have been shown to stabilize blood sugar levels – and they are very satisfying.

1½ tablespoons extra virgin olive oil
1 large onion, finely chopped
2 cloves garlic, crushed
½ teaspoon turmeric
1 teaspoon curry powder
½ teaspoon cayenne pepper
1½ litres (2½ pints) water
350ml (12fl oz) chicken or vegetable stock
200g (7oz) red lentils
100g (3½oz) pearl barley
400g (14oz) canned chopped tomatoes
salt and pepper
chopped fresh parsley

Heat the oil in a large saucepan over moderate heat, add the onion and garlic and fry for about 1 minute. Add the spices and stir to mix. Add the water, stock, lentils, barley and tomatoes.

Bring to the boil, then cover the pan and leave the soup to simmer for 45 minutes.

Season to taste and serve hot, sprinkled with parsley.

PER SERVING: GLYCAEMIC LOAD 10; PROTEIN 11G; CARBOHYDRATE 38G; FAT 4G (OF WHICH 0.5G SATURATES); FIBRE 3G

Watercress would work well in this vivid green soup instead of spinach.

1 tablespoon clarified butter (ghee) or extra virgin olive oil
6–8 spring onions, chopped
1 clove garlic, crushed
500g (1lb 2oz) fresh spinach, or 300g (10oz) frozen spinach
1 litre (1¾ pints) chicken or vegetable stock
1 ripe avocado, chopped
2 tablespoons chopped fresh parsley
freshly ground nutmeg
salt and pepper
2–4 tablespoons natural yogurt or soya cream

Heat the butter in a saucepan over low heat, add the spring onions and garlic and cook for 1 minute. Add the spinach and the stock, bring to the boil and simmer for 10 minutes.

Add the avocado and parsley, then purée the soup in a blender or food processor and return to the saucepan. Add nutmeg, salt and pepper to taste and heat through. Serve in bowls, with a swirl of yogurt or soya cream.

PER SERVING: GLYCAEMIC LOAD 1; PROTEIN 6G; CARBOHYDRATE 4G; FAT 11G (OF WHICH 2G SATURATES); FIBRE 4G

5 SHELLFISH AND FISH PLATTER
SERVES 4

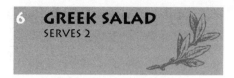

Get a bit of luxury out of your leftovers! You can use almost any cooked fish: peppered mackerel, smoked salmon, pickled herring, leftovers from a fish dinner earlier in the week, or fresh, frozen or canned shellfish.

   400–600g (14–21oz) cooked fish and
      shellfish
   raw vegetables, e.g. carrots,
      cauliflower, cucumber, fennel, cut
      into bite-sized pieces

Sauce:
150g (5oz) natural yogurt
1 tablespoon mayonnaise
1 teaspoon mustard
1 teaspoon chopped fresh dill
pepper

Arrange the shellfish and fish on a plate together with the prepared vegetables. Mix all the sauce ingredients until smooth and serve in a small bowl.

PER SERVING: GLYCAEMIC LOAD 1; PROTEIN 23G; CARBOHYDRATE 3G; FAT 15G (OF WHICH 3G SATURATES); FIBRE 0G

6 GREEK SALAD
SERVES 2

Greeks call this *horiatikisalata*, meaning 'peasant salad'; it has been named 'Greek' by foreigners, because it is ubiquitous – you will find it on every Greek table, in homes, tavernas and restaurants.

   1 Cos (Romaine) lettuce, roughly
      chopped
   2 tomatoes, quartered
   1 small red onion, thinly sliced
   ½ small cucumber, peeled and sliced
   1 green pepper (capsicum), cut into
      strips
   10–20 black olives (optional)
   100–170g (3½–6oz) feta cheese,
      diced
   2 tablespoons extra virgin olive oil
   dried (or fresh) oregano

Gently toss all the vegetables with the feta cheese in a large bowl. Sprinkle with olive oil and plenty of oregano.
   If you wish, mix 1 tablespoon of lemon juice or balsamic vinegar with the olive oil.

PER SERVING: GLYCAEMIC LOAD 0; PROTEIN 12G; CARBOHYDRATE 15G; FAT 22G (OF WHICH 8G SATURATES); FIBRE 5G

7 MIXED BEAN SALAD
SERVES 2

Any beans can be used in this recipe, either canned or ones you have soaked and cooked yourself.

150g (5oz) red kidney beans
150g (5oz) cannellini beans
3 spring onions, finely chopped
1 tablespoon chopped fresh parsley
120–150g (4–5oz) mixed salad leaves
1 red pepper (capsicum), seeded and chopped
1/2 cucumber, chopped
2 tomatoes, cut into wedges
200g (7oz) lean cooked ham, turkey or chicken breast, or cottage cheese
2 tablespoons fresh basil, shredded

Dressing:
1 tablespoon extra virgin olive oil
1 tablespoon wine vinegar or balsamic vinegar
1 clove garlic, finely chopped
1 teaspoon Dijon mustard
salt and pepper

Whisk all the dressing ingredients together. Mix the beans with the spring onions and parsley, and stir in half the dressing.

Chop the salad leaves, if large, and mix with the red pepper, cucumber and tomatoes. Arrange the salad on plates, with the bean salad on top. Add the ham, turkey or cottage cheese and pour the remaining dressing over the salad. Sprinkle the basil on top.

PER SERVING: GLYCAEMIC LOAD 10; PROTEIN 40G; CARBOHYDRATE 35G; FAT 11G (OF WHICH 2G SATURATES); FIBRE 12G

8 FRESH TUNA SALAD
SERVES 2

You could also make this with canned tuna; drain well before use and do not sear. Look for tuna packed in water rather than brine, sunflower or soya oil.

2 x 150g (5oz) fresh tuna steaks
2 tablespoons extra virgin olive oil
2 tablespoons lemon juice
2 celery sticks, diced
1 red pepper (capsicum), seeded and diced
100–120g (3 1/2–4oz) rocket, or mixed salad leaves
1 egg, hardboiled and sliced (optional)
salt and pepper

Marinate the tuna in 1 tablespoon oil and 1 tablespoon lemon juice for at least 20 minutes.

Chop the celery and red pepper. Pile the rocket on two plates and top with the celery and red pepper.

Whisk the remaining oil and lemon juice; season to taste. Spoon over the salad.

Sear the tuna in a hot non-stick frying pan for 1–2 minutes on each side (do not overcook or it will become tough). Place on the salad and serve at once. If using canned tuna, you may like to add sliced hardboiled egg.

PER SERVING: GLYCAEMIC LOAD 0; PROTEIN 40G; CARBOHYDRATE 6G; FAT 15G (OF WHICH 3G SATURATES); FIBRE 3G

9 CHICKEN SALAD
SERVES 2

Leftover grilled (or even roast) chicken or turkey is the basis for this colourful main-course salad.

300g (10oz) mixed salad leaves
2 tomatoes, cut into wedges
2 small leeks, sliced
1 avocado, sliced
350g (12oz) grilled chicken, skinned and diced
2–3 tablespoons sweetcorn, boiled

Dressing:
150g (5oz) natural yogurt
1 teaspoon tomato purée (concentrate)
2 teaspoons Dijon mustard
2 teaspoons curry powder
2 teaspoons turmeric
pinch of ground cinnamon
pinch of ground allspice
1/2 teaspoon fructose (optional)

Arrange the salad leaves in a bowl. Add the tomatoes, leeks, avocado and chicken, and sprinkle with sweetcorn.

Whisk together all the ingredients for the dressing and drizzle over the salad.

PER SERVING: GLYCAEMIC LOAD 4.5; PROTEIN 57G; CARBOHYDRATE 27G; FAT 19G (OF WHICH 5G SATURATES); FIBRE 8G

10 CHILLI LIME CHICKEN SALAD
SERVES 4

A blend of Mediterranean and South American flavours, and some of the healthiest ingredients from both ancient worlds, this tangy, high-protein salad will keep you satisfied.

4 skinless, boneless chicken breasts
oil for frying
salt and pepper
2 courgettes (zucchini)
100–120g (3½–4oz) rocket
200g (7oz) boiled red lentils
12 cherry tomatoes

Dressing:
3 tablespoons extra virgin olive oil
1 tablespoon balsamic vinegar
1 tablespoon capers
2 tablespoons finely grated lime zest
1 small red chilli pepper, finely chopped

Fry the chicken breasts for 3–4 minutes on each side, season, then leave them to rest for 3–4 minutes. Cut each breast diagonally into 1cm (½in) slices.

Slice the courgettes lengthways into 3mm (⅛in) slices. Drop into a saucepan of boiling water for 30 seconds, then drain and rinse under cold running water. Drain well and pat dry on paper towels.

Divide the courgettes and rocket between four plates. Put the lentils, chicken slices and tomatoes on top.

Mix the oil, balsamic vinegar, capers, lime and chilli together and sprinkle over the salad.

PER SERVING: GLYCAEMIC LOAD 3; PROTEIN 31G; CARBOHYDRATE 11G; FAT 18G (OF WHICH 3G SATURATES); FIBRE 2G

11 PRAWN, AVOCADO AND FETA SALAD
SERVES 2

Not only does this taste great, it's also a healthy source of monounsaturated fat, protein, fibre and several antioxidants, including vitamins C and E and lycopene.

1 avocado
200g (7oz) large cooked prawns
4–6 tomatoes, quartered
2 spring onions, thinly sliced
1 head of lettuce or other salad leaves
50g (1¾oz) feta cheese, diced, or cottage cheese
1 tablespoon extra virgin olive oil
1 tablespoon lemon juice
2 teaspoons dried oregano
salt and pepper

Peel and dice the avocado.

Put the avocado, prawns, tomatoes, spring onions, lettuce and feta or cottage cheese in a bowl.

With a fork, whisk together the olive oil, lemon juice and oregano in a small bowl. Season to taste. Pour over the salad and toss to mix.

PER SERVING: GLYCAEMIC LOAD 0; PROTEIN 30G; CARBOHYDRATE 11G; FAT 24G (OF WHICH 7G SATURATES); FIBRE 5G

12 ASPARAGUS AND PRAWN SAUTÉ
SERVES 1

Good news for our blood sugar and cholesterol levels, as well as your tastebuds. With 9g of fibre per serving, this dish provides you with more than one-third of your recommended daily fibre intake.

1 teaspoon extra virgin olive oil
250g (9oz) asparagus, chopped
1 onion, finely chopped
1 green pepper (capsicum), cut into thin strips
2 cloves garlic, chopped
50ml (1¾fl oz) white wine (optional)
1–2 teaspoons lemon juice
150g (5oz) prawns, preferably uncooked

Heat the oil in a non-stick pan, add the vegetables and garlic and cook over moderate heat, stirring frequently. Add the white wine (if using) and lemon juice and continue to cook for about 5 minutes, stirring frequently.

Add the prawns, mix well and cook for a further 3–4 minutes.

Note: if you are using cooked prawns, they should be heated through for 1–2 minutes only; do not overheat or they will become tough.

PER SERVING: GLYCAEMIC LOAD 0; PROTEIN 45G; CARBOHYDRATE 23G; FAT 8G (OF WHICH 1.5G SATURATES); FIBRE 9G

13 HERB-BAKED FISH
SERVES 4

This fragrant dish will work with any white-fleshed fish; you could also use other herbs, such as thyme.

4 tomatoes, quartered
20 olives, pitted
3 cloves garlic, chopped
1 tablespoon extra virgin olive oil
4 x 200g (7oz) white fish fillets
8 sprigs of oregano
6 sprigs of parsley
2 sprigs of sage
2 sprigs of rosemary
salt and pepper

1 lemon, quartered, to serve

Preheat the oven to 100°C/200°F/gas ¼ or its lowest setting. Put the tomato quarters, olives and garlic in an ovenproof dish and sprinkle with the olive oil. Put the fish on top, then add the herbs and a little salt and pepper. Bake for 30 minutes, or until a cooking thermometer reaches 55–60°C.

Serve with lemon wedges and a mixed salad, with brown basmati rice if this is your reward meal.

PER SERVING: GLYCAEMIC LOAD 0; PROTEIN 37G; CARBOHYDRATE 4G; FAT 9G (OF WHICH 1G SATURATES); FIBRE 1.5G

14 FISH CASSEROLE WITH PESTO
SERVES 4

You can use ready-made pesto, but there's nothing quite like the heady aroma of fresh basil.

400g (14oz) white fish fillet
1 large onion, sliced
200g (7oz) broccoli florets
1 red or green pepper (capsicum), sliced
500g (1lb 2oz) mushrooms, sliced
2 tablespoons grated Parmesan cheese
2 tablespoons basil pesto (below)

Basil pesto:
1 basil plant
3 tablespoons toasted pine nuts or walnuts
3–4 cloves garlic, chopped
1 tablespoon grated Parmesan cheese
100–200ml (3½–7fl oz) extra virgin olive oil

For the pesto, cut the basil leaves off the plant and place in a food processor. Add the rest of the ingredients and blend until evenly mixed. Pesto keeps well in the refrigerator for about a week.

Preheat the oven to 100°C/200°F/gas ¼ or its lowest setting. Put the fish in an ovenproof dish. Add the vegetables and cover with a lid. Bake for 40 minutes, or until a cooking thermometer reaches 55–60°C.

Sprinkle with Parmesan cheese towards the end of the baking time. Divide 1–2 tablespoons basil pesto over the fish. Serve with red lentil purée (recipe 34) and a green salad.

PER SERVING: GLYCAEMIC LOAD 0; PROTEIN 28G; CARBOHYDRATE 7G; FAT 13G (OF WHICH 3G SATURATES); FIBRE 4G

15 BAKED FISH ON A BED OF SPINACH
SERVES 2

Trout works well in this dish, but you could use any fish.

2 x 200g (7oz) fish fillets
soy sauce
salt and pepper
500g (1lb 2oz) fresh spinach or 300g
   (10oz) frozen spinach, defrosted
1 tablespoon cold-pressed rapeseed oil
1 teaspoon Dijon mustard
1 teaspoon dried dill

Preheat the oven to 100°C/200°F/gas ¼ or its lowest setting. Put the fish in an ovenproof dish and sprinkle with soy sauce, salt and pepper. Cover with a lid and bake for about 40 minutes, or until a cooking thermometer reaches 55–60°C.

If using fresh spinach, wash it thoroughly, then place in a large saucepan over medium heat. Stir frequently until it wilts, 2–3 minutes.

Heat the spinach in a little oil. Add the mustard and dill and season to taste. Arrange the spinach on two plates and put the fish on top.

PER SERVING: GLYCAEMIC LOAD 0; PROTEIN 52G; CARBOHYDRATE 2G; FAT 16G (OF WHICH 2.5G SATURATES); FIBRE 3G

16 GRILLED MACKEREL
SERVES 2

Mackerel are a good source of essential omega-3 fats.

2 whole mackerel, 250–300g (9–10oz)
   each
4 tablespoons extra virgin olive oil
juice of 1 lemon
2 cloves garlic, crushed
1 tablespoon chopped parsley
1 teaspoon paprika
freshly ground black pepper

Score the fish two or three times on either side. Mix the remaining ingredients in a shallow glass dish, add the fish and leave for 1–2 hours, turning once or twice.

Line a grill pan with foil and preheat the grill for 5 minutes. Grill the mackerel for 4–6 minutes, about 10cm (4in) away from the grill. Turn and cook for a further 4–5 minutes. When cooked, the flesh will be opaque; test with a skewer or small knife. Serve at once, with a green salad.

PER SERVING: GLYCAEMIC LOAD 0; PROTEIN 38G; CARBOHYDRATE 3G; FAT 21G (OF WHICH 4G SATURATES); FIBRE 0.5G

17 SALMON BURGERS WITH GREEN TARTARE SAUCE
SERVES 6

Get together with friends and serve these heart-healthy burgers that contain omega-3 -6 and -9 essential fatty acids.

Green tartare sauce:
1 small onion
3 tablespoons capers
150g (5oz) gherkin, finely chopped
150ml (5fl oz) mayonnaise
3 tablespoons finely chopped fresh chives
3 tablespoons finely chopped fresh parsley
1 teaspoon lemon juice
1/2 teaspoon Dijon mustard
1/2 teaspoon pepper
3 tablespoons extra virgin olive oil

Salmon burgers:
600g (1lb 5oz) skinless salmon, finely chopped with a knife
200g (7oz) red or green pepper (capsicum), finely chopped
90g (3oz) onion, finely chopped
3 tablespoons single cream or soya cream
2 teaspoons Tabasco sauce
2 teaspoons salt
pepper
1 egg white
2 1/2 tablespoons extra virgin olive oil

To serve:
12 thick tomato slices
600g (1lb 5oz) salad leaves

To make the green tartare sauce: put the onion, capers and gherkin in a food processor and chop finely. Add the rest of the ingredients and process until smooth and creamy. You can prepare this in advance and keep it chilled for up to 3 days. Serve at room temperature.

To make the salmon burgers: mix the salmon, red or green pepper, onion, cream, Tabasco, salt and pepper together in a large bowl. In another bowl beat the egg white until stiff. Carefully combine the salmon mixture and the egg white. Shape into 6 burgers, about 1cm (1/2in) thick. These can be made in advance and kept cool for up to 6 hours.

Cook the burgers in a non-stick frying pan over medium heat for about 3 minutes on each side.

Serve each burger with 1 tablespoon green tartare sauce, 2 slices tomato and plenty of green salad.

PER SERVING: GLYCAEMIC LOAD 0; PROTEIN 21G; CARBOHYDRATE 8G; FAT 40G (OF WHICH 7G SATURATES); FIBRE 2G

18 GRILLED SESAME SALMON WITH ASPARAGUS
SERVES 4

An elegant, teriyaki-style dish that is equally good for a gourmet dinner or an everyday supper.

4 skinless salmon fillets, about 150g (5oz) each
1 tablespoon sesame seeds
1 small onion, finely chopped
600g (1lb 5oz) fresh asparagus

Marinade:
3 tablespoons soy sauce
1½ tablespoons brown rice vinegar or wine vinegar
1 teaspoon fructose
1 tablespoon lemon juice
½ teaspoon grated fresh ginger

Stir all the ingredients for the marinade together in a small bowl.

Put the salmon in a dish, pour the marinade over and turn the salmon to coat with the marinade. Cover and refrigerate for at least 1 hour.

Heat the grill. Line the grill pan with aluminium foil and spray with oil. Grill the salmon for 2 minutes, about 10cm (4in) from the grill.

Pour the marinade into a small saucepan and boil for 2 minutes. Turn the salmon and spoon a little marinade over it. Sprinkle with sesame seeds and grill for another 2 minutes, or until the fish is just cooked through.

Meanwhile, steam or boil the asparagus for about 5 minutes, or until just tender. Drain well.

Serve the salmon with some of the marinade and the asparagus.

PER SERVING: GLYCAEMIC LOAD 1; PROTEIN 33G; CARBOHYDRATE 7G; FAT 20G (OF WHICH 4G SATURATES); FIBRE 3G

19 STIR-FRIED SALMON
SERVES 2

The wonderful colours tell you this dish is packed with antioxidants.

1 tablespoon cold-pressed rapeseed oil or extra virgin olive oil
200–300g (7–10oz) skinless salmon fillet, cut into chunks
1 small fennel bulb, cut into strips
1 small leek, thinly sliced
90g (3oz) broccoli florets
90g (3oz) cauliflower florets
1 red pepper (capsicum), cut into strips
1 tablespoon soy sauce, Indonesian ketjap manis, chilli sauce or chopped red chilli
2 teaspoons sesame seeds

Heat a wok or large frying pan, add the oil, then the salmon and cook over medium-high heat for a few minutes. Remove from the wok and set aside.

Stir-fry the vegetables for a few minutes. Put the salmon back in the wok and add the sauce. Give it a quick stir, then serve immediately, sprinkled with sesame seeds.

PER SERVING: GLYCAEMIC LOAD 4; PROTEIN 25G; CARBOHYDRATE 10G; FAT 21G (OF WHICH 3G SATURATES); FIBRE 6G

20 CHINESE STIR-FRIED CHICKEN
SERVES 2

Try this with other vegetables, such as courgette, peas or Chinese leaves.

300g (10oz) skinless, boneless chicken, cut into strips
4 tablespoons cold-pressed rapeseed oil or extra virgin olive oil
1 small fennel bulb, cut into strips
1 red or green pepper, cut into strips
1 onion, thinly sliced
1 spring onion, thinly sliced
10 mushrooms, sliced
10–12 small broccoli florets
chopped fresh parsley or chives

Marinade:
100ml (3½fl oz) chicken stock
2 tablespoons soy sauce
1 clove garlic, crushed
2cm (1in) fresh ginger, thinly sliced
pepper

Mix all the marinade ingredients and add the chicken. Refrigerate overnight.

Take the chicken out of the marinade; reserve the marinade. Heat a wok or large frying pan, add 2 tablespoons oil, then add the chicken and cook over medium-high heat, stirring often. When the chicken is cooked, remove from the pan and keep warm. Discard excess oil.

Add the remaining oil to the pan and stir-fry the vegetables for 2–3 minutes. Return the chicken to the pan together with the marinade. Stir over medium-high heat for about 30 seconds, until the chicken is hot.

Serve at once, sprinkled with herbs.

PER SERVING: GLYCAEMIC LOAD 0; PROTEIN 51G; CARBOHYDRATE 14G; FAT 30G (OF WHICH 3G SATURATES); FIBRE 8G

21 MOROCCAN CHICKEN
SERVES 2

This dish is aromatic with cinnamon, a spice with hidden powers (see page 26).

4 chicken thighs
1 teaspoon ground cinnamon
1 teaspoon ground ginger
½ teaspoon ground allspice
pinch of saffron
pinch of cayenne pepper
freshly ground black pepper
2 tablespoons extra virgin olive oil
2 cloves garlic, crushed
juice of ½ lemon

Put the chicken in a glass dish and rub the spices into the flesh. Add the olive oil, garlic and lemon, cover with cling film and leave in the refrigerator for at least 2 hours, turning occasionally.

Preheat the oven to 275°F/140°C/gas 1. Bring the chicken back to room temperature, then bake for about 1 hour, until cooked through.

Serve with green beans and couscous if this is your reward meal.

PER SERVING: GLYCAEMIC LOAD 0; PROTEIN 24G; CARBOHYDRATE 1G; FAT 16G (OF WHICH 3G SATURATES); FIBRE 0.5G

22 CHICKEN WITH SPINACH AND YOGURT SAUCE
SERVES 4

If this is your reward meal, serve it with boiled basmati rice – but remember the palm of hand measurement (page 145): 1 palm chicken with 1/2 palm rice.

2–3 tablespoons extra virgin olive oil
2 onions, finely chopped
4 cloves garlic, finely chopped
1 small fresh chilli, finely chopped
1 teaspoon grated fresh ginger
600g (1lb 5oz) fresh spinach
600g (1lb 5oz) skinless, boneless chicken breasts
2 teaspoons ground coriander
1 tablespoon Dijon mustard
300g (10oz) natural yogurt
1 teaspoon salt

Heat 1–2 tablespoons oil in a non-stick pan, add the onions, garlic, chilli and ginger, cover the pan and cook until the onions are softened, about 15 minutes.

Rinse the spinach well, chop, then set aside.

While the onions are cooking, cut the chicken into small cubes and fry in 1 tablespoon oil in a non-stick pan, stirring frequently, until cooked through.

Add the coriander and mustard to the onions and stir together for about 1 minute. Add the spinach and cook for 1–2 minutes. Add the yogurt a little at a time, until everything is blended well together. Add the chicken and serve hot.

PER SERVING: GLYCAEMIC LOAD 5; PROTEIN 50G; CARBOHYDRATE 14G; FAT 14G (OF WHICH 3G SATURATES); FIBRE 4G

23 COLOURFUL CHICKEN AND COUSCOUS
SERVES 4

An all-in-one 'reward' meal, this is a healthy variation on plain couscous.

4 skinless, boneless chicken breasts
2 tablespoons extra virgin olive oil
400ml (14fl oz) chicken stock
200g (7oz) couscous
1/2 teaspoon turmeric
2 apples, sliced, pips removed
1 red onion, thinly sliced
120g (4oz) rocket, coarsely chopped
200g (7oz) feta cheese, chopped

Dressing:
200g (7oz) natural yogurt
100g (3 1/2oz) sun-dried tomatoes, chopped
1 tablespoon chopped fresh basil
1 tablespoon chopped fresh tarragon
1 tablespoon chopped toasted almonds
1 teaspoon white wine vinegar
salt and pepper

Fry the chicken in 1 tablespoon oil for 3–4 minutes on each side. Leave to rest for a few minutes, then slice.

Bring the chicken stock and the remaining oil to the boil. Remove from the heat and add the couscous and turmeric. Cover and leave the couscous to swell for 5 minutes. Stir gently to separate the couscous grains.

In a small bowl, stir together all the dressing ingredients; season to taste.

Mix the apples and onion with the couscous, then stir in the rocket and feta cheese. Divide the couscous among four plates. Serve the chicken on top, with the dressing on the side.

PER SERVING: GLYCAEMIC LOAD 22; PROTEIN 47G; CARBOHYDRATE 50G; FAT 27G (OF WHICH 10G SATURATES); FIBRE 4G

24 LEMON CHICKEN WITH CHICKPEAS
SERVES 4

You can use canned chickpeas – add them towards the end of cooking time, just long enough to warm them through.

200g (7oz) chickpeas
2 tablespoons extra virgin olive oil
1 onion, finely chopped
1 teaspoon turmeric
4 chicken legs
approx. 300ml (10fl oz) chicken stock
juice of 1 lemon
3–4 cloves garlic, crushed
1 tablespoon dried rosemary
1 tablespoon dried oregano or thyme
1 tablespoon Dijon mustard
pinch of chilli powder (optional)
pepper
salt (optional)

Soak the chickpeas in water overnight.
Heat the oil in a large saucepan and cook the onion over low heat until softened. Sprinkle with turmeric and stir well. Add the chicken and brown on both sides. Add chicken stock to half-cover the chicken. Add the chickpeas, lemon juice and the rest of the ingredients and bring to the boil. Simmer over very low heat for about 1 hour, or until the chickpeas are tender and the chicken is cooked through. Serve with a green salad.

PER SERVING: GLYCAEMIC LOAD 9; PROTEIN 30G; CARBOHYDRATE 31G; FAT 14G (OF WHICH 3G SATURATES); FIBRE 6G

25 CHICKEN FAJITAS
SERVES 2

Following the ABC plate model (page 143) the tortilla forms the C part of this meal; serve with plenty of shredded lettuce as the B part.

2 skinless, boneless chicken breasts
1 red pepper (capsicum), in thin strips
1/2 onion, cut into thin strips
2 tortillas, approx. 20cm (8in) diameter
2 tomatoes, chopped
guacamole (avocado dip) or fresh avocado, sliced

Marinade:
3 tablespoons Mexican salsa (ready-made)
3 tablespoons lime or lemon juice
approx. 3 tablespoons water
pepper

Cut the chicken into thin strips, about 2cm (1in) long. Put them in a bowl and add the marinade. Make sure the marinade covers the chicken completely. Add more water if necessary. Cover with cling film and refrigerate overnight.
Pour the marinade into a hot non-stick pan and simmer until reduced by half. Add the chicken and simmer, turning often. When the chicken is cooked, add the pepper and onion and continue to cook, stirring frequently, until all the liquid has evaporated.
Put the chicken mix onto the tortillas and roll up. Serve with tomatoes and guacamole or avocado.

PER SERVING: GLYCAEMIC LOAD 7; PROTEIN 31G; CARBOHYDRATE 22G; FAT 15G (OF WHICH 5G SATURATES); FIBRE 5G

26 CHICKEN IN APRICOT CURRY SAUCE
SERVES 4

27 TURKEY WITH NUT SAUCE
SERVES 4

Apricots add natural sweetness to this fruity curry, the light acidity of the yogurt balances the sweetness.

4 skinless, boneless chicken breasts
salt and pepper
2 tablespoons cold-pressed rapeseed
    oil

Apricot sauce:
1 onion, chopped
1 clove garlic, chopped
2 bay leaves
2 tablespoons curry powder
4 dried apricots, cut in small pieces
3 tablespoons unsweetened apple
    sauce or juice
100ml (3½fl oz) chicken stock
100ml (3½fl oz) soya cream or single
    (pouring) cream
4 tablespoons Greek (strained) natural
    yogurt, or low-fat sour cream

Cut each chicken breast into 3 or 4 pieces, season, and cook in the oil for 3–4 minutes on each side, turning occasionally. Remove the chicken from the pan and keep warm.

Add the onion and garlic to the pan with the bay leaves and cook over low heat until the onion is softened. Add the rest of ingredients (except the yogurt or sour cream) and simmer for a few minutes.

Return the chicken to the pan and add the yogurt or sour cream. Do not let it boil. Season to taste.

Serve with green beans and brown basmati rice if this is your reward meal.

PER SERVING: GLYCAEMIC LOAD 4; PROTEIN 30G; CARBOHYDRATE 12G; FAT 17G (OF WHICH 6G SATURATES); FIBRE 2G

This delicious recipe couldn't be easier to prepare. You could also make it with a roasted chicken from the supermarket.

4 tablespoons walnuts, hazelnuts or
    almonds
1 clove garlic, finely chopped
1 teaspoon ground cumin
2 teaspoons Dijon mustard
300g (10oz) natural yogurt
lemon juice
salt and pepper
about 500g (1lb 2oz) leftover roast
    turkey (or chicken)

Preheat the oven to 180°C/350°F/gas 4.

Blanch the nuts in boiling water for 2 minutes. Drain well and rub off the skins. Chop the nuts finely and mix with the chopped garlic, cumin, mustard and yogurt. Add lemon juice, salt and pepper to taste.

Cut the turkey into thin slices and place in an ovenproof dish. Pour the yogurt sauce over and bake in the oven for 20 minutes, or until the sauce is bubbling hot.

PER SERVING: GLYCAEMIC LOAD 2; PROTEIN 44G; CARBOHYDRATE 7G; FAT 16G (OF WHICH 2G SATURATES); FIBRE 1G

28 KEFTEDES (GREEK MEATBALLS)
SERVES 4

In Greece these meatballs often include soaked bread; this is a healthier version, using oats, a valuable source of heart-healthy fibre.

600g (1lb 5oz) minced lean lamb or
 beef
2 tablespoons extra virgin olive oil
1 large onion, finely chopped
3 cloves garlic, finely chopped
1 tablespoon dried oregano
1 tablespoon dried mint
1 egg
100g (3½oz) oats or oatmeal
1 tablespoon balsamic vinegar
1 teaspoon ground anise seeds
1 tablespoon paprika
salt and pepper

To serve:
tzatziki (recipe 2)
Greek salad (recipe 6)

Put the meat in a bowl, add 1 tablespoon oil and the remaining ingredients and knead until everything is thoroughly mixed. Place in the refrigerator for a couple of hours to allow the flavours to blend.

While the mixture is chilling, make a tzatziki dip and a Greek salad.

Shape the mixture into walnut-sized meatballs. Heat a large, non-stick frying pan and add the remaining oil. Cook the meatballs (in batches if necessary to prevent overcrowding), turning occasionally, for 6–8 minutes or until browned. Serve hot, with tzatziki and Greek salad.

PER SERVING: GLYCAEMIC LOAD 12; PROTEIN 36G; CARBOHYDRATE 23G; FAT 17G (OF WHICH 4G SATURATES); FIBRE 3G

29 CHILLI CON CARNE
SERVES 4

This is better if made in advance and reheated.

2 tablespoons extra virgin olive oil
300g (10oz) minced beef
1 onion, sliced
2 cloves garlic, chopped
1 red or green pepper (capsicum),
 chopped
200g (7oz) sweetcorn (canned or
 frozen)
420g can chilli beans or red kidney
 beans
420g can white beans
1 tablespoon chilli sauce
1 beef stock cube
salt and pepper

Heat the oil in a large saucepan over medium heat. Add the beef, onion and garlic and cook until the meat browns. Add the remaining ingredients, including the liquid from the canned beans, and bring to the boil. Simmer for 20 minutes. Season to taste. Serve with green salad and rice, if this is your reward meal.

PER SERVING: GLYCAEMIC LOAD 18; PROTEIN 31G; CARBOHYDRATE 50G; FAT 11G (OF WHICH 2G SATURATES); FIBRE 13G

30 DR LINDBERG'S MOUSSAKA
SERVES 10

Known to most tourists as Greece's national dish, 'moussakas' can be stodgy and disappointing if badly made. This is a lighter, healthier version. Freeze leftovers in individual portions for an easy meal another day.

600g (1lb 5oz) aubergines (eggplants)
3 tablespoons extra virgin olive oil
red lentil purée (recipe 34)

Meat sauce:
1 tablespoon extra virgin olive oil
1 onion, chopped
400g minced beef, lamb or chicken
1 red pepper (capsicum), chopped
4 cloves garlic, crushed
400g (14oz) canned chopped
    tomatoes
1 tablespoon Dijon mustard
4 tablespoons finely chopped fresh
    parsley
1 tablespoon Worcestershire sauce
1 tablespoon dried oregano
1 tablespoon balsamic vinegar
2 tablespoons tomato purée
    (concentrate)

White sauce:
500g (1lb 2oz) natural fat-free yogurt
300g (10oz) cottage cheese
1/2 teaspoon grated nutmeg
2 tablespoons grated Parmesan cheese
2 tablespoons grated Cheddar cheese
    or Swiss cheese
2 eggs
salt and pepper

First make the lentil purée; set aside.
    For the meat sauce: heat the oil in a saucepan, add the onion and cook until softened. Add the meat and stir over medium-high heat until opaque. Add the remaining ingredients and leave to simmer over low heat until almost all the liquid has evaporated.

Cut the aubergines into thin (3–4 mm/1/8in) slices and fry them (in batches if necessary) in olive oil in a non-stick pan until golden. Drain on paper towels.

For the white sauce: place all the ingredients in a food processor and process until well blended.

Preheat the oven to 200°C/400°F/gas 6. Oil an ovenproof dish and cover the base with a 2cm (1in) thick layer of lentil purée. Pour half of the meat sauce evenly on top. Add the aubergines in a layer, then cover with the rest of the meat sauce. Finally, pour the white sauce over. Bake in the oven for about 30–40 minutes, or until the surface is golden. Leave to cool slightly before serving. A green salad makes the perfect accompaniment.

PER SERVING: GLYCAEMIC LOAD 14; PROTEIN 35G; CARBOHYDRATE 46G; FAT 20G (OF WHICH 5G SATURATES); FIBRE 6G

31 MEAT SAUCE
SERVES 4

Traditional meat and tomato spaghetti sauce can be made much more nutritious with the addition of beans. Don't serve a plateful of spaghetti with some sauce on top: this sauce is so filling you won't need very much spaghetti. It is also good with steamed or boiled green beans.

    1 tablespoon extra virgin olive oil
    400g (14oz) lean minced beef
    1 onion, chopped
    2 teaspoons dried oregano or thyme
    1 courgette (zucchini), chopped
    10 mushrooms, sliced
    1 red or green pepper, chopped
    4 cloves garlic, crushed
    400g (14oz) can tomatoes
    300g (10oz) can chilli beans
    200g (7oz) canned red or white beans
    4 tablespoons chopped fresh parsley

Heat the oil in a large saucepan and brown the meat. Add all the other ingredients (except the parsley) and simmer for 10–15 minutes. Finito!

Serve hot, sprinkled with parsley, with spaghetti on the side. A fresh salad is a natural accompaniment.

PER SERVING: GLYCAEMIC LOAD 10; PROTEIN 31G; CARBOHYDRATE 29G; FAT 9G (OF WHICH 2G SATURATES); FIBRE 9G

32 LAMB WITH ROSEMARY
SERVES 8–10

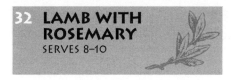

Cooking at this low temperature keeps the meat succulent and full of flavour.

    1 leg of lamb, about 2kg (4½lb)
    2 branches of fresh rosemary
    4 garlic cloves
    pepper
    2 tablespoons extra virgin olive oil
    4 tablespoons red wine
    100ml (3½fl oz) stock or water

Preheat the oven to 275°F/140°C/gas 1.

Strip the leaves from the rosemary and chop together with the garlic; mix with freshly ground black pepper. Loosen the skin from the lamb and push the rosemary mixture under the skin. Put the lamb in a roasting pan and pour the olive oil all over. Place in the oven for about 2 hours, until a cooking thermometer reaches 68–70°C.

Leave the meat to rest in a warm place. Place the roasting pan over heat, add the wine, then the stock, and boil until slightly thickened. Season to taste.

Carve the lamb and serve with the sauce, and steamed or sautéed spinach.

PER SERVING: GLYCAEMIC LOAD 0; PROTEIN 44G; CARBOHYDRATE 0.5G; FAT 16G (OF WHICH 6G SATURATES); FIBRE 0G

33 LAMB CASSEROLE WITH CABBAGE
SERVES 4

Lamb is a rather fatty meat, so try to buy lean pieces or trim off excess fat. Serve with red lentil purée (recipe 34) rather than potatoes.

1kg (2lb) lamb, cubed
1.5kg (3lb) cabbage, chopped
2 teaspoons salt
1–2 teaspoons whole peppercorns
approx. 400ml (14fl oz) boiling water
2 tablespoons finely chopped parsley

Layer the meat and cabbage in a large flameproof casserole dish, beginning with the meat, and seasoning each layer with salt and peppercorns. The top layer should be cabbage. Pour boiling water over the meat and cabbage. Bring to the boil, cover with a lid and leave to simmer gently until the meat is tender, about 1½ hours. Do not stir, but turn the casserole dish every now and then to prevent sticking.

Serve hot, sprinkled with parsley.

PER SERVING: GLYCAEMIC LOAD 0; PROTEIN 58G; CARBOHYDRATE 15G; FAT 23G (OF WHICH 10G SATURATES); FIBRE 9G

34 RED LENTIL PURÉE
SERVES 8

This is a very versatile vegetarian recipe. It keeps well in the fridge for about 4–5 days and freezes well, so it's worth making a big batch. Instead of the celery, you could use leek, fennel or spring onion. For further variations, add chilli, pesto, Dijon mustard, horseradish, chopped toasted nuts, chopped sun-dried tomatoes or fresh herbs.

1½ litres (2½ pints) vegetable stock
500g (1lb 2oz) red lentils
½ onion, finely chopped
200g (7oz) celery, finely chopped
3 cloves garlic, finely chopped
4 tablespoons extra virgin olive oil
4 tablespoons lemon juice
salt and pepper

Bring the stock to the boil. Add the lentils, onion, celery and garlic and simmer over low heat for 20–30 minutes, stirring occasionally.

The lentils should be really tender. If you want a smooth texture, purée in a food processor or with a hand blender. If you want a thicker purée, cook it a little longer. Just before serving, stir in the olive oil, lemon juice, freshly ground pepper and a little salt to taste if necessary.

PER SERVING: GLYCAEMIC LOAD 9; PROTEIN 16G; CARBOHYDRATE 36G; FAT 6G (OF WHICH 1G SATURATES); FIBRE 3G

35 LENTIL STEW
SERVES 2–3

'Lentils again?' was my standard reaction every Monday and Thursday during my childhod in Athens when I came home from school and smelt what was cooking, and my brothers nodded supportively. Lentils, beans or chickpeas were a twice-a-week ritual. Complaining didn't help: either eat lentil stew or go hungry. Funny how things change: this lentil stew is now one of my favourite dishes.

3 tablespoons extra virgin olive oil
1 large onion, finely chopped
3–4 tablespoons tomato purée or 200g (7oz) canned tomatoes
400–500ml (14–18fl oz) chicken or vegetable stock
200g (7oz) green or brown lentils, rinsed
1 teaspoon dried sage
3–4 cloves garlic, crushed
2 tablespoons lemon juice
2 teaspoons soy sauce
salt and pepper

Heat the oil in a saucepan, add the onion and cook gently until golden. Add the tomato purée or tomatoes and stock. Add the lentils, stir well, then add the sage, garlic, lemon juice and soy sauce. Leave to simmer for 30–40 minutes, until the lentils are tender.

Season to taste and serve hot, with a mixed salad.

PER SERVING: GLYCAEMIC LOAD 18; PROTEIN 29G; CARBOHYDRATE 61G; FAT 19G (OF WHICH 2G SATURATES); FIBRE 11G

36 SPANISH OMELETTE WITHOUT POTATOES
SERVES 1

A low-glycaemic makeover of the traditional Spanish omelette. Eggs, although they are high in cholesterol, do not increase blood cholesterol, so you can enjoy them regularly – they are one of nature's superfoods.

4 egg whites
2 egg yolks
1 tablespoon skimmed milk
1/2 teaspoon chilli powder
olive oil cooking spray
1/2 small onion, chopped
1/2 green pepper (capsicum), cut into strips
1 teaspoon extra virgin olive oil
3 tablespoons red or white beans (boiled or canned), drained
1 tablespoon grated Cheddar cheese or Parmesan
1 tablespoon salsa (optional)

In a bowl, whisk together the egg whites, egg yolks, milk and chilli powder. Set aside.

Spray a non-stick frying pan with cooking spray and place over medium heat. Add the onion and green pepper and sauté for about 3 minutes. Transfer the vegetables to a bowl. Add the beans.

Pour the olive oil into the pan and add the beaten egg mixture. Cook over low heat until the eggs begin to set.

Put the vegetables and grated cheese on top of the omelette, fold over and continue to cook until it is golden.If you wish, serve with salsa.

PER SERVING: GLYCAEMIC LOAD 8; PROTEIN 28G; CARBOHYDRATE 23G; FAT 20G (OF WHICH 6G SATURATES); FIBRE 7G

37 DR LINDBERG'S RATATOUILLE
SERVES 4–6

Serve ratatouille as a vegetarian main course or as an accompaniment to meat, fish or chicken.

3 aubergines (eggplants), cut into cubes
1 tablespoon salt
8 tablespoons extra virgin olive oil
2 onions, chopped
2 fennel bulbs, cut into thin strips
4 courgettes (zucchini), cut into cubes
2 green and 2 red peppers (capsicums), cut into large pieces
2 x 400g (14oz) cans plum tomatoes
1 x 300g (10oz) can red kidney beans
8 cloves garlic, crushed
20 leaves fresh basil (or 2 teaspoons dried basil)
2 tablespoons fresh chervil
2 tablespoons fresh thyme leaves (or 1–2 teaspoons dried thyme)
1 tablespoon Dijon mustard
1 tablespoon Worcestershire sauce (optional)
1 tablespoon soy sauce
2 tablespoons vegetable, chicken or beef stock
freshly ground black pepper

Put the aubergines in a large bowl, add the salt and leave for about 30 minutes. Rinse and pat dry with kitchen towels.

Heat 2 tablespoons oil in a large frying pan over medium heat. Add the onions and fennel and sauté until they are translucent. Transfer to a bowl.

Add another 2 tablespoons oil to the pan, increase the heat and fry the aubergines until golden, about 15 minutes. Put the aubergines into a large saucepan and add half of the onions and fennel.

Add another 2 tablespoons oil to the frying pan and sauté the courgettes until golden, about 10 minutes. Add the courgettes to the saucepan with the aubergines and cover them with the remaining onion and fennel.

Add 1 tablespoon oil to the frying pan and fry the peppers until they begin to brown, about 15 minutes. Add them to the saucepan.

Put the remaining 1 tablespoon oil in the frying pan and add the tomatoes, beans, garlic, basil, chervil, thyme, mustard, Worcestershire sauce, soy sauce, stock and pepper. Bring to the boil and simmer until the mixture starts to thicken, about 15 minutes. Transfer everything to the saucepan and leave to simmer over low heat for about 30 minutes, stirring occasionally. Taste and add a little more salt if necessary.

PER SERVING: GLYCAEMIC LOAD 11; PROTEIN 14G; CARBOHYDRATE 39G; FAT 24G (OF WHICH 3G SATURATES); FIBRE 14G

38 INDIAN-SPICED BEANS AND VEGETABLES
SERVES 3

To give this vegetarian dish a Mediterranean flavour, replace the spices with two or three sprigs of fresh thyme.

2 tablespoons extra virgin olive oil
1/2 onion, sliced
3 cloves garlic, chopped
1 green or yellow courgette (zucchini), cubed
1 aubergine (eggplant), cubed
1/2 celeriac, cubed
1/2 fennel bulb, chopped
400g (14oz) canned chopped tomatoes
300g (10oz) canned chilli beans
200g (7oz) canned borlotti beans
1 tablespoon tomato purée (concentrate)
pinch of ground cinnamon
pinch of ground allspice
1 teaspoon fructose (optional)
salt and pepper

Heat the oil in a large saucepan, add the onion and garlic and cook over medium heat until the onion is tender.

Add the rest of the vegetables, tomato purée, spices and fructose, if using, and cook until heated through. Season to taste and serve hot.

PER SERVING: GLYCAEMIC LOAD 15; PROTEIN 16G; CARBOHYDRATE 44G; FAT 10G (OF WHICH 1G SATURATES); FIBRE 14G

39 STUFFED MUSHROOMS
SERVES 4

Serve as a first course, or to accompany a main course instead of potatoes.

12 large flat mushrooms
1 tablespoon butter
2 shallots, finely chopped
1 clove garlic, crushed
2 tablespoons finely chopped fresh parsley
salt and pepper
150g (5oz) cooked lentils
100g (3 1/2 oz) finely chopped almonds
100g (3 1/2 oz) grated Parmesan or Cheddar cheese

Preheat the oven to 180°C/350°F/gas 4.
Remove the stalks from the mushrooms and chop finely. Heat the butter in a non-stick pan, add the mushroom stalks, shallots, garlic and parsley and cook for 5 minutes, until softened. Season to taste.

Coat a large baking sheet with cooking oil spray. Arrange the mushrooms in the tray and fill with the lentil mixture. Sprinkle with the grated cheese and bake for 10–15 minutes, or until the mushrooms are tender when tested with a knife.

PER SERVING: GLYCAEMIC LOAD 3; PROTEIN 17G; CARBOHYDRATE 11G; FAT 26G (OF WHICH 8G SATURATES); FIBRE 5G

40 VEGETABLE AND CASHEW NUT STIR-FRY
SERVES 2

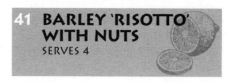

This colourful stir-fry is chock-full of antioxidants, vitamins and minerals.

- 1 tablespoon cold-pressed rapeseed or extra virgin olive oil
- 1 clove garlic, crushed
- 5cm (2in) fresh ginger, grated
- 4 spring onions, sliced
- 1 red pepper (capsicum), cut into strips
- 1 yellow pepper (capsicum), cut into strips
- 90g (3oz) broccoli florets
- 2 courgettes (zucchini), sliced
- 2 tablespoons light soy sauce
- 60g (2oz) water chestnuts, sliced
- 1 teaspoon sesame oil
- 90g (3oz) cashew nuts

Heat a wok or large frying pan over medium-low heat, add the oil, then add the garlic, ginger and spring onions and stir-fry for 30 seconds.

Increase the heat to medium-high and add the vegetables, soy sauce and water chestnuts. Stir-fry for 2–3 minutes. Add the sesame oil and cashew nuts and stir-fry for a further 30 seconds. Serve at once.

PER SERVING: GLYCAEMIC LOAD 4; PROTEIN 16G; CARBOHYDRATE 20G; FAT 31G (OF WHICH 5G SATURATES); FIBRE 6G

41 BARLEY 'RISOTTO' WITH NUTS
SERVES 4

A low-glycaemic risotto makeover, using pearl barley instead of high-glycaemic Arborio rice.

- 2 tablespoons butter ghee (or cold-pressed rapeseed oil)
- 1 spring onion, finely chopped
- 150g (5oz) pearl barley
- 100ml (3½fl oz) dry white wine
- approx. 500ml (18fl oz) strong, hot chicken stock
- 100g (3½oz) fromage frais or sour cream
- 50g (1¾oz) unsalted cold butter
- salt and pepper
- 2 tablespoons roasted almonds or walnuts or hazelnuts, coarsely chopped

Melt the ghee in a wide saucepan. Add the spring onion and sauté until translucent. Add the barley and stir until all the grains are covered with butter. Add the wine and reduce until most of the liquid has evaporated.

Add about a third of the hot stock and simmer, stirring frequently, adding more stock as it gets absorbed by the barley.

When the barley is cooked through and tender, remove from the heat and add the butter and fromage frais or sour cream and stir thoroughly. Season to taste. Serve at once, sprinkled with chopped nuts.

PER SERVING: GLYCAEMIC LOAD 9; PROTEIN 7G; CARBOHYDRATE 36G; FAT 25G (OF WHICH 9G SATURATES); FIBRE 0.5G

42 OATMEAL AND ALMOND PORRIDGE
SERVES 2

Oats are an excellent source of fibre, and cinnamon is a powerful antioxidant and anti-inflammatory spice that substantially reduces high blood sugar, cholesterol and triglyceride levels.

450ml (15fl oz) skimmed milk
150g (5oz) fine oatmeal or oat bran
4 teaspoons fructose (optional)
1 tablespoon chopped almonds
1/2 teaspoon vanilla extract
pinch of salt
pinch of ground cinnamon

Put all the ingredients (except the cinnamon) in a saucepan and bring to the boil. Simmer for 2–3 minutes, then pour into bowls and sprinkle the cinnamon on top.

PER SERVING: GLYCAEMIC LOAD 33; PROTEIN 17G; CARBOHYDRATE 60G; FAT 11G (OF WHICH 2G SATURATES); FIBRE 6G

43 PEACH MERINGUE
SERVES 4

A delicate dessert, with almonds to add healthy fat.

4 fresh peaches
4 egg whites
4 tablespoons fructose
60g (2oz) almonds, sliced and slightly toasted

Preheat the oven to 160°C/325°F/gas 3.
    Peel each peach and cut in half; remove the stones.
    Beat the egg whites until stiff, then gradually sprinkle in the fructose, beating all the time.
    Place the peach halves, cut side up, on a baking sheet. Put a large spoonful of egg white into each half peach and sprinkle the almonds on top. Bake until the meringue is golden, 10–15 minutes. Serve straight from the oven.

PER SERVING: GLYCAEMIC LOAD 9; PROTEIN 7G; CARBOHYDRATE 29G; FAT 8G (OF WHICH 1G SATURATES); FIBRE 2G

44 BLUEBERRY PANCAKES
SERVES 4–6

Blueberries are not only rich in fibre and vitamin C, they are also a good source of anthocyanins and other antioxidant compounds, which help prevent many chronic diseases and premature ageing. Frozen blueberries are just as healthy as fresh ones.

60g (2oz) soya flour
100g (3½oz) wholemeal flour
½ teaspoon bicarbonate of soda
½ teaspoon ground cinnamon
2 teaspoons fructose
1 egg
250ml (8fl oz) skimmed milk
½ teaspoon vanilla extract
100g (3½oz) blueberries
cold-pressed rapeseed oil

Put the dry ingredients in a bowl and mix well. Add the egg, milk and vanilla extract and beat until smooth. Stir in the blueberries.

Heat a non-stick frying pan over medium-high heat and add a little oil. Drop 2 tablespoons of the mixture into the pan to form small pancakes, about 8cm (3in) in diameter. When the batter begins to set and small bubbles appear, flip the pancakes over and cook until light brown.

Serve hot, with low-fat sour cream or yogurt, sweetened with fructose if you like.

PER SERVING: GLYCAEMIC LOAD 9; PROTEIN 14G; CARBOHYDRATE 26G; FAT 4G (OF WHICH 1G SATURATES); FIBRE 8G

45 DR LINDBERG'S LEMON MOUSSE
SERVES 4

A light, tangy, low-glycaemic dessert to enjoy without guilt!

3 lemons
5 egg yolks
1 whole egg
150g (5oz) fructose
3 leaves of gelatine
200ml (7fl oz) full-fat milk or soya milk
200ml (7fl oz) double cream or 38% soy cream

Grate the zest of 1 lemon and squeeze the juice from all three. Beat the egg yolks and the egg together with the fructose, lemon zest and juice. Leave the gelatine to soak in plenty of cold water.

Bring the milk to simmering point, then let it cool down to lukewarm. Pour the milk over the egg mixture, whisking constantly. Pour the mixture back into the saucepan over low heat or over a pan of simmering water. Keep whisking.

Take the gelatine strips out of the water and let them dissolve in the milk mixture. Stir gently until the gelatine is completely dissolved. Leave to cool.

Whip the cream until stiff and fold it gently into the mixture. Pour the mousse into ramekins or one big bowl. Cover with cling film and place in the refrigerator for 6 hours before serving.

PER SERVING: GLYCAEMIC LOAD 9; PROTEIN 8G; CARBOHYDRATE 44G; FAT 34G (OF WHICH 18G SATURATES); FIBRE 0G

46 DR LINDBERG'S CHEESECAKE
SERVES 10

Instead of a crumb or pastry base, this has a base of nuts and oats – rich in protein and fibre.

Nut base:
150g (5oz) nuts (almonds, walnuts or peanuts)
100g (3¹/₂oz) oats or oatmeal
2 tablespoons fructose
1 teaspoon ground cinnamon
3 tablespoons butter (at room temperature)

Filling:
450g (1lb) cottage cheese
250g (9oz) low-fat cream cheese
3 eggs, separated
2 tablespoons cornflour
150g (5oz) fructose
1 teaspoon lemon zest, grated
1 teaspoon vanilla extract
500g (1lb 2oz) low-fat sour cream

Preheat the oven to 180°C/350°F/gas 4. Put the nuts and oats in a food processor and process until finely ground. Add the fructose, cinnamon and butter and process just until the mixture comes together. Spread the mixture evenly in a 20cm (8in) diameter springform cake tin. Put the tin in the oven and bake for 4–5 minutes, until pale golden. Reduce the oven temperature to 125°C/250°F/gas ¹/₂.

To make the filling, put the cottage cheese and cream cheese in a food processor and blend until creamy. Add the egg yolks, cornflour, fructose, grated lemon zest, vanilla sugar and sour cream. Blend well.

Whisk the egg whites until they are stiff, then blend into the cheese mixture. Pour over the nut base and bake in the oven for about 1¹/₂ hours, or until the centre of the cheesecake is firm to the touch.

Turn off the oven and leave the oven door open to allow the cake to cool down to room temperature.

Serve with mashed fresh berries blended with some fructose.

The cake keeps well in the refrigerator.

PER SERVING: GLYCAEMIC LOAD 9; PROTEIN 16G; CARBOHYDRATE 37G; FAT 27G (OF WHICH 12G SATURATES); FIBRE 2G

47 DR LINDBERG'S 8-GRAIN BREAD
2 LOAVES

You can vary this recipe by replacing the sesame seeds with finely chopped walnuts, almonds or hazelnuts. Spelt is an ancient type of wheat; spelt flour is available in health food shops and some supermarkets.

- 2 teaspoons (or 1 x 7g sachet) dried yeast
- 2 tablespoons extra virgin olive oil or cold-pressed rapeseed oil
- 1 tablespoon fructose or honey
- 500–700ml (18–25fl oz) lukewarm water
- 500g (1lb 2oz) stoneground wholemeal wheat or spelt flour
- 80g (2¾oz) barley flour
- 80g (2¾oz) spelt flour
- 80g (2¾oz) buckwheat flakes
- 80g (2¾oz) fine wholemeal rye
- 80g (2¾oz) oats
- 80g (2¾oz) sesame seeds
- 50g (1¾oz) fine durum wheat (pasta flour)
- 2 teaspoons carob powder (optional)
- 2 teaspoons salt

Mix the yeast with the oil, fructose and the smaller quantity of water. Add the rest of the ingredients and knead until the dough is firm and elastic (use a food processor or the dough hook of a mixer if you like); you may need to add more water, especially if you are using a food processor. Leave to rise in a warm place until the dough has doubled in size, about 1½ hours.

Knead the dough for 2–3 minutes, then shape into two loaves. Put the loaves in two lightly oiled 1kg (2lb) loaf tins (or use non-stick tins).

Alternatively make 16 to 20 rolls and place on a lightly oiled baking sheet.

Cover with a cloth and leave to rise for a further 30–40 minutes.

Preheat the oven to 180°C/350°F/gas 4. Bake the bread for about 40–50 minutes, or rolls for 15–20 minutes. Test by turning out and knocking the base with your knuckles; if it is done, the bread will sound hollow. Transfer the bread to a wire rack to cool.

Note: some types of dried yeast need to be blended with water (and sugar or honey) and left for 15 minutes until frothy; others are mixed with the dry ingredients first. Follow the directions on the packet.

PER SLICE: GLYCAEMIC LOAD 8; PROTEIN 4G; CARBOHYDRATE 15.5G; FAT 2.5G (OF WHICH 0.5G SATURATES); FIBRE 2.5G

48 DR LINDBERG'S SUNFLOWER RYE BREAD
2 LOAVES

In this recipe you can use cold-pressed rapeseed oil, walnut oil or extra virgin olive oil. The carob powder (carob flour) stabilizes the large particles in wholegrain breads such as this one, and helps to retain moisture. These ingredients can be found at health food shops.

25g (7/8oz) fresh yeast
700ml (1 1/4 pints) lukewarm water
1 1/2 tablespoons vegetable oil
2 teaspoons molasses, fructose or honey
400g (14oz) wholemeal rye flour
200g (7oz) stoneground wholemeal (wheat) flour
60g (2oz) wheat flakes
60g (2oz) sunflower seeds
60g (2oz) ground flaxseed
50g (1 3/4oz) rye flakes
50g (1 3/4oz) oatmeal
2 teaspoons carob powder (optional)
2 teaspoons salt
cooking spray

Dissolve the yeast in a little of the lukewarm water, then add the vegetable oil and molasses.

Put the rest of the water in a large bowl and add the remaining dry ingredients and the yeast mixture. Knead the dough for 5–10 minutes (use a food processor or the dough hook of a mixer if you like). Add more flour if the mixture is too sticky. Divide the dough into two.

Spray two 1kg (2lb) loaf tins with cooking spray (or use non-stick loaf tins) and divide the dough between the two tins. Cover with a cloth and leave to rise for about 1 1/2 hours.

Preheat the oven to 200°C/400°F/ gas 6. Bake the bread for 45–55 minutes. Test by turning out and knocking the base with your knuckles; if it is done, the bread will sound hollow. Turn the loaves out on to a wire rack to cool.

PER SLICE: GLYCAEMIC LOAD 7; PROTEIN 2.5G; CARBOHYDRATE 13.5G; FAT 2.5G (OF WHICH 0.5G SATURATES); FIBRE 2.5G

Glycaemic Load List

These tables are compiled from information supplied by laboratories in various countries. There are many variables in testing methods, calculation data and composition of food, and sometimes the result is the mean of several studies. Rice, for example, shows a large range of GI values; this variation is due to botanical differences in rice from country to country. The type of starch could explain much of the variation in the GI values of rice (and other foods), because amylose is digested more slowly than amylopectin starch. GI values for rice cannot be reliably predicted on the basis of the size of the grain or the type of cooking method.

There are no GI values given for meat, poultry, fish, avocados, salad vegetables, cheese or eggs because these foods contain little or no carbohydrate and it would be difficult for anyone to consume a portion of the foods containing 50g of carbohydrate. Even in large amounts, these foods when eaten alone are not likely to induce a significant rise in blood sugar.

The GI of nuts is the same whether they are salted or unsalted; I recommend that you avoid salted and roasted nuts and choose raw nuts – the healthiest option.

Glycaemic Load (GL)
Food of reference: Glucose, GI 100

Foods	GI	Amount of food in grams containing 50g carbohydrate	Carbohydrate per 100g of food	GL per 100g of food
All-Bran (Kellogg's)	42	100	50	21
Apples	38	400	13	5
Apples, dried	29	88	57	16
Apple juice, unsweetened	40	431	12	5
Apricots	57	667	8	4
Apricots, dried	31	107	47	14
Apricots, tinned, in light syrup	64	316	16	10
Bagel	72	100	50	36
Baguette	95	100	50	48
Banana	52	250	20	10
Banana bread, made without sugar	55	138	36	20
Barley, pearl	25	179	28	7
Barley porridge/wholemeal barley flour	68	179	28	19
Beans, baked	48	500	10	5

Foods	GI	Amount of food in grams containing 50g carbohydrate	Carbohydrate per 100g of food	GL per 100g of food
Beans, black, dried, boiled	20	300	17	3
Beans, black-eyed, dried, boiled	42	250	20	8
Beans, brown/borlotti, dried, boiled	24	100	50	12
Beans, fava/broad, boiled	79	364	14	11
Beans, green, boiled	29	1667	8	2
Beans, haricot/navy, dried, boiled	38	242	21	8
Beans, kidney, dried, boiled	28	300	17	5
Beans, kidney, tinned	52	441	11	6
Beans, lima/butter beans, dried, boiled	32	250	20	6
Beans, mung, dried, boiled	31	441	11	4
Beans, mung, pressure cooked	42	441	11	5
Beans, mung, sprouts	25	441	11	3
Beans, pinto, dried, boiled	39	288	17	7
Beans, soya, dried, boiled	18	1250	4	1
Beans, soya, tinned	14	1250	4	1
Beetroot	64	571	9	6
Bran flakes cereal	74	83	60	44
Bread, flat Middle Eastern	97	94	53	52
Bread, gluten free, white	76	100	50	38
Bread, gluten free, white, added bran	73	115	43	32
Bread, hamburger bun	61	100	50	31
Bread, multigrain	43	108	46	20
Bread, nan	30	625	8	2
Bread, oatbran	47	83	60	28
Bread, pitta	57	88	57	32
Bread, pumpernickel	50	125	40	20
Bread, rice	66	116	43	28
Bread, rye, dark (100% wholemeal)	58	107	47	27
Bread, sourdough, dark, barley	53	75	67	35
Bread, sourdough, white flour	54	107	47	25
Bread, soya and linseed	36	166	30	11
Bread, spelt, dark	63	79	63	40
Bread, sunflower and barley	57	151	37	21
Bread, stoneground wholewheat	49	94	53	26
Bread, white	70	98	51	36
Bread, white flour, 80% whole grain	52	75	67	35
Breadfruit	68	222	23	15
Buckwheat	54	250	20	11
Bulgur wheat	48	288	17	8
Carrot, boiled	58	667	8	4
Carrot, raw	16	500	10	2

Foods	GI	Amount of food in grams containing 50g carbohydrate	Carbohydrate per 100g of food	GL per 100g of food
Carrot juice	43	543	9	4
Cashew nuts	22	192	26	6
Cassava	46	185	27	12
Cheerios cereal	74	75	67	49
Cherries	22	500	10	2
Chickpeas, dried, boiled	28	250	20	6
Chickpeas, chana dal	11	208	24	3
Chickpeas, tinned	42	341	15	6
Chocolate, dark, 70% cocoa solids	22	156	32	7
Chocolate, M & Ms, peanut	33	88	57	19
Chocolate, Mars	65	75	67	43
Chocolate, milk	43	89	56	24
Chocolate, milk (low-sugar, with malitol)	35	114	44	15
Chocolate, Snickers	55	88	57	31
Chocolate, Twix	44	77	65	29
Coca Cola	58	481	10	6
Coco Pops (Kellogg's)	77	58	87	67
Corn, chips	63	96	52	33
Cornflakes cereal	81	58	87	70
Couscous, boiled	58	431	12	7
Cranberry juice	56	431	12	6
Crispbread	64	78	64	41
Croissant	67	110	46	31
Dates, dried	103	75	67	69
Digestive biscuits	55	73	68	37
Doughnut	76	102	49	37
Fanta, orange	68	368	14	9
Frosties (Kellogg's)	55	58	87	48
Fruit cocktail	55	375	13	7
Fructose	19	50	100	19
Grapefruit	25	545	9	2
Grapefruit juice, unsweetened	48	625	8	4
Grapenuts cereal	71	71	70	50
Grapes	46	333	15	7
Glucose	100	50	100	100
Honey	55	69	72	40
Hummus	6	300	17	1
Ice cream, premium (15% fat)	37	278	18	7
Ice cream, low-fat (1.2% – 7.1% fat)	43	227	22	9
Kiwi fruit	53	500	10	5
Lactose	46	50	100	46

Foods	GI	Amount of food in grams containing 50g carbohydrate	Carbohydrate per 100g of food	GL per 100g of food
Lentils, green, dried, boiled	30	441	11	3
Lentils, green, tinned	52	454	11	6
Lentils, red, dried, boiled	26	417	12	3
Lucozade	95	312	16	15
Maltose	105	50	100	105
Mango	51	353	14	7
Marmalade, orange	48	75	67	32
Melon, orange-fleshed	65	1000	5	5
Milk, buttermilk	11	1136	4	0
Milk, full-fat	27	1042	5	1
Milk, semi-skimmed	29	1000	5	1
Milk, skimmed	32	962	5	2
Milk, soya	42	714	7	3
Millet, boiled	71	208	24	17
Muffin	57	102	49	28
Muesli (Alpen)	55	79	63	35
Muesli, unsweetened	49	76	66	32
Noodles, instant	47	225	22	10
Noodles, mung bean/transparent	33	200	25	8
Noodles, rice	61	231	22	13
Noodles, Chinese vermicelli	58	231	22	13
Nutella chocolate and nut spread	33	83	60	20
Oranges	42	545	9	4
Orange juice, unsweetened	46	481	10	5
Pancakes, from packet mix	67	69	73	49
Papaya	59	353	14	8
Parsnip, boiled	97	333	15	15
Pasta, brown rice, boiled	92	237	21	19
Pasta, corn, boiled	54	214	23	13
Pasta, fettucine (durum wheat), boiled	40	196	26	10
Pasta, gnocchi (potato-based)	68	188	27	18
Pasta, linguine (durum wheat), boiled	50	196	26	13
Pasta, macaroni, boiled	47	188	27	13
Pasta, spaghetti, al dente	39	191	26	10
Pasta, spaghetti, boiled 10–15 mins	43	188	27	11
Pasta, spaghetti, protein-rich/low-carb, boiled	27	173	29	8
Pasta, spaghetti, wholewheat, boiled	37	214	23	9
Peaches	42	545	9	4
Peaches, tinned, in juice	38	545	9	3
Peaches, tinned, in syrup	57	353	14	8

Foods	GI	Amount of food in grams containing 50g carbohydrate	Carbohydrate per 100g of food	GL per 100g of food
Peanuts	14	417	12	2
Pears	38	545	9	3
Pears, tinned, unsweetened	43	545	9	4
Peas, green, dried, boiled	22	833	6	1
Peas, green, fresh	48	571	9	4
Pineapple	59	462	11	6
Pineapple juice, unsweetened	46	357	14	6
Pizza (approx. 5 toppings, GI varies from 30 to 80)	60	185	27	16
Plums	39	500	10	4
Polenta, boiled	68	577	9	6
Popcorn	72	91	55	40
Porridge, made from oatbran	55	100	50	28
Porridge, made from stoneground oatmeal	74	78	64	47
Porridge, made from rolled oats	58	568	9	5
Porridge, instant	66	481	10	7
Potato, boiled, peeled	88	417	12	11
Potato, boiled, unpeeled	80	441	11	10
Potato, crisps (chips)	54	102	42	23
Potato, chips/French fries	75	259	19	15
Potato, instant, mashed	85	375	13	11
Potato, jacket	85	250	20	17
Potato, mashed	74	375	13	10
Potato, new, boiled in skin	57	357	14	8
Potato, new, tinned	63	417	12	8
Potatoes, steamed	65	278	18	18
Pretzels	83	75	67	55
Prunes, pitted, ready-to-eat	29	91	55	16
Puffed wheat cereal	74	71	70	52
Pumpernickel bread	50	125	40	20
Pumpkin, boiled	75	1000	5	4
Raisins	64	68	73	47
Ravioli, with meat	39	237	21	8
Rice, basmati, white	58	197	25	15
Rice, basmati, precooked in pouch	57	185	27	15
Rice, brown	55	227	22	12
Rice, jasmine	109	179	28	31
Rice, parboiled/converted (Uncle Ben's)	47	208	24	11
Rice, risotto/arborio	69	143	35	24
Rice, white, long-grain	56	183	27	15
Rice, white, long-grain, Bangladeshi	38	192	26	10

Foods	GI	Amount of food in grams containing 50g carbohydrate	Carbohydrate per 100g of food	GL per 100g of food
Rice, wild	57	238	21	12
Rice cakes	91	60	83	76
Rye, whole grain, boiled	34	66	76	26
Scones	92	139	36	33S
Shredded Wheat cereal	75	76	66	49
Special K (Kellogg's)	54	71	70	38
Sponge cake	54	95	53	29
Sports drink, Gatorade	78	833	6	5
Sports drink, Isostar	70	694	7	5
Strawberries	40	2000	3	1
Sugar (sucrose)	68	50	100	68
Sultanas	56	66	75	42
Swede	72	750	7	5
Sweet potatoes, cooked	61	268	19	11
Sweetcorn, fresh	53	234	21	11
Taco shells, corn	68	83	60	41
Tapioca	70	694	7	5
Tomato juice	38	1389	4	1
Tortilla, Mexican	52	104	48	25
Watermelon	72	1000	5	4
Weetabix cereal	70	79	63	44
Wheat, wholegrain, boiled	41	74	68	28
Yakult	46	278	18	8
Yam	66	208	24	16
Yogurt, fat-free, natural, unsweetened	33	625	8	3
Yogurt, fat-free, soya, with fruit and sugar	50	385	13	7
Yogurt, fat-free, with aspartame	14	769	7	1
Yogurt, fat-free, with fruit and sugar	33	323	16	5

Bibliography

Books

Brand-Miller, JC. *The G.I. Factor: The Glycaemic Index Solution. The Scientific Answer to Weight Reduction and Blood Sugar Control.* Hodder & Stoughton, 1997, Australia.

Crawford, M and D Marsh. *The Driving Force: Food, Evolution and the Future.* Harper & Row, 1989, New York.

Eaton, SB, M Shostalle and M Konner. *The Paleolithic Prescription.* Harper & Row, 1988, New York.

Erzin, C and RE Kowalski. *The Endocrine Control Diet.* Harper & Row, 1990, New York.

Heller, RF. *The Carbohydrate Addict's Diet.* Penguin, 1991, New York.

Hills, AP and ML Wahlquist. *Exercise and Obesity.* Smith-Gordon, 1994.

Lands, WEM. *Fish and Human Health.* Academic Press, 1986, New York.

Sinclair, A and R Gibson. *Essential Fatty Acids and Eicosanoids.* American Oil and Chemical Society Press, 1992, Champaign, IL, USA.

WHO. *Obesity Preventing and Managing the Global Epidemic.* 1998.

Articles

Adrian, F. 'Divergent trends in obesity and fat intake patterns: the American paradox.' *Am J Med* 102 (1997): 259–64.

Amano, Y, K Kawakubo, JS Lee, AC Tang, M Sugiyama, K Mori. 'Correlation between dietary glycemic index and cardiovascular disease risk factors among Japanese women.' *Eur J Clin Nutr* Nov 2004; 58(11):1472–8.

American Heart Association Journal. Report. 'High blood levels of insulin possible independent predictor of heart attack risk.' (Circ/Pyörälä) no. 98–4937.

Anderson, R, N Cheng, NA Bryden et al. 'Beneficial effects of chromium for people with type 2 diabetes.' *Diabetes* 45 (1996): 124A.

Anderson, RA, N. Cheng, NA Bryden, MM Polansky, N Cheng, J Chi and J Feng. 'Elevated intakes of supplemental chromium improve glucose and insulin variables in individuals with type 2 diabetes.' *Diabetes* 46, no.11 (1997): 1786–91.

Atrens, DM. 'The questionable wisdom of a low-fat diet and cholesterol reduction.' *Social Science Medicine* 39, no.3 (1994): 433–47.

Augustin, LS, S Gallus, E Negri, C La Vecchia. 'Glycemic index, glycemic load and risk of gastric cancer.' *Ann Oncol.* Apr 2004; 15(4): 581–84.

Augustin, LS, C Galeone, L Dal Maso, C Pelucchi, V Ramazzotti, DJ Jenkins, M Montella, R Talamini, E Negri, S Franceschi, C La Vecchia. 'Glycemic index, glycemic load and risk of prostate cancer.' *Int J Cancer.* Nov 10 (2004); 112(3): 446–50.

Bao, W, S Srinivasan and G Berenson. 'Persistent elevation of plasma insulin levels is associated with increased cardiovascular risk in children and young adults.' *Circulation* 93 (1996): 54–59.

Barclay AW, Brand-Miller JC, Mitchell P. 'Glycemic index, glycemic load and diabetes in a sample of older Australians.' *Asia Pac J Clin Nutr* 2003; 12 Suppl: S11.

Behan, PO, WMH Behan and DF Horrobin. 'Effect of high doses of essential fatty acids on postviral fatigue syndrome.' *Acta Neurology Scandinavia* 82 (1990): 209–16.

Berne, C. 'Insulin in hypertension – A relationship with consequences?' *Journal of Internal Medicine* 735, suppl. (1991): 65–73.

Bittiner, BS, I Cartwright, WFG Tucker and SS Bleehen. 'A double-blind, randomized, placebo-controlled trial of fish oil in psoriasis.' *Lancet* 1 (1988): 378–80.

Björck, I, Y Granfeldt, H Liljeberg, J Tovar and NG Asp. 'Food properties affecting the digestion and absorption of carbohydrates.' *Am J Clin Nutr* 59 (1994): 699S–705S.

Bjørneboe, A, E Søyland, GEA Bjørneboe, G Rajha and G Drevon. 'Effect of dietary supplementation with eicosapentaenoic acid in treatment of atopic dermatitis.' *Brit J Dermatology* 117 (1987): 436–69.

Black, HR. 'The coronary artery disease paradox: The role of hyperinsulinemia and insulin resistance and its implications for therapy.' *Journal of Cardiovascular Pharmacology* 15, suppl.5 (1990): S26–38.

Brand-Miller, JC. 'Glycemic index in relation to coronary disease.' *Asia Pac J Clin Nutr* 2004; 13(Suppl): S3.

Brand-Miller, JC. 'Importance of glycemic index in diabetes.' *Am J Clin Nutr* 59 suppl. (1994): 747S–52S.

Brands, MW and JE Hall. 'Insulin resistance, hyperinsulinemia, and obesity-associated hypertension.' *J Am Soc Nephrol* 3, no. 5 (1992): 1064–77.

Bruning, PF, MG Bonfrer, PAH van Noord, AAM Hart, M de Jong-Bakken and WJ Nooijen. 'Insulin resistance and breast cancer.' *Int J Cancer* 52 (1992): 511–16.

Burr, GO and MR Burr. 'A new deficiency disease produced by rigid exclusion of fat from the diet.' *Journal of Biology and Chemistry* 82 (1929): 345–67.

Cerami, A. 'Hypothesis: Glucose as a mediator of aging.' *Journal of the American Geriatric Society* 33 (1985): 626–34.

Chen, YD, AM Coulston, Z Ming-Yue, CB Hollenbeck and GM Reaven. 'Why do low-fat high-carbohydrate diets accentuate postprandial lipemia in patients with NIDDM?' *Diabetes Care* 18 (1995): 10–16.

Chew, I et al. 'Application of glycemic index to mixed meals.' *Am J Clin Nutr* 47 (1988): 53–56.

Chiles, R. 'Excessive serum insulin response to oral glucose in obesity and mild diabetes.' *Diabetes* 19 (1970): 458.

Colombani PC. 'Glycemic index and load-dynamic dietary guidelines in the context of diseases. *Physiol Behav* (2004) Dec 30; 83(4): 603–10.

Coulston, AM, CB Hollenbeck, ALM Swislocki, Y-DI Chen and G Reaven. 'Deleterious metabolic effects of high-carbohydrate, sucrose-containing diets in patients with non-insulin-dependent diabetes mellitus.' *Am J Med* 82 (1987): 213–20.

Crapo, PA 'Comparison of serum glucose-insulin and glucagon responses to different types of carbohydrates in non insulin dependent diabetic patients.' *Am J Clin Nutr* 34 (1981): 84–90.

Crapo, PA 'The effects of oral fructose, sucrose and glucose in subjects with reactive hypoglycemia.' *Diabetes Care* 5 (1982): 512–17.

Davis MS, CK Miller, DC Mitchell. 'More favorable dietary patterns are associated with lower glycemic load in older adults.' *J Am Diet Assoc* (2004) Dec; 104(12): 1828-35.

Diabetes for 10 milliarder! *Diabetikeren* nr. 7 (1999).

Dreon, DM et al. 'The effects of polyunsatured fat versus monounsatured fat on plasma lipoproteins.' *JAMA* 263 (1990): 2462–66.

Dyerberg, J et al. 'Eicosapentaenoic acid and prevention of thrombosis and atherosclerosis.' *Lancet* 2 (1978): 117–19.

Eaton, SB and MJ Konner. 'Stone age nutrition: implications for today.' *ASDC J Dent Child* 53, no. 4 (1986): 300–3.

Eaton, SB, MJ Konner and M Shostak. 'Stone agers in the fast lane: chronic degenerative diseases in evolutionary perspective.' *Am J Med* 84, no.4 (1988): 739–49.

Eriksson, KF and F Lindgärde. 'Prevention of type 2 (non-insulin-dependant) diabetes mellitus by diet and exercise. The 6-year Malm feasibility study.' *Diabetologia* 34 (1991): 891–98.

Folsom, AR, Z Demissie, L Harnack. 'Glycemic index, glycemic load, and incidence of endometrial cancer: the Iowa women's Health Study.' *Nutr Cancer.* (2003); 46(2): 119–24.

Food and Agriculture Organization / World Health Organization. 'Energy and protein requirements.' WHO *Technical Report* (1985): 724.

Foster-Powell, K, SA Holt, JC Brand-Miller. 'Intake of glycemic index and glycemic load values.' *Am J Clin Nutr* (2002) 76: 5–56.

Geiselman, PJ and D Novin. 'The role of carbohydrates in appetite, hunger and obesity.' *Appetite: J Intake Res* 3 (1982): 203–23.

Gwinup, G and AN Elias. 'Hypothesis: Insulin is responsible for the vascular complications of diabetes.' *Medical-Hypotheses* 34, no.1 (1991): 1–6.

Higginbotham, S, ZF Zhang, IM Lee, NR Cook, JE Buring, S Liu. 'Dietary glycemic load and breast cancer risk in the Women's Health Study.' *Cancer Epidemiol Biomarkers Prev* (2004) Jan; 13(1): 65–70.

Higginbotham, S, ZF Zhang, IM Lee, NR Cook, E Giovannucci, JE Buring, S Liu. 'Dietary glycemic load and risk of colorectal cancer in the Women's Health Study.' *J Natl Cancer Inst* (2004) Feb 4; 96(3): 229–33.

Hill, EG, SB Johnson, LD Lawson, MM Mahfouz and RT Holman. 'Perturbation of the metabolism of essential fatty acids by dietary partially hydrogenated vegetable oil.' *Proceedings of the National Academy of Science USA* 79 (1982): 953–57.

Hodge, AM, DR English, K O'Dea, GG Giles. 'Glycemic index and dietary fiber and the risk of type 2 diabetes.' *Diabetes Care* (2004) Nov (11): 2701–6.

Hofeldt, FD 'Reactive hypoglycemia.' *Metab* 24 (1975): 1193–208.

Holmes MD, S Liu, SE Hankinson, GA Colditz, DJ Hunter, WC Willett. 'Dietary carbohydrates, fiber, and breast cancer risk.' *Am J Epidemiol* (2004) Apr 15; 159(8): 732–39.

Jenkins, DJA. 'Dietary carbohydrates and their glycemic responses.' *JAMA* 251/21 (1984): 2829–31.

Jenkins, DJA et al. 'Glycemic index of foods: a physiological basis for carbohydrate exchange.' *Am J Clin Nutr* 34 (1981): 362–66.

Jenkins, DJA. 'Low glycemic index; lente carbohydrates and physiological effects of altered food frequency.' *Am J Clin Nutr* 56 suppl. (1994): 706S–9S.

Jenkins, DJA. 'Metabolic effects of low glycemic index diet.' *Am J Clin Nutr* 46 (1987): 968–75.

Jenkins, DJA, TMS Wolever, S Vukson, F Brighenti, SC Cunnane, AV Rao, AL Jenkins, G Buckley and W Singer. 'Nibbling versus gorging: Metabolic advantages of increased meal frequency.' *New England J Med* 321 (1989): 929–34.

Kaplan, N. 'The deadly quartet: upper body obesity, glucose intolerance, hypertriglyceridemia, and hypertension.' *Archives of Internal Medicine* 149 (1989): 1514–20.

Kemp, K. 'Carbohydrate addiction.' *Practitioner* 190 (1963): 358–64.

Kremer, JM, W Jubiz, A Michaslek, RI Rynes, LE Bartholomew, J Bigavo, M Timchalk, D Beeler and L Linnger. 'Fish-oil supplementation in active rheumatoid arthritis.' *Annual Internal Medicine* 106 (1987): 497–503.

Krumhout, D, EB Bosschieter and C Lezenne-Coulander. 'The inverse relation between fish consumption and 20 year mortality from coronary heart disease.' *New Engl J Med* 312 (1985): 1205–9.

Ludwig, DS, JA Majzoub, A Al-Zahrani, GE Dallal, I Blanco and S Roberts. 'High glycemic index foods, overeating, and obesity.' *Pediatrics* (1999); 103: e26.

Luo, J, SW Rizkalla, J Boillot et al. 'Dietary polyunsaturated (n-3) fatty acids improve adipocyte insulin action and glucose metabolism in insulin resistant rats; relation to membrane fatty acids.' *J Nutr* 126 (1996): 1951–58.

Mitchinson, MJ. 'Possible role of deficiency of selenium and vitamin E in atherosclerosis.' *J Clin Pathol* 37 (1984): 7–837.

Molnar, D. 'Insulin secretion and carbohydrate tolerance in childhood obesity.' *Klin Padiatr* 202, no. 3 (1990): 131–35.

Nader, S. 'Polycystic ovary syndrome and the androgen-insulin connection.' *American Journal of Obstetrics and Gynecology* 165, no. 2 (1991): 346–48.

Neel, JV. 'The 'thrifty genotype' in 1998,' *Nutr Rev* 57(5) (1999): S2–S9.

Odeleye, OE, M de Courten, D Pettitt and E Ravussin. 'Fasting hyperinsulinemia is a predictor of increased body weight gain and obesity in Pima Indian children.' *Diabetes* 46 (1997): 1341–45.

Oh, K, FB Hu, E Cho, KM Rexrode, MJ Stampfer, JE Manson, S Liu, WC Willett. 'Carbohydrate intake, glycemic index, glycemic load, and dietary fiber in relation to risk of stroke in women.' *Am J Epidemiol* (2005) Jan 15; 161(2): 161–9.

Oh, K, WC Willett, CS Fuchs, EL Giovannucci. 'Glycemic index, glycemic load, and carbohydrate intake in relation to risk of distal colorectal adenoma in women.' *Cancer Epidemiol Biomarkers Prev* (2004) Jul; 13(7): 1192–98.

Paolisso, G, A D'Amore, D Giugliano et al. 'Pharmacologic doses of vitamin E improve insulin action in healthy subjects and non-insulin-dependent diabetic patients.' *Am J Clin Nutr* 57 (1993): 650–56.

Paolisso, G, M Barbagallo. 'Hypertension, diabetes, and insulin resistance: the role of intracellular magnesium.' *Am J Hypertens* 10(3) (1997): 346–55.

Paolisso, G, S Sambato, G Pizza, et al. 'Improved insulin response and action by chronic magnesium administration in aged type 2 diabetes subjects.' *Diabetes Care* 12 (1989): 265–69.

Parillo, M, AA Rivellese, AV Ciardullo, B Capaldo, A Giacco, S Genovese and G Riccardi. 'A high-monounsaturated-fat/low-carbohydrate diet improves peripheral insulin sensitivity in non-insulin dependent diabetic patients.' *Metabolism* 41 (1992): 1373–78.

Pereira, MA, J Swain, AB Goldfine, N Rifai, DS Ludwig. 'Effects of a low-glycemic load diet on resting energy expenditure and heart disease risk factors during weight loss.' *JAMA* (2004) 292 (20).

Pyörälä, M, H Miettinen, M Laakso and K Pyörälä. 'Hyperinsulinemia predicts coronary heart disease risk in healthy middle-aged men: The 22-year follow-up results of the Helsinki policemen study.' *Circulation* 98 (1998): 398–404.

Racette, SB, DA Schoeller, RF Kushner, KM Neil and K Herling-Iaffaldano. 'Effects of aerobic exercise and dietary carbohydrate on energy expenditure and body composition during weight reduction in obese women.' Am J Clin Nutr 61 (1995): 486–94.

Reaven, GM and BB Hoffman. 'Hypertension as a disease of carbohydrate and lipoprotein metabolism.' Am J of Medicine 87, no. 6A (1989): 2S–6S.

Sadur, CN and RH Eckel. 'Insulin stimulation of adipose tissue lipoprotein lipase.' J Clinical Investigation 69 (1982): 1119–23.

Salonen, JT 'Serum fatty acids, apolipoproteins, selenium and vitamin antioxidants and risk of death from coronary artery disease.' Am J Cardiol 56, no.2 (1985): 226–31.

Sanchez, A and RW Hubbard. 'Plasma amino acids and the insulin/glucagon ratio as an explanation of the dietary protein modulation of atherosclerosis.' Medical Hypotheses 35, no. 4 (1991): 324–29.

Saris, WHM. 'Fit, fat and fat free: the metabolic aspects of weight control.' Int J Obes 22, suppl. 2 (1998): S15–S21.

Scaglioni, S, G Stival, M Giovannini. 'Dietary glycemic load, overall glycemic index, and serum insulin concentrations in healthy schoolchildren.' Am J Clin Nutr (2004) Feb; 79(2): 339–40.

Schaumberg, DA, S Liu, JM Seddon, WC Willett, SE Hankinson. 'Dietary glycemic load and risk of age-related cataract.' Am J Clin Nutr (2004) Aug; 80(2): 489–95.

Scholl, TO, X Chen, CS Khoo, C Lenders. 'The dietary glycemic index during pregnancy: influence on infant birth weight, fetal growth, and biomarkers of carbohydrate metabolism.' Am J Epidemiol (2004) Mar 1; 159(5): 467–74.

Schulze, MB, S Liu, EB Rimm, JE Manson, WC Willett, FB Hu. 'Glycemic index, glycemic load, and dietary fiber intake and incidence of type 2 diabetes in younger and middle-aged women.' Am J Clin Nutr (2004) Aug; 80(2): 348–56.

Schwartz, MW, D Figlewicz, DG Baskin, SC Woods and D Porte: 'Insulin in the brain: a hormonal regulation of energy balance.' Endocrine Review 43 (1992): 387–414.

Sears, B. 'Essential fatty acids and dietary endocrinology.' Journal of Advanced Medicine 6 (1993): 211–24.

Shang, H, K Osada, M Maebasi et al. 'A high biotin diet improves the impaired glucose tolerance of long term spontaneously hyperglycemic rats with non-insulin-dependent diabetes mellitus.' J Nutr Sci Vitamin 42 (1996): 517–26.

Silvera, SA, M Jain, GR Howe, AB Miller, TE Rohan. 'Dietary carbohydrates and breast cancer risk: A prospective study of the roles of overall glycemic index and glycemic load.' Int J Cancer (2004) Dec 17

Simopoulos, A. 'Fatty acid composition of skeletal muscle membrane phospholipids, insulin resistance and obesity.' Nutrition Today Jan/Feb (1994): 12–16.

Simpson, HCR. 'A high carbohydrate leguminous fibre diet improves all aspects of diabetic control.' Lancet 1 (1981): 1–5.

Tamburrano, G. 'Increased insulin sensitivity in patients with idiopathic reactive hypoglycemia.' J Clin Endocr Metab 69 (1989): 885.

Thaw, KT, N Wareham, R Luben, S. Bingham, S Oakes, A Welch and N Day. 'Glycated haemoglobin, diabetes, and mortality in men in Norfolk cohort of European prospective investigation of cancer and nutrition (EPIC Norfolk).' BMJ 322 (2001): 15–18.

Thomas, DE, JR Brotherhood and JC Brand. 'Carbohydrate feeding before exercise: effect of glycemic index.' Int J of Sports Medicine 12, no. 2 (1991): 180–86.

Westerterp, KR et al. 'Body mass, body composition and sleeping metabolic rate before, during and after endurance training.' Eur J Appl Physiol 69 (1994): 203–208.

WHO/FAO Expert Consultation. 'Carbohydrates in human nutrition: interim report.' Rome, April 1997.

Willett, WC. 'Dietary fat and obesity: an unconvincing relation.' Am J Clin Nutr 8 (1998): 1149–50.

Yale, J. 'Taming the hunger hormone: is insulin the key to weight control?' American Health, Jan/Feb (1984).

Zavaroni, I, S Mazza, P Dall'aglio et al. 'Prevalence of hyperinsulinaemia in patients with high blood pressure.' J Int Med 231 (1992): 235–40.

Zavaroni, I, P Couzzi, L Bonini et al. 'Association between salt sensitivity and insulin concentrations in patients with hypertension.' Am J Hypertens 8 (1995): 855–58.

Index

Recipe index

OTHER RODALE BOOKS
AVAILABLE FROM PAN MACMILLAN

1-4050-7744-1	The Abs Diet	*David Zinczenko*	£12.99
1-4050-2101-2	8 Minutes in the Morning	*Jorge Cruise*	£12.99
1-4050-4180-3	8 Minutes in the Morning for Maximum Weight Loss	*Jorge Cruise*	£12.99
1-4050-0668-8	Banish Your Belly, Butt and Thighs	*The Editors of* Prevention	£10.99
1-4050-4099-8	Before the Heart Attacks	*Dr H. Robert Superko*	£12.99
1-4050-3335-5	Picture Perfect Weight Loss	*Dr Howard Shapiro*	£14.99
1-4050-7739-5	Picture Perfect Weight Loss 30-Day Plan	*Dr Howard Shapiro*	£12.99
1-4050-6715-2	South Beach Diet Good Fats/Good Carbs Guide	*Dr Arthur Agatston*	£4.99
1-4050-6717-9	The South Beach Diet Cookbook	*Dr Arthur Agatston*	£20

All Pan Macmillan titles can be ordered from our website, *www.panmacmillan.com,* or from your local bookshop and are also available by post from:

Bookpost, PO Box 29, Douglas, Isle of Man IM99 1BQ
Tel: 01624 677237; fax: 01624 670923; e-mail: *bookshop@enterprise.net*;
or visit: *www.bookpost.co.uk*. Credit cards accepted. Free postage and packing in the United Kingdom

Prices shown above were correct at time of going to press.
Pan Macmillan reserve the right to show new retail prices on covers which may differ from those previously advertised in the text or elsewhere.

For information about buying *Rodale* titles in **Australia**, contact Pan Macmillan Australia.
Tel: 1300 135 113; fax: 1300 135 103; e-mail: *customer.service@macmillan.com.au*;
or visit: *www.panmacmillan.com.au*

For information about buying *Rodale* titles in **New Zealand**, contact Macmillan Publishers New Zealand Limited. Tel: (09) 414 0356; fax: (09) 414 0352; e-mail: *lyn@macmillan.co.nz*; or visit: *www.macmillan.co.nz*

For information about buying *Rodale* titles in **South Africa**, contact Pan Macmillan South Africa. Tel: (011) 325 5220; fax: (011) 325 5225; e-mail: *roshni@panmacmillan.co.za*

RODALE

MACMILLAN